Managing for Change

For Joanna, Sarah Jane, Morgan and Gavin

Managing for Change

Leadership, Strategy and Management in Asian NGOs

Ian Smillie and John Hailey

AGA KHAN FOUNDATION CANADA - FONDATION AGA KHAN CANADA

Earthscan Publications Ltd, London and Sterling, VA

First published in the UK and USA in 2001 by
Earthscan Publications Ltd

A catalogue record for this book is available from the British Library

ISBN: 1 85383 722 9 paperback
       1 85383 721 0 hardback

Typesetting by JS Typesetting, Wellingborough, Northants
Printed and bound by Creative Print and Design, Ebbw Vale
Cover design by Yvonne Booth

For a full list of publications please contact:

Earthscan Publications Ltd
120 Pentonville Road
London, N1 9JN, UK
Tel: +44 (0)20 7278 0433
Fax: +44 (0)20 7278 1142
Email: earthinfo@earthscan.co.uk
http://www.earthscan.co.uk

22883 Quicksilver Drive, Sterling, VA 20166–2012, USA

Earthscan is an editorially independent subsidiary of Kogan Page Ltd
and publishes in association with WWF-UK and the International
Institute for Environment and Development

This book is printed on elemental chlorine-free paper

TABLE OF CONTENTS

LIST OF TABLES

FOREWORD

Over the past three decades, the growth of non-governmental organiz-ations (NGOs) in many parts of the world has been nothing short of phenomenal. What were once small charities have become large, going concerns, some of them rivalling government departments and private sector firms in their scope and ambition. In South Asia, this growth has been especially impressive because of the cultural, political and economic challenges that many of these organizations have faced and overcome successfully.

A new body of study has emerged, focusing on the rise of the NGO in the South, but one area which has received virtually no serious attention is the issue of Southern NGO management. This is surprising, since NGOs enter the 21st century with growing amounts of influence and exposure, and they do so at a time of increasingly complex developmental challenges – and opportunities.

Why should the management of NGOs be of interest? First, the NGO sector has grown in size, importance and in the scope of its activities. It has also had to grow in sophistication, although none of this has been easy. Second, the first generation of NGOs has reached a significant level of experience and success, and they are now in a position to 'teach' younger counterparts about the pitfalls associated with growth and change, both in an organizational sense and with regard to the world in which they live. Third, within the voluntary sector, a new generation of managers is emerging – a generation that will require the full wealth of advice and experience that its predecessors have to offer.

For these reasons, Aga Khan Foundation Canada (AKFC) concept-ualized and directed the NGO Management Research Programme. This initiative aimed to explore how some of the most successful NGOs are managed, and to share Asian experiences with organizations in other parts of the world, both in the South and the North, as well as those that work with them, including bilateral and multilateral donors and governments. *Managing for Change* is an important component of this programme, one that makes a substantial contribution to research on the management practices of NGOs, and one that will be of value to 'veterans' of the business and newcomers alike.

The NGOs in our study – which include the Aga Khan Rural Support Programme (AKRSP), India, AKRSP, Pakistan, the Bharatiya Agro Industries Foundation (BAIF), the Bangladesh Rural Advancement Committee (BRAC), the International Union for the Conservation of Nature (IUCN) in Pakistan, Mafatlal Sadguru Water and Development

Foundation (Sadguru), PROSHIKA, the Sungi Development Foundation and the Sarhad Rural Support Corporation (SRSC) – were invited to participate in the research because they have been successful at what they do. They are well respected in the development community for their contribution to poverty alleviation, the quality of their work and their management skills, and they are organizations that AKFC has collaborated with or learned from.

In commissioning this research, we were interested to find out what, in management terms, made these organizations the success stories that they are. Was it simply the availability of friendly donors? Was it the strong and charismatic leadership of a few individuals? Was it the strength of their vision and values, and their success in inculcating these throughout their respective organizations? Was it participatory management techniques, or careful strategic planning, or just plain luck? We wanted to find out if there are common management themes across the three countries in our study, and to know whether the prescriptions in standard Western management texts have any bearing on the reality of our case study organizations. *Managing for Change* is an enquiry into successful management; although the success of these organizations is apparent, this book attempts to shed some light on the *why* and the *how*.

This has been an exciting and challenging endeavour for AKFC, and we are proud of the fact that this book is the product of case studies researched and written by individuals who are indigenous to the countries in which the participating NGOs are based. The study, of course, benefited immensely from the encouragement, assistance and input of many others, and from the participating organizations who took a risk in exposing themselves to the scrutiny of outsiders. We believe that their courage has paid off, not only for them, but for others who will read about their work and benefit from it.

We would like to thank the Canadian International Development Agency (CIDA) for its generous support and encouragement – a testimony to CIDA's historical commitment to the non-governmental sector in the developing world, as it was among the first bilateral agencies to recognize the value of working with NGOs. Thanks are also due to the authors, Ian Smillie and John Hailey, who expended considerable time and effort collecting and compiling facts and figures, working with the independent local researchers on their respective case studies, and interviewing current and former staff in the participating NGOs. The experience, insights and expertise they brought to this book in particular, and to the NGO Management Research Programme in general, have been invaluable. We are especially grateful for the commitment and patience they have displayed from the programme's inception.

Nazeer Aziz Ladhani
Chief Executive Officer, Aga Khan Foundation Canada

PREFACE

This book is the result of a six-year process. Following a 1994 consultation with the leaders of several South Asian NGOs in Dhaka, AKFC established a South Asian NGO Development Research Programme to examine some of the key challenges facing the non-profit sector on the subcontinent. One of the first products of the programme was *Speaking Out: Women's Economic Empowerment in South Asia*, edited by Marilyn Carr, Martha Chen and Renana Jhabvala (IT Publications, London, 1996). Co-sponsored by the United Nations Development Fund for Women (UNIFEM), the study examined the experience of NGOs in four South Asian countries in creating sustainable income generation opportunities for women.

In 1997, AKFC shifted the programme's focus to issues of management. Over the past two decades, the NGO sectors in Pakistan, India and Bangladesh have grown in size, complexity and influence. An increasing number of NGOs face the difficulties of managing a diverse range of staff who are working in different communities on a variety of projects. Concurrently, they must balance complex financial and operational demands while meeting the requirements of government and the multifarious conditions of different donors. Although they confront a multitude of management and organizational problems, a number of NGOs have successfully overcome these hurdles to grow and thrive.

The original idea behind this book was that participating organizations would each nominate one researcher to conduct a case study of another organization. This would draw on 'insider' NGO insights, and would also serve a 'cross-fertilization' purpose. A 1997 planning meeting in Lahore brought the participating organizations and researchers together, and, as a result of that meeting, a detailed research manual was prepared. The plan did not work as well as envisaged. It proved more difficult than expected to arrange for researchers to work across international borders. Some of the participating organizations were nervous about being exposed to the scrutiny of a counterpart. Nevertheless, an IUCN researcher carried out the case study of Sungi; AKRSP, India and BAIF carried out case studies of each other, while BRAC and PROSHIKA did the same in Bangladesh. (For readers who are unfamiliar with the organizations and the acronyms, explanations and descriptions are given in Chapter 1.) Independent researchers carried out the other studies. Research for the case studies was detailed and intensive, based on field visits and interviews conducted with field staff and mid-level and senior managers.

The results, completed by the end of 1998, were in some cases contentious: there was a feeling in one or two instances that a particular case study looked too much like an evaluation, and there were efforts (happily short-lived) to 'sanitize' points with which the subject disagreed. The exercise was decidedly not an evaluative one in the sense of passing judgement. It aimed rather to draw out lessons that might confirm, debunk or refine standard operating perceptions about Southern NGO management. In the chapters that follow, therefore, there is a search for myths about NGO management as well as for the realities.

Managing for Change represents a synthesis of the nine case studies, which together comprise over 600 pages of commentary and hundreds of hours of interviews with at least 120 staff members at all levels of the participating organizations. Additional interviews were conducted with donor agencies, academics and government representatives. After the case studies were completed, three members of the Project Steering Committee spent time between 1998 and 2000 with the participating NGOs, conducting further interviews and gathering data to fill in gaps. Zafar Qureshi visited Pakistani organizations, John Hailey spent time with the three Indian participants, and Ian Smillie worked with BRAC and Proshika in Bangladesh, and with Sungi in Pakistan.

The views expressed, of course, are those of the two authors of this book who owe a strong vote of thanks to the nine organizations involved in the study, all of which sustained considerable intrusive poking and prodding. A special vote of thanks is also offered here to the individual case study writers: Sara Ahmed (Sadguru), Saneeya Hussain (Sungi), Shandana Khan (AKRSP, Pakistan), Apoorva Oza (BAIF), Zia Ahmed Khan and Muhammad Azam (SRSC), Wasif A Rizvi (IUCN, Pakistan) and Girish G Sohani (AKRSP, India). The Bangladesh studies were team efforts: Mohammed N E Fatmi was principal researcher on the BRAC study, working with Mohammed Azmal Kabir, Asgar Ali Sabri and Mohammed Shahabuddin. The study of PROSHIKA was carried out by M G Sattar, Neena Afreen and M G Samdani Fakir.

The authors would also like to thank a number of readers who commented helpfully and constructively on an early draft. These included David Bonbright, Michael Edwards, Alan Fowler, Veronica Hope-Hailey, Stella Jafri, Rick James, Kamal Malhotra, Peter Morgan and John Saxby. We are grateful to Nazeer Ladhani who prodded us with insightful questions and long discussions on three continents, and to Fayaz Manji who provided invaluable back-up support throughout the long and exhaustive, and mostly enjoyable process. Naturally, errors or omissions and views expressed in the book are the responsibility of the authors alone.

Finally, a word on words. Preliminary readers persuaded us to remove a number of words and expressions that they did not like or understand, but two remain, both derived from other languages. The first is *dirigisme*, which comes from the French, 'to direct'. The second is more complicated. Grigori Potemkin, a Russian General, frequently disguised the weak points of his work from Catherine the Great, resulting in an apocryphal tale about his creation of artificial villages that could be seen by the Empress as she passed. 'Potemkin village', therefore, came to denote any pretentious façade designed to cover up a shabby or undesirable condition. The purpose of retaining these expressions will become clear in the text.

Ian Smillie, Ottawa
John Hailey, Oxford

October 2000

ACRONYMS AND ABBREVIATIONS

ADAB	Association of Development Agencies in Bangladesh
ADC	Area Development Centre
AKFC	Aga Khan Foundation Canada
AKRSP (I)	Aga Khan Rural Support Programme, India
AKRSP (P)	Aga Khan Rural Support Programme, Pakistan
BAIF	Bharatiya Agro Industries Foundation
BRAC	Bangladesh Rural Advancement Committee (formerly Bangladesh Rehabilitation Assistance Committee)
CAPART	Council for Advancement of People's Action and Rural Technology
CBO	Community-based Organization
CEO	Chief Executive Officer
CIDA	Canadian International Development Agency
CUSO	Canadian University Service Overseas
DFID	Department for International Development (UK)
DLO	Donor Liaison Office
GRCC	Gender Resource and Co-ordination Cell
HDT	Human Development Training
IDPAA	Institute for Development Policy Analysis and Advocacy
IFAD	International Fund for Agricultural Development
IMEC	Impact Monitoring and Evaluation Cell
IUCN	International Union for the Conservation of Nature (The World Conservation Union)
JMM	Joint Monitoring Mission
LFA	Logical Framework Analysis
MBO	Management by Objectives
NCS	National Conservation Strategy
NFPE	Non-formal Primary Education (programme)
NFRs	Note for Records
NGO	Non-governmental Organization
NORAD	Norwegian Agency for Development Cooperation
NOVIB	Netherlands Organization for International Development Cooperation
NRSP	National Rural Support Programme
NWFP	Northwest Frontier Province (Pakistan)
ODA	Official Development Assistance
OECD	Organization for Economic Cooperation and Development
ORAP	Organization for Rural Associations for Progress

ORT	Oral Rehydration Therapy
ORW	Oral Rehydration Worker
PRA	Participatory Rural Appraisal
PSDT	Practical Skills Development Training
PVP	Participatory Video Programme
RBM	Results-based Management
RED	Research and Evaluation Division
SAPRI	Structural Adjustment Participatory Review
SDC	strategic development committee
SRSC	Sarhad Rural Support Corporation
TARC	Training and Resource Centre
TQM	Total Quality Management
UNDP	United Nations Development Programme
UNIFEM	United Nations Development Fund for Women
USAID	United States Agency for International Development
WID	Women in Development

CHAPTER 1

INTRODUCTION

Sweet dreams are made of this . . .

The Eurythmics

This book is about how some of the most successful non-governmental development organizations in the world are managed. It is about learning and change and growth. It is about leading and following; and it is about survival in hostile environments where politics and tradition compete for pride of place with bureaucracy and international donor agendas. It is about risk, ambition and humility. It is about the management of growth – often spectacular and very rapid growth – among organizations holding strong views about poverty and participation. Most of the story takes place during the last third of the 20th century, but it demonstrates the tremendous potential of the non-governmental sector for the 21st. It also covers a vast sweep of territories and people, ranging from the high mountain passes of the Karakoram to the Ganges–Brahmaputra Delta, 2500 kilometres to the south-east. Mostly, *Managing for Change* is about individuals, people who have taken on large tasks and who have found ways to reach important objectives.

The book is also about myths and realities in NGO management, and about whether the nostrums and prescriptions for good management contained in Western texts travel well. *Managing for Change* is the result of a long, occasionally difficult, but rarely dull process. It is the product of many hands and many minds, applied to the exceedingly complex topic of NGO management – a topic shrouded in considerable mystery, sophistry and debate.

At one level, NGOs are the envy of both government and business in the way that they mobilize resources and motivate staff – with low overheads and minimalist administrative structures. However, their very success, and the rapid growth in the size and complexity of some NGOs during the 1990s, has uncovered management problems that threaten their distinctiveness and their effectiveness. As they scale up, it is apparent that some NGOs suffer from an uncertain strategic focus, unclear governance structures, weak leadership, ill-developed structures and systems, limited investment in staff development, erratic funding, the contradictory influences of overseas donors and local politicians, and growing demands from their beneficiaries. It is against such a background that this study aimed to analyse how a sample of successful NGOs overcame these problems, continuing to develop and grow. We felt that by looking in depth at a small sample of successful NGOs, we could begin to analyse the key characteristics of the growth process, and to understand what strategies, management styles and organizational structures have led to their success.

CHANGE MANAGEMENT AND MANAGEMENT FOR CHANGE

Everywhere, in all walks of life, today's managers are concerned about change within their organizations, and about their ability to respond to the increasingly complex demands of an increasingly complex world. This accounts for the growing library of books about change, re-engineering and transformation, as well as books that go 'beyond change', 'beyond re-engineering' and 'beyond transformation' (eg *Beyond Reengineering: How the Process-Centered Organization is Changing Our Work and Our Lives*, Michael Hammer, 1996, or *Beyond the Basics of Reengineering: Survival Tactics for the 90s*, Ellen Snodgrass, 1996). Under 'change management', in fact, Amazon.com offered, in February 2000, over 50 books on the subject published between 1993 and 2000, whose titles started with either 'a' or 'b' alone.

This book, therefore, finds itself in something of a generic crowd, because it is partly about change management – about how successful organizations adapt their work to the challenges posed by their beneficiaries, by donors, governments and critics. It is also about how they have dealt with growth. More importantly, however, it is about how they have understood and adapted or invented new ways of working towards the economic and social empowerment of the disempowered. It is also about the building of organizations that aim to make changes in the lives of poor people. In other words, it is about the management *of* change within organizations, as well as management *for* change in the societies and in the lives of the people they work with.

Balancing diverse challenges is the key to NGO management. Yet, there is a surprising lack of research on the subject. A well established body of knowledge exists on the design and implementation of development projects, and there is also a growing amount of literature on the issues that surround advocacy and NGO–state relations. There is also a growing body of research on the management of Northern non-profit organizations. But Northern organizations exist in a setting shaped by a long history of philanthropy, constructive government interaction with civil society, and by relatively stable social conditions. Surprisingly, little has yet been written about the dynamics of Southern NGO management and the strategic and organizational issues involved, let alone the skills and competencies needed by hands-on Southern NGO managers. It is as though the approaches to leadership, strategic planning, personnel and resource mobilization that might make sense in London or New York are fully transferable to Karachi, New Delhi and Dhaka; or, more pointedly, to Kohat, Surendranagar and Noakhali.

Our study aimed to discover to what extent this might or might not be true. We did not set out to show that the logical framework analysis, say, was a good thing or a bad thing in a South Asian setting. Rather, we aimed to see whether 'standard' management tools and concepts were being applied, and, if so, how well they work. Of greater interest were the tools, concepts and practices that might have been developed and applied *beyond* the standard Northern idea of good management, whether non-profit or otherwise. Current development literature, for example, is awash with chapters about the importance of participation. We wanted to find out what participation actually means to the management of an organization with a fast-growing, and therefore necessarily formulaic approach to health, or education, or natural resource management or savings and credit. How compatible are growth and participation? What kinds of hierarchies are used? How are teams formed and how important are they? Where does commitment come from? Is it a luxury among South Asian NGOs? Who makes strategy? Are formal strategies useful? Are they important? Do they even exist? What are the realities of dealing with government? Are the much vaunted 'partnerships' between South Asian NGOs and Northern supporters genuine? Readers may find some of the answers, spelled out in the following chapters, surprising.

Concerns are often expressed about Southern NGO leadership (usually by Northern donors). Is management genuinely participatory? Is charismatic leadership appropriate to modern NGO management needs? What would happen if the founder disappeared? These questions are relevant for Southern NGOs as well as for Northern donors, and four of the organizations invited to participate in the project were included, in part, because they had already gone through leadership change. As the study was being completed, two more leadership changes occurred.

SUCCESS, GROWTH AND DEVELOPMENT

Before going further, it may be useful to give some consideration to the word 'success' and to the expression 'successful NGO'. The organizations discussed in this book were invited to participate because they have all become going concerns. All have survived at least one decade and some have survived almost four. Survival, therefore, in a complex and often hostile environment was one of our criteria. All have become sizeable organizations and some have become huge, against all expectations that such growth was possible or even appropriate for NGOs in developing countries.

Growth, therefore, was another factor in our selection. Success, of course, is not only about growth and survival. These might be criteria enough if we were looking only at car manufacturers, but even there, the product would be an essential part of the definition of, or the reason for, success. Where NGOs are concerned, the 'product' is complex. It may be a reduction in poverty or work that leads to a new government policy on environmental protection. Or it may be a process that allows these things to happen – greater awareness by women of their potential, more literacy, or the ability of people to work for the first time with neighbours on community improvement. However they define it and however well they accomplish it, the intended 'product' of the NGOs described in this book is development. Readers should keep in mind, however, that this is a book about management, not about development per se. In other words, the book, of necessity, deals with the broad brush-strokes of the NGO product, rather than with the details.

There is more to say on this point, however. Where South Asian NGOs are concerned, the debate about 'success' has several strands, many of them antipathetic to the basic concepts of growth or even survival. 'Success', according to many writers, can *only* be defined in terms of product, and in much of the serious literature about South Asian NGOs, the product is found wanting. Accused during the 1970s and 1980s of being unable to 'go to scale' with successful but tiny initiatives, those NGOs that eventually did scale up then found themselves accused of creating 'parallel systems' to those of the state. They were thus accused of undermining the state by fragmenting service delivery, and thereby fragmenting the public voice, sidelining more legitimate civic institutions such as political parties and trade unions. In this way, says Bangladesh commentator Geof Wood, 'accountability is diluted at both ends: source and destination. The function of resource allocation and public expenditure is performed by disaggregated, non-public, non-transparent agencies, insulated from a universal system of accountability'.[1]

As if accusations of poor development were not enough, the work of many NGOs is denied the development label altogether. The favoured critique of larger South Asian NGOs, especially those in Bangladesh, is that in their quest for survival and growth, they have become fat and lazy, focusing on 'service delivery' because that is what donors will pay for, and adopting microcredit operations because, in addition to being favoured by donors, microcredit has the added benefit of financial sustainability (if managed well, of course). 'Most NGOs in Bangladesh,' writes Syed Hashemi, 'have given up strategies to organize the poor, sanitized their activities (if not their rhetoric), and chosen the path of delivering economic assistance.'[2] This critique leads logically to Michael Edwards' conclusion that 'among Bangladeshi NGOs, there is a tendency to concentrate on the sustainability of the NGO itself . . . This is especially true of credit providers'.[3] In other words, NGOs that followed the advice of earlier dependency critics got it wrong in pursuing financial sustainability.

As incorrect as it is dramatic, the suggestion has been made by some writers that there has been a general NGO shift away from grassroots mobilization towards service delivery, or even welfarism, and that NGO activity outside of these areas is actively and successfully discouraged by the government of Bangladesh. Further, it is said that NGOs have become little more than stooges for donor agencies who erroneously but deliberately equate them with 'civil society', using them as part of a master plan orchestrated by USAID. Hashemi writes that USAID

> *is gearing up to provide funding to strengthen civil society, perceiving this strategy as a logical element in its open market and open society program . . . Donor funding is therefore provided to groups in society that pursue 'democratic' agendas. Explicitly (and deliberately) missing from this definition of civil society are the political parties, trade unions and peasant organizations that have consistently fought against exploitation in Bangladesh.*[4]

It would be churlish to observe that many of these organizations have also fought against just about everyone else as well, including each other. This, of course, does not detract from the issue of selective donor interest in civil society. It is worth noting, however, that in fact most donors have gone to great lengths to make a clear distinction between developmental NGOs and other forms of civil society, often treating NGOs as fraudulent interlopers and civil society impersonators. Contrary to what Hashemi says, the civil society debate has not helped most development NGOs; it has actually increased the competition for funding as donors search for new partners, including political parties and trade unions, if not peasant organizations. And it may be noted here, because it will not arise in the text again, that USAID has actually provided no funding whatsoever to most of the case study organizations in this book. In one of the two examples where it did (see Chapter 2), the result was nearly fatal for the NGO concerned.

These issues will arise again on occasion throughout the book, but it is perhaps worth repeating that they are not its primary focus. The book is primarily about the management of NGOs rather than the work that they do. We need not be overly apologetic about this, except, perhaps, for one further observation. There is an idea that most NGOs start out as small welfare organizations. Some then move on to larger development efforts. As they mature, they see that there are broader systemic problems that require systemic change, and so they become involved in more strategic and often political activities. These three 'generations' of NGO life were popularized by David Korten and have been widely and uncritically accepted in much NGO-related literature.[5] The thesis is simple: as organizations become more sophisticated in their understanding of, say, poverty or environmental problems, they will move from welfare to activism; from band-aids to meaningful activity.

The thesis is perhaps a little too simple. If an NGO wants to be a welfare organization, what is wrong with that? If it wants to provide 'service delivery', what is wrong with that? The industrialized world is full of service NGOs: the Red Cross, the Salvation Army, day-care centres, hostels, counselling services, homes for the elderly. Some are large and mature and have not moved, nor are they expected to move, from 'first generation' to generations two and three, challenging the systemic problems of society. Some may move, but many will not. It is equally true that their counterparts in developing countries – welfare agencies and service delivery organizations – may not be appropriate partners for progressive and forward-thinking donor agencies. This does not invalidate their success in their chosen field, nor does it invalidate the lessons they may have to teach about management. For they too must manage priorities, resources, people and the pressures of the environment in which they work.

'Success', therefore, is something of a movable feast, or at least a moving target, in the eye – if not the cross-hairs – of the beholder. Criticized for not going to scale, many South Asian NGOs are accused of supplanting the state when they do. Criticized for a lack of financial sustainability, they are charged with thinking only of themselves when they create self-financing credit operations. Accused of working against the state, they are then condemned for abandoning the poor when they actually engage the state. Regardless of their grassroots mobilization, their rights-based adult education, the risks they take in confronting vested economic, social, political and religious interests, regardless of their engagement of government on large and controversial development and environmental issues, somehow they are, for their critics, little more than 'service providers' and pliant proxies for manipulative donors. While there is some truth in some of the criticism, there is a great body of evaluative material to substantiate contrary conclusions. That aside, it is perhaps misplaced to assume that South Asian NGOs are less adept at managing their priorities and their relationships than those they work with. As the Eurythmics song *Sweet Dreams Are Made of This* puts it, 'Some want to use you; some want to be used by you'. Such sentiments cut both ways.

As a background for our work, we reviewed most of the well-known and many less well-known management texts. We were struck by how few make specific reference to gender. This is as true of the books on the voluntary sector as it is of those on the private sector. A search through the indexes of the works of Mintzberg, Drucker, Senge, Handy and others reveals little or nothing under women or gender. This is odd, not least because during the 1990s many books were published on the subject of women and management. There were more than two dozen with the words 'glass ceiling' in the titles alone.

We do not claim that *Managing for Change* deals with the subject as completely or as well as we (or you) might like. That said, several of the organizations in our study have made women the focal point of their work, learning over the years that empowerment is a gender issue relating as much to men as to women, and that women's reproductive health is less important to them and to development writ large than their social and productive health. While their gender-related development programming evolved over the years, our case study NGOs were slower to understand and adopt gender-related management policies. We deal with their struggle on this issue from a management (rather than a development) perspective in Chapters 3 and 5, and in Chapter 6 where we consider the achievements of the only woman among our 16 past and present chief executive officers (CEOs).

THE PARTICIPATING ORGANIZATIONS

Nine South Asian NGOs took part in the study. The youngest is Sungi, founded in 1989, and the oldest is BAIF which, although formally founded in 1967, actually has roots that go back to 1946. Being the youngest, it is not surprising that Sungi is also the smallest in terms of its income, while BRAC, probably the largest development NGO in the world, had a 1998 turnover of US$262 million.* In between, they came in all shapes and sizes. There are two Bangladeshi organizations, three Indian organizations and four Pakistani NGOs in our study. This may appear to make it somewhat unbalanced in that the Indian NGO movement is the oldest in the region, while the Bangladeshi NGO movement is the largest, at least in terms of impact and proportionate spending levels. But then PROSHIKA and BRAC, our two Bangladeshi participants, are each larger than all the others combined, and while the study gains from Indian NGO maturity, it also benefits from the exuberance of Pakistani NGO youth.

---

* Some international NGOs such as World Vision and CARE, with global incomes close to US$500 million in cash and kind are, of course, larger in dollar terms and geographic reach. But they are considerably smaller than BRAC in terms of their real spending power, the number of people that they reach and their staffing complement. In 2000, BRAC had over 24,000 full-time and more than 34,000 part-time employees.

The origins of the participating organizations represent a cross-section of initiatives. Two were inspired or founded by men who were gurus in the true Indian sense of the word – Sadguru was named for Ranchhod Dasji Maharaj, while BAIF was founded by Shri Manibhai Desai, a disciple and follower of Mahatma Gandhi. BRAC and Sungi were founded by young social activists, while PROSHIKA grew out of a donor project that was also staffed, and eventually taken over, by young social activists. Three others in the group had external origins and one, the Sarhad Rural Support Corporation, had strong initial support from the government of the Northwest Frontier Province in Pakistan.

Table 1.1 *Participating NGO size and milestones*

Organization	Founding date	Leadership change	Number of staff	1997 Financial turnover
BAIF	1967	1993	1700	Rs 250m – US$6.4m
BRAC	1972	No	58,700 (24,700 full time)	Tk 10.9bn – $237m
Sadguru	1974	No	86	Rs 74.5m – $1.9m
PROSHIKA	1976	No	2988	Tk 2.6bn – $56.5m
AKRSP (P)	1982	1992, 1994	368	Rs 525.1m – $11.93m
AKRSP (I)	1984	1993	169	Rs 63.7m – $1.63m
IUCN (P)	1985	2000	200+	Rs 148.9m – $3.38m
SRSC	1989	1995, 1996	211	Rs 125m – $2.84m
Sungi	1989	1999	100	Rs 21m – $0.48m

Note: Exchange rates to US dollar for 1997: India Rs 39.02; Pakistan Rs 44.0; Bangladesh Tk 46 (June 1998)

Six of the participating organizations are purely indigenous, while three are hybrids of a sort. The Aga Khan Rural Support Programmes in Pakistan and India were created by the Aga Khan Foundation, which continues to play a role as mentor and funder, even though both organizations are independently incorporated with their own trustees in their respective countries. The Sarhad Rural Support Corporation (SRSC) was included in the study in part because it was initially an attempt to replicate the AKRSP (P) model in a very different Pakistani setting. That experience brings interesting lessons and contrasts to the study. IUCN Pakistan (P) looks like the odd man out, although this is not, in fact, the case. IUCN (P) – the only NGO in our study that has been headed by a woman – is the Pakistani programming branch of the International Union for the Conservation of Nature (IUCN), headquartered in Switzerland.

Although not strictly speaking a Pakistani organization, therefore, it exhibits, nevertheless, all the traits of a successful South Asian NGO. Its Country Representative, Aban Marker Kabraji, developed the programme 'from scratch', as the case study puts it, generating virtually all of its funding and programming initiatives within Pakistan. IUCN in Switzerland provided the name, as well as moral support and consultants as required, but IUCN (P) soon began to provide the same sort of support to other IUCN offices, becoming the biggest IUCN country programme in the world.

Details on the organizations will emerge through the text, but in order to set the scene, brief thumbnail sketches of the nine organizations follow.

BAIF (founded 1967)

The BAIF Development Research Foundation (formerly known as the Bharatiya Agro Industries Foundation) was formalized in 1967, although it actually began in 1946, when Mahatma Gandhi visited Urulikanchan, a poverty-stricken village near Pune, with a young follower named Manibhai Desai. Manibhai stayed behind to work on social reforms, education and rural development. His work on the cross-breeding of cattle led to the creation of BAIF, whose mission today is

> *to create opportunities of gainful self-employment for rural families, especially disadvantaged sections, ensuring sustainable livelihoods, enriched environment, improved quality of life and good human values. This will be achieved through development research, effective use of local resources, extension of appropriate technologies, and upgrading of skills and capabilities with community participation. BAIF is a non-political, secular and professionally managed organization.*

The blend of research, training and development is a unique characteristic of BAIF's work. 'BAIF believes that any development without research becomes outdated, and any research programme without development becomes academic.' In addition to cattle, BAIF has worked in wasteland development, horticulture, water development, forestry, tribal rehabilitation and the empowerment of women. Its 725 cattle-breeding centres are spread over seven states, providing service to over half a million families.

BRAC (founded 1972)

Founded as a post-war relief effort, BRAC (once an acronym for 'Bangladesh Rural Advancement Committee') is today one of the biggest

NGOs in the world, with over 58,000 full- and part-time staff, and an annual turnover in excess of US$260 million. It works in more than 40,000 villages. BRAC focuses primarily on rural women, in part because they are the most socially and economically deprived, but also because their limited resources make them better household managers than men. Its programmes in education, health, fish, livestock, savings and credit, and capacity building overlap so that there can be an integrated approach at the village level. To complement and finance its village activities, BRAC has created a large handcraft development and marketing operation, a cold-storage plant, a printing press and a fully equipped modern dairy. Its savings and credit operation was formalized as a bank in 1999 and it has plans to open a BRAC university in the near future:

> *BRAC works with people whose lives are dominated by extreme poverty, illiteracy, disease and other handicaps. With multifaceted development interventions, BRAC strives to bring about positive change in the quality of life of these people. BRAC is committed to making its programmes socially, financially and environmentally sustainable using new methods and technologies. BRAC firmly believes and is actively involved in promoting human rights and dignity, and gender equity. (BRAC Annual Report 1998, Dhaka, p4)*

Although its emphasis is at the individual level, 'BRAC will continue its efforts to bring about change in the macro-level policy environment.

Sadguru (founded 1974)

Navinchandra Mafatlal Sadguru Water and Development Foundation – 'Sadguru' – works in the tribal areas of Dahod and other districts in North Eastern Gujarat. Its broad objectives are to improve the living conditions of rural and tribal people, chiefly by developing environmentally sound land and water resources programmes. It works to improve the environment and social development through programmes that enhance the natural resource base. According to Sadguru:

> *The aim is to help the tribal people break away from the vicious circle of poverty ... By making best use of available water resources and demonstrating the economic and environment benefits of afforestation and watershed development, [Sadguru] has reversed the exodus of tribal people forced out from their land by drought and erosion, thereby bringing new prosperity and ... impetus to environmental improvement.*

By 1999, it had reached more than 75,000 families and a tribal population of 465,000 people. With the establishment of a training institute in natural resource management, Sadguru added an important dimension to its activities, building its own capacity and helping other agencies to replicate similar programmes in other parts of India.

PROSHIKA (founded 1976)

Today, PROSHIKA is one of the largest NGOs in Bangladesh. The name is derived from the first syllables of three Bangla words: *proshikhan*, *shiksha* and *kaj* which mean training, education and action. Its mission is 'to conduct an extensive and intensive participatory development process through empowerment of the poor. Its objectives include:

1 achieving structural poverty alleviation;
2 environmental protection and regeneration;
3 improvement in the status of women;
4 increasing people's participation in public institutions; and
5 increasing people's capacity to gain and exercise democratic and human rights.

By mid-1999, PROSHIKA had established over 87,000 village groups with a membership of 1.7 million people, more than half of them women. It had widespread programmes in ecological agriculture, adult literacy, non-formal primary education, social forestry, house construction, and savings and credit. PROSHIKA was one of the first NGOs to begin working among the urban poor, and now has programmes in all the cities and major towns of the country. An integral part of the PROSHIKA approach is its Institute for Development Policy Analysis and Advocacy (IDPAA). IDPAA builds linkages between the organization's grassroots development efforts and macro-level policy advocacy. IDPAA, for example, has been involved in the Structural Adjustment Participatory Review (SAPRI), an international NGO–World Bank initiative aimed at understanding the impact of structural adjustment programmes on the poor. IDPAA is based on the idea that satisfactory development will not occur without making concrete links between grassroots issues and macro-economic policies.

Aga Khan Rural Support Programme, Pakistan (founded 1982)

AKRSP (P) was formed to increase the capacity of people in the Northern Areas and Chitral to become involved in their own development, so that they can improve their income and welfare in a sustainable and equitable manner. Key elements in the approach have been the establishment of village-level organizations to manage the development process, the use of physical productive infrastructure projects with a grant element to support economic development and to provide the initial incentive for community organization, the introduction of a savings and credit scheme, and training programmes to support self-help activities. AKRSP works in a difficult mountainous terrain, covering 75,000 square miles. As of mid-1997, it had mobilized more than 80 per cent of the population into village organizations, introducing a variety of new income-generating activities and technologies. Up to 17,000 people had benefited from AKRSP training programmes, and it is estimated that incomes in the region had doubled in real terms between 1982 and 1994, in part because of AKRSP's interventions.

Aga Khan Rural Support Programme, India (founded 1983)

AKRSP (I) 'exists to enable the empowerment of rural communities and groups, particularly the underprivileged and women, to take control over their own lives and manage their environment, to create a better and more equitable society'. Founded in 1983 with a grant from the Aga Khan Foundation, AKRSP (I) works in Gujarat State, with its headquarters in Ahmedabad and three field offices that cover 'macro-watersheds' of approximately 10,000 hectares each. 'The key to eradicating poverty,' according to AKRSP (I), 'is to recognize the linkages between development needs – not just conceptually, but through the application of an integrated plan that can impact the whole of people's lives.' For this reason, since 1995 AKRSP (I) has followed a 'Watershed Approach'. This approach takes the physical linkages of the ecological territory served by a particular river and considers them in a coordinated fashion, tying them to a variety of development interventions, including agriculture, soil and water conservation, water resource development, forestry and biogas energy development. At the core of the programme is the creation of village institutions that serve as a focal point, inter alia, for savings and credit, agricultural input supply and marketing, and programmes related to gender and development. AKRSP (I) has conducted pioneering work in joint forestry management, participatory irrigation management, gender issues in natural resource management, and participatory rural appraisal. It is not distinguished so much by its size, as by its innovative approaches to natural resource management.

IUCN Pakistan (founded 1985)

The International Union for the Conservation of Nature, also known as 'IUCN – The World Conservation Union', was founded in 1948, bringing together states, government agencies and a diverse range of NGOs in a unique partnership of 900 members in 138 countries. Pakistan became a state member of IUCN in 1976, but it was not until 1985 that a first tentative programming office was opened in Karachi, with a mandate to begin working on the creation of a National Conservation Strategy (NCS) for Pakistan. The NCS was completed in 1992 and, since then, IUCN (P) has worked closely with federal and provincial governments, NGOs and the private sector on projects and strategies related to NCS implementation. While clearly part of an international organization, IUCN (P) is also 100 per cent Pakistani. With 24 institutional members in Pakistan and over 250 employees at the end of 1998, it had become the largest IUCN operation in the world. IUCN (P)'s vision is as follows:

> *Equity among all groups within human society is both an organizational value and a principle. It is a value that runs across the psyche of the organization and cannot be compromised. It is a principle on which IUCN Pakistan strives to base its programme and management systems. The organization's mission will only be achieved if there is a continuous push for a process of societal and behavioural change. The building blocks of this change are justice and the empowerment of societies, through information and knowledge that enables people to influence the decisions that will affect them and their children's quality of life.*

Sarhad Rural Support Corporation (founded 1989)

SRSC was established in 1989 in the Northwest Frontier Province of Pakistan with the objective of promoting development through a participatory approach to social organization and networking in community-based organizations. It was a deliberate attempt to replicate the approach that had been taken in the Northern Areas of Pakistan by AKRSP (P), with initial support from USAID and the government of the province. By 2000, it had broadened its approach, working in seven districts through more than 2887 community-based men's and women's organizations. It aims to raise the income and quality of life of rural people through improved economic and food security, and to evolve sustainable structures for the productive management of available natural, human and financial resources. These objectives manifest themselves in a variety of agricultural and education programmes, a savings and credit operation, and, in recent years, a much more focused emphasis on gender integration and planning.

Sungi Development Foundation (founded 1989)

Sungi, which is the word for 'companion' in Hindko, was established in 1989 to work on grassroots mobilization in the Hazara Division of Pakistan's Northwest Frontier Province. Its initial efforts focused on advocacy, but it became involved in relief activities during a period of flooding in 1992. Sungi realized that rehabilitation would bring only temporary relief, however, and it decided that if there were to be real changes in people's lives, poverty would have to be tackled through more permanent institution-building mechanisms. Since then the organization has grown rapidly, with almost 100 staff at the end of 1998 working in two zonal and three cluster offices. While its advocacy work has continued (on forestry reform, for example), the organization now works as well on sustainable natural resource management, health and sanitation, livestock, and savings and credit. Sungi's Founder and first Executive Director, Omar Asghar Khan, was appointed Pakistan's Minister of Environment, Local Government and Rural Development, as well as Minister for Labour, Manpower and Overseas Pakistanis in 1999.

ORGANIZATION OF THE BOOK

The 'right' way to structure a book on NGO management might be to start with organizational mission, moving on through strategy, governance and structures. Somewhere early in the journey, one might expect to find a discussion about teamwork, institutional culture and leadership. We have chosen a slightly different structure, in part because of the different origins of our case study NGOs, and in part because of the environment in which they work. Many of the NGOs in this study are what we call 'accidental NGOs'. They were formed as a short-term response to an emergency, or as small experimental efforts with uncertain life expectancies. There were no mission statements, no strategic plans, and there were many more ideas than there was money to pay for them. Few expected to become large; even fewer expected to become role models for others. In this category we place the Indian NGO, BAIF, along with BRAC and PROSHIKA in Bangladesh, and Sungi in Pakistan. Others in our collection – the two AKRSPs in India and Pakistan, SRSC in Pakistan, and to some extent Sadguru in India – are what we call, for want of a better term, 'premeditated NGOs'. They were established from the outset with a clear mission, start-up strategies and workplans, and a healthy amount of donor support. To start this book, therefore, with a discussion about vision, mission or strategies when half our sample had articulated few of these at the beginning, would be like setting out on a journey with two flat tyres.

Chapter 2, therefore, begins with the setting. It describes the intractable nature and the monstrous scale of the poverty that South Asian NGOs seek to end. It also describes the complex political and financial environment in which they have functioned over the past two decades, the changing attitudes of changing governments, the regulatory frame-work, and the efforts of NGOs to work with government, while at the same time maintaining enough distance and legitimacy to act as advocates when necessary. Part of the environmental discussion has to do with donors – how they have related to NGOs over time and how the NGOs have alternately resisted or been influenced by them.

Organizational behaviour is partly the product of the local environ-ment, partly of mission and values, but it is also shaped by the way people work and socialize together. Chapter 3 explores the dynamics of this process, examining the role of symbols and formal systems in creating effective and purposive organizational cultures. Much development writing deals with 'capacity building', usually from the perspective of outsiders (such as donor agencies) who aim to 'build' the capacity of people or institutions elsewhere. Chapter 4 focuses on how South Asian NGOs have built their own capacities, in part through clear and determined investments in formal learning structures. Because formal structures and systems are so important where learning and capacity building are concerned, it might be expected that the same formality would pertain to strategy development. We have found throughout the study, however, that there is a constant struggle within South Asian NGOs between the formal and the informal. Chapter 5 demonstrates that where strategy is concerned, caution, incrementalism and selective opportunism coexist with the formal strategies advocated in much management writing. Where strategic plans do exist, the study asks if they are 'Potemkin villages', erected to satisfy the expectations of donors, evaluators and other passers-by. Or are they key ingredients of successful management as practised in real life?

Chapter 6 deals with the issues of power, participation, hierarchy and governance, examining the evolution of these concepts over time as the case study NGOs grow from small groups of like-minded friends into large institutions advocating governmental policy change and operating in dozens, and in some cases, thousands of villages. While many of our participating NGOs were the brainchild of a single charismatic individual, we have left the issue of leadership to the end. The leaders and questions of leadership, of course, are a leitmotif throughout the book, so in a sense Chapter 7 is a drawing together of what has been said about leadership in the first six chapters. Had the book been written ten years ago, some of the leadership discussion would have been more tentative. The organizations, of course, were all much younger then, their future less secure. But there has always been talk about 'the guru syndrome' and whether institutions built by strong, dynamic individuals can survive their passing. Building on earlier chapters, Chapter 7 studies the extent to which our case study NGOs actually *were* built by an individual, whether leaders run true to indigenous and external ideas about the 'guru', and what has happened to the organizations that have passed through a leadership change. A final chapter draws together some of the lessons and cross-cutting issues that have been gleaned from the book, offering thoughts about their relevance to other organizations in South Asia and further afield.

Managing for Change is about how some of the most successful NGOs in the world are managed. Drawing on evidence from detailed case studies, it explores the reality of NGO management and shows how real people respond to real challenges. We root the story in the historical and social context of the region, examining the impact of the external environment and internal organizational culture. We then explore the systems and processes used by NGOs to promote organizational learning and to develop strategies. We conclude the story by looking at the way such organizations balance governance and strong leadership with decentralized operations and participative processes. *Managing for Change* is an evolving story about mistakes and success, vision and commitment. Most of all, it is about the people who made these important organizations what they are today.

CHAPTER 2

A DANGEROUS SEA: MANAGING THE EXTERNAL ENVIRONMENT

Ye gentlemen of England
That live at home at ease,
Ah! Little do you think upon
The dangers of the seas.

Martin Parker (*c* 1600–1656)

INTRODUCTION

South Asian NGOs, especially the older and larger ones, are often regarded as strong, stand-alone entities, institutions that in some ways operate outside the complex political and economic environments in which they work. Many seem to have risen above their external environment in order to grow and succeed. Nothing could be further from the truth, although the ways in which our case study NGOs have managed, and been shaped by, their environments offer important lessons that may not be readily apparent to the casual observer.

The first thing to note about the international environment in which both Northern and Southern NGOs work is that it has changed dramatically over the past two decades, and continues to change. The Mexican debt crisis of the early 1980s and subsequent debt crises elsewhere led to a restructuring of aid and aid thinking, and to far-reaching structural adjustment programmes throughout the developing world. As government social safety nets shrank or collapsed, new roles emerged for both Northern and Southern NGOs as service providers. The end of the Cold War and transitions from command to market economies added to already strong forces that were pushing back the state, offering further challenges and new dilemmas for NGOs.

The advent of new technologies – computers and the Internet – dramatically altered the speed of change and the ability of people to communicate with the rest of the world – if they had the money and the connectivity. And although not a new phenomenon, the pace of globalization picked up dramatically, with far-reaching and still unquantified impacts on the lives of people throughout the region. A dramatic decline in Official Development Assistance (ODA) throughout the 1990s brought additional pressures: while in some countries there was more money for NGOs, it was often at the expense of bilateral assistance, placing Southern NGOs in competition with their own governments. Growing international concern about human rights abuse in the 1980s, a rapid escalation of civil wars and complex emergencies, and an unexpected flowering of discourse on civil society – with the money to go along with it – created further challenges and opportunities, especially for Southern NGOs.

These things did not 'just happen', of course; they were the product of policies and choices that were mostly made by governmental donor agencies. Much of the environment that shaped NGOs during these years, in other words, was deliberately shaped by Northern donors, Northern policies and Northern bureaucrats.

Albert Einstein once defined the environment as 'everything that isn't me'. This chapter will reduce the definition somewhat, focusing primarily on the relationship between NGOs and their governments, their benefactors and the community of NGOs in which they play a role. It will consider the domestic political environment, as well as elements of the natural environment that have helped to shape them. First, however, it will be important to consider the social context in which NGOs ply their trade.

POVERTY

Poverty can be defined in many ways – by the levels of income, assets, calorie intake, per capita gross national product, or combinations of factors such as the United Nations Development Programme's (UNDP's) Human Development Index. Some years ago, Robert Chambers divided deprivation into different dimensions or conditions: poverty proper (lack of income and assets); physical weakness (undernutrition, sickness, disability, lack of strength); isolation (ignorance, illiteracy, lack of access to government services, remote location); vulnerability (to contingencies, to becoming poorer); and powerlessness:

> *To varying degrees these are tackled by government programmes, but vulnerability and powerlessness are neglected compared with the rest . . . Members of elites find physical weakness, isolation and poverty more acceptable and less threatening aspects of deprivation to tackle. They also appear more measurable than vulnerability and powerlessness which are less tangible, and more social and political. So there is a convergence between elite interests in limiting interventions to physical aspects of deprivation, and professional interests in measurability. Together they conspire to concentrate planning, programmes, policy and debate on physical weakness, isolation and poverty, and to neglect vulnerability and*

*powerlessness. Not surprisingly, normal professional and elite paradigms of
deprivation are predominantly physical.*[1]

Working on background for the World Bank's 2000 *World Development Report*,
Chambers refined his thinking further, interviewing a vast range of people
living in poverty, and exploring their concepts of well-being and 'ill-being'.
Freedom of choice and action, good social relations, security, enough for
a good life and physical well-being were paramount. Violence, corruption
and lawlessness were key contributors to ill-being. 'Illness, especially
catastrophic illness, stands out as a trigger for the downward slide into
poverty.'[2]

Many South Asians have never been on this slide; they have always
resided permanently at the bottom. According to the World Bank, over
500 million people in the region live in absolute poverty, on less than
US$1 a day. This represents 40 per cent of the world's absolute poor.
Hopeful reductions in poverty throughout the region during the 1970s
and 1980s were slowed or reversed in the 1990s. Poverty rates in Bangladesh and Pakistan increased, and while the rate of poverty continued
to fall in India, absolute numbers did not. Approximately 300 million
Indians continue to live in poverty, giving India the world's largest backlog
of poor people.

In South Asia, primary school enrolment is high, but staying power
is not; in East Asia, children get an average of 6.2 years of education; in
South Asia they get less than a year and a half. Health statistics are dismal
and environmental degradation is endemic. For poor women, life is
appreciably worse than it is for men. The maternal mortality rate is twice
what it is in East Asia, and the South Asian adult female literacy rate is
36 per cent, compared with 44.6 per cent in sub-Saharan Africa. UNDP's
1995 Gender-Related Development Index for South Asia was more than
40 per cent lower than for East Asia, demonstrating the huge gaps in
opportunities for women.

The rural landscape in which most South Asian NGOs work has
changed dramatically over the past four decades, and even more in the
past two. The combined populations of India, Pakistan and Bangladesh
almost doubled between 1980 and 2000, and while there has been a great
shift in the rural–urban population balance, most people remain in the
countryside. New technologies, new cropping patterns and yields, and
changes in labour intensity have resulted in tremendous change. While
feudal agricultural practices and landholding patterns are changing and
agricultural yields have increased, few of the benefits have trickled down
to the poorest. Self-employment and wage labour has grown of necessity
in most rural areas, along with increases in landlessness. In 1960 there
were a million landless people living in Pakistan. By the mid-1990s, the
number had increased to 5 million. In Bangladesh, 75 per cent of the

households were landless or near landless. In India the number was over 72 per cent, and in Pakistan it was more than 88 per cent.

Human Development in South Asia 1999 summed it up in this way:

> *South Asia remains a region divided – divided between the hopes of the rich and the despair of the poor. A region where the richest one-fifth earns almost 40 per cent of the income, and the poorest one-fifth makes do with less than 10 per cent. A region where today begins with the struggle of survival for 515 million poverty-ridden destitutes, and tomorrow threatens the future of 395 million illiterate adults. Where women are often denied basic human rights and minorities continue their struggle against prejudice and discrimination.*[3]

Poverty, environmental degradation, urban bias, the growing pressure of population, corruption, high levels of military spending and recurrent crises in governance: these are the issues that South Asian NGOs live with on a daily basis.

GOVERNMENT

The Political and Regulatory Environment

The rise of the modern South Asian NGO in the last three decades of the 20th century coincided with a period of great political turmoil in the region. India and Pakistan each had nine different governments (not counting brief interim arrangements in both countries) and Bangladesh had six. The pace of change increased in the 1990s, with five different governments each in India and Pakistan, and three in Bangladesh. Over the past 30 years, Pakistan and Bangladesh have alternated between military and civilian rule. India went through a period of 'emergency rule' in the 1970s, and several Indian states have endured severe political turmoil. Each of the countries has experienced long periods of concentrated political disorder, marked by strikes, demonstrations and civil unrest.

During this period, NGOs occasionally rose to prominence in the political consciousness, although for most politicians, NGOs have represented little more than a minor distraction. Politicians, however – and more importantly, civil servants – can be a major preoccupation for NGOs. The frequent changes of government throughout the region have resulted in a changing, uncertain and sometimes volatile regulatory environment for NGOs. Many of these regulatory changes have been considerably more than a reflection of governmental caprice. Some resulted from changes in the NGO world that seemed threatening to new governments, many of them unstable and uncertain of themselves.

One change that South Asian governments could not fail to notice was the tremendous growth in the number of NGOs and community-based organizations (CBOs). By 2000, there were an estimated 12,000 NGOs and CBOs in Bangladesh, more than 1000 of them registered with the umbrella Association of Development Agencies in Bangladesh (ADAB). Although a relatively late starter where formal NGOs are concerned, Pakistan caught up quickly in the 1990s, with several hundred registered NGOs and thousands of CBOs. In India, 10,963 NGOs received contributions from abroad in 1994[4] and these represent only a small fraction of the total NGO population.

Growth in the number of NGOs was accompanied by their increasing capacity to work effectively with the poor, often providing services that were promised, but not delivered by government. If this was not embarrassing enough for civil servants and politicians, some NGOs actively encouraged their beneficiaries to stand up to government in demanding their rights. This phenomenon took a variety of forms, from localized human rights demonstrations to national campaigns aimed at thwarting massive infrastructure projects. Indian NGOs fought a running battle with their government for many years over the Narmada Dam project; in Bangladesh NGOs fought the massive Flood Action Plan for a decade; and in Pakistan there have been a variety of skirmishes over environmentally disruptive dams and highways built by the government. While governments and donors might well have frowned on NGO criticism of specific projects, the NGO capacity for advocacy has become an important, although sometimes shaky reason for the increase in donor funding. Civil society, of which NGOs are a part, is sometimes seen as a buffer, even as an antidote to anti-democratic state behaviour. Support for the creation of a strong and vocal civil society, therefore, became part of the donor arsenal for better governance throughout the South in the late 1980s and the 1990s.

While overt political behaviour among our case study NGOs has been the exception rather than the rule, many have been directly involved in coordinated NGO efforts to resist the imposition of regulations that would impede their work. A few have taken more explicitly political positions. In Pakistan, Sungi became involved in a major advocacy campaign demanding compensation for those affected by the Ghazi Barotha Hydro Power project, and worked with community organizations to pressure the government to ban the commercial harvesting of timber. PROSHIKA organized landless groups that came into conflict with vested interests when they occupied unused land. PROSHIKA also took an overt political stand in the early 1990s during the waning days of an unpopular and undemocratic government, calling openly for its resignation. It did so again in 1996, calling for new elections during a period of civil unrest, earning itself a good name with some politicians and a bad name with

Table 2.1 *A political chronology of India, Pakistan and Bangladesh, 1971–1999*

Year	India	Pakistan	Bangladesh
1971	Civilian government in India; military in Pakistan. War: in East Pakistan the Awami League declares the independence of Bangladesh following electoral confusion. Pakistan army crackdown results in civil war; massive refugee crisis; India invades East Pakistan, resulting in the creation of Bangladesh		
1973		Election of civilian government; Zulfikar Ali Bhutto becomes Prime Minister	
1975	Indira Gandhi convicted of corruption; declares state of emergency		Sheikh Mujib killed in a coup; second coup results in military takeover
1977	Janata Party takes office following general elections	Bhutto government overthrown in military coup; General Zia ul-Haq takes power	General Ziaur Rahman takes power
1980	Indira Gandhi returns to power in general election		Zia forms political party, holds elections and is elected president
1981			Zia assassinated in abortive coup
1982			General Mohammad Ershad takes power, declaring martial law
1984	Indira Gandhi assassinated; her son, Rajiv Gandhi becomes Prime Minister		
1988		General Zia dies in plane crash. General elections; Benazir Bhutto becomes Prime Minister	
1989	Gandhi loses majority; National Front forms minority government under VP Singh		

Table 2.1 contd *A political chronology of India, Pakistan and Bangladesh, 1971–1999*

Year	India	Pakistan	Bangladesh
1990	Singh resigns and is succeeded by Janata Dal; Chandra Shekar becomes Prime Minister	President sacks Bhutto government; Nawaz Sharif becomes Prime Minister	Massive political unrest; Ershard resigns
1991	Gandhi assassinated; PV Narasimha Rao becomes Prime Minister following election of Congress-I		Khaleda Zia, widow of General Zia, becomes Prime Minister following general elections
1993		President sacks Nawaz Sharif; Bhutto re-elected as Prime Minister	
1996	General elections: Bharatiya Janata Party government resigns after 13 days; United Front under Deve Gowda forms coalition government	President sacks Bhutto; caretaker government appointed	Opposition denounces results of general elections; widespread unrest; new elections; Sheikh Hasina becomes Prime Minister
1997		Elections; Nawaz Sharif becomes Prime Minister	
1998	General elections: BJP forms coalition government		
1999	BJP coalition collapses; general elections; new BJP coalition formed	Military coup; Parvez Musharraf becomes Chief Executive	

others. While such an overt political stance was not common among Bangladeshi NGOs, **PROSHIKA** believes that development cannot be separated from obvious and clear issues of governance. This, of course, reflects the language of most bilateral and multilateral donors, all of whom put governance close to the top of the development agenda, but usually without naming names and almost never calling for governments to resign.

While for politicians some NGOs appeared to be 'going political', others seemed to be encroaching on equally sensitive government territory–money. The growth of the modern South Asian NGO was made possible in the first instance by support from Northern NGOs. By the mid-1980s, however, many Asian NGOs were receiving support from bilateral and multilateral agencies, a trend that was to grow through the 1990s. NGOs were seen by some official development agencies as a more effective way of reaching the poor than traditional funding routes through government departments. This put NGOs in a more favoured financial position, but it did little for their popularity with governments, for obvious reasons.

Government concerns about NGOs were not all fashioned from pique and jealousy, however. Many NGOs have been the creation of opportunists whose activities bear little relationship to their funding proposals. There is a joke in Pakistan about dowries. Ten years ago, it is said, a typical dowry might have included cash and some livestock. Today it is more likely to include cash, some livestock and an NGO. A Bangladeshi father is said to have written to his son studying in Europe. 'Come home', wrote the father, 'and start an NGO before it is too late.' While obviously apocryphal, such stories underline widespread concern about the bona fides of many NGOs. And in the past decade or so, a further, more sinister problem has arisen. A number of NGOs have been formed, both locally and internationally, to support fundamentalist religious causes and separatist political movements. Regulations aimed at catching sharks like these, however, have also served to catch dolphins. Many South Asian NGOs believe, in fact, that changes in the regulatory environment in all three countries have been designed to capture, or at least to tame, as many dolphins as sharks.

India, Pakistan and Bangladesh have a common colonial history, and consequently a common regulatory environment for voluntary organizations. The Indian Societies Registration Act of 1861, which predates voluntary organization legislation in almost all other countries of the world, North and South, remains the basis for NGO regulation in all three countries. Even though national and state regulations have been added, the act of 1861 continues to loom large, and there are other commonalities, including a surprising amount of shared legislative watchfulness among the three governments: when one changes, there tend to be similar changes in the others.

Few of the changes, however, have made life easier for NGOs. As an Indian study puts it, 'Each successive amendment to the Society Registration Act in different states of the country has been an attempt to further tighten the "noose around the neck" of voluntary organizations by giving unilateral and inordinate powers to the agents of the state to intervene, regulate and check the fates of voluntary organizations'.[5] India

Table 2.2 *A Chronology of South Asian NGO legislation*

Year	India	Pakistan	Bangladesh
1861	---------- The Societies Registration Act ----------		
1882	-------------- The Trust Act --------------		
1925	---------- Cooperative Societies Act ----------		
1961		Voluntary Social Welfare ----- Agencies (Registration and ----- Control) Ordinance	
1976	Foreign Contributions (Regulation) Act (FC(R)A)		
1978			Foreign Donations (Voluntary Activities) Regulation Ordinance
1982			Foreign Contributions (Regulation) Ordinance
1985	Amendment to the FC(R)A gives greater power to states		
1994	Social Welfare Agencies Registration and Regulation Act (draft)		Voluntary Social Welfare Organizations (Registration and Control) Draft Act
1999		New government regulations lead to dissolution of 1941 NGOs and CBOs in Punjab	

was the first to impose controls on international donations, an arbitrary decision made during the 1976 Emergency. India was followed by Bangladesh two years later. A series of prominent Indian cases over the years in which the foreign contributions registration of an NGO has been suspended or cancelled, have encouraged others to pay close attention to government sensitivities. A 1991 study observed that 'the Act has been amended several times since [1976] with a view to further tightening it . . . Over the last 20 years, the state has been tightening its role as a regulator and using it more often than not for limiting space, work and those types of voluntary organizations which go beyond mere provision of help and charity and welfare of the poor'.[6]

Having already imposed Indian-style regulations on NGOs during the 1980s, the government of Bangladesh introduced efforts to toughen the controls even further in 1993, giving the Ministry of Social Welfare full powers over the registration and survival of NGOs, with added authority to check undefined 'anti-state or anti-social' NGO behaviour by cancelling an organization's registration without allowing any process of appeal. In drafting a similar NGO ordinance in 1994, the government of Pakistan took as its starting point an already stringent 1961 Social Welfare Ordinance and attempted to tighten it further, giving the federal government the authority to amend an NGO's charter, dismiss its board, freeze its funds and transfer its assets. Most damaging was a proposal that would have prevented NGOs from receiving foreign funds that were not channelled directly through the government. In both Bangladesh and Pakistan, the legislation was eventually modified, but only after lengthy and concerted protest from the NGO communities and donors. A similar process took place in Pakistan during 1999. The Government of Punjab alone dissolved 1941 NGOs[7] and community-based organizations, and similar plans elsewhere were not shelved until donors protested.

In an odd reversal of fortune, the military government that took power in Pakistan at the end of 1999 appointed Omar Asghar Khan, the Executive Director of Sungi, Minister of Environment, Local Government and Rural Development. In appointing him, said the Islamabad *News*, the new government was 'sending a strong message to . . . the timber mafia in remote areas who had in the past tried to stop Sungi from functioning'.[8] What message, however, was it sending about civil society? More to the point, what was a prominent member of civil society doing in the cabinet of a military regime? Omar tried to answer the question himself, saying that the new situation offered both challenges and opportunities for civil society. But he warned against pinning too many hopes on the new government:

> *It is critical to reassert the role of civil society, which by definition is in fact the antithesis of an authoritarian state . . . The expectation that the present government will play a lead role in the process of rejuvenating democratic institutions absolves civil institutions of responsibility in this process. Civil society . . . needs to develop critical engagement with the state so that the voices of the deprived and marginalized are heard and included in developing a new social contract.*[9]

Working *with* Government

Much of the literature on Southern NGOs deals with the confrontational nature of their relationship with government. Depending on which side of the bed a writer emerges on a particular morning, the confrontational role may be seen as a good thing, an expression of civil society functioning as an antidote to the state, a key component in building democracy. Even if 'building democracy' is not uppermost in the mind of an NGO working in health or education or agricultural development, the idea of working with inefficient, autocratic government departments may be inimical to its very reason for existence. Many, if not most NGOs were formed to do things that government could not, or would not do, and they aimed to influence indirectly, by demonstration and example, rather than by direct contact. For many observers, this is the NGO's great asset: its independence from the old ways of doing things and from rigid, bureaucratic structures. It is precisely why the negative term 'non-governmental organization' has resisted all attempts at change – because NGOs are, or aspire to be, what governments are not – not rigid, not bureaucratic, not slow, not distant from the people they work with.

But the NGO detachment from government has been criticized as well. Sheldon Annis' much quoted critique of NGOs is still relevant and in the face of extreme poverty:

- 'small scale' can merely mean 'insignificant';
- 'politically independent' can mean 'powerless' or 'disconnected';
- 'low cost' can mean 'underfinanced' or 'poor quality';
- 'innovative' can mean simply 'temporary' or 'unsustainable'.[10]

In the late 1980s, in fact, 'scale' was the stick that NGOs were most often beaten with. It was argued that they could never be more than small exemplars of good practice and innovation, and that sooner or later they would have to work with government. As Edwards and Hulme put it:

> There are sound reasons for NGOs to enter into a positive and creative relationship with the institutions of both state and government. Governments remain largely responsible for providing the health, education and agricultural and other services on which people rely . . . The state remains the ultimate arbiter and determinant of the wider political changes on which sustainable development depends. Some would argue that only governments can do these things effectively and equitably . . .[11]

Some, but not all. Our case study NGOs have varied dramatically over time in their approach to working with government, ranging from a complete and deliberate detachment characterized by outright hostility, to close relationships that might be described more as marriages than anything else. Sadguru's Harnath Jagawat says that '99 per cent of NGOs complain about the government, but this is one NGO where there are no complaints on either end'.[12]

For some NGOs the relationship actually began as a marriage. The Sarhad Rural Support Corporation was founded on the initiative of individuals within the government of the Northwest Frontier Province (NWFP) of Pakistan, and if anything, it looked more like a GONGO* in its early years than an NGO. Its first executive director was seconded from the government and the chairman of its board was a senior government official. The government's purpose in helping to establish SRSC was to replicate, or to attempt to replicate, some of the impressive achievements of AKRSP (P). Taking advice from AKRSP, however, the NWFP government acknowledged and accepted its own limitations in social mobilization, flexibility and innovation. It provided start-up funding and an executive director, but from the outset, it took a remarkable hands-off approach to SRSC, treating it in much the same way as it treated other NGOs. One of SRSC's organizing techniques – the creation of linkages between village organizations and government line departments – was a major attraction for government. SRSC did not seek to supplant or avoid government; it sought to make departments more effective in their mandates. This approach was also a key feature of the Aga Khan Rural Support Programmes in both India and Pakistan. Where government services existed, attempts were made to help them to reach the target group in ways that had not been possible before.

Is SRSC an NGO? A Johns Hopkins University study of the global non-profit sector defines voluntary organizations as those which make 'a reasonable showing' in each of five categories:

1   *Formal* – the organization is institutionalized to at least some extent: probably incorporated, but at least formalized in the sense of having regular meetings, office bearers and some degree of organizational permanence.
2   *Private* – it is institutionally separate from government, although perhaps it receives government support.
3   *Non-profit-distributing* – the organization may generate a financial surplus, but this does not accrue to the owners or directors.
4   *Self-governing* – able and equipped to control and manage its own activities.
5   *Voluntary* – there is some meaningful degree of voluntary participation in the conduct or management of the organization. 'This does not

---

* GONGO: government-organized NGO

mean that all or most of the income of an organization must come from voluntary contributions or that most of its staff must be volunteers'.[13]

A 1996 evaluation found that by these standards, SRSC 'certainly qualifies as an NGO', most notably in its demonstrated financial and policy-related independence from government. Independence notwithstanding, SRSC's origins make it unique – not because it was initiated by government, but because the government of the NWFP understood that if the organization was to do the job for which it was created, it would *have* to be independent of government.

IUCN, on the other hand, is a deliberate hybrid. Founded in Europe in 1948, its members include 74 governments, 105 government agencies, more than 700 NGOs, as well as thousands of scientists and experts committed to the protection of nature. Through its council, commissions and meetings, it is accountable to a broad cross-section of institutions and individuals. Neither fish nor fowl – neither government nor pure NGO – on occasion it can take on the characteristics of an NGO, while retaining strong links with government. In Pakistan, IUCN membership includes federal and provincial government bodies as well as NGOs, including SRSC and Sungi. This unique arrangement means that IUCN has the ear of a wide range of actors. This, in turn, gave it a special advantage in developing the National Conservation Strategy (NCS), a process initiated by government in 1986, but one that would probably have been stillborn without IUCN's assistance. By devoting virtually all of its energy to the NCS, IUCN was able to make formal and informal partnerships between a wide cross-section of Pakistani NGOs, academics, business people and government institutions. The final product, adopted by the Cabinet in 1992, was regarded as 'one of the most comprehensive and thoughtful documents of its kind in the world'.[14] A 1993 review of IUCN found that both government and NGOs regarded it as highly professional, unbureaucratic and catalytic. Because its senior staff have always been Pakistani, and because it has always raised its own funding, mainly from international donor sources located in Pakistan, it is viewed by many as a thoroughly Pakistani NGO, although its international status and its relationship with government are somewhat ambiguous. This lack of clarity actually serves it well, allowing it to swim in the sea with the fishes when this makes sense, and to fly in the air with the birds when this is more appropriate.

AKRSP, India was established in part to augment and work with government service agencies in rural Gujarat. Its first Executive Director was a retired senior civil servant who had excellent ties with government and a good reputation. This gave AKRSP access to senior and working-level officials from its inception, and it attracted invitations to participate in government committees on training, forest management and water supply. Similarly, Sadguru participates in a variety of government committees and receives a significant proportion of its income from government. In 1995, a senior government official asked why Sadguru did not expand in a certain area. When he was told that the limitation was funding, the official solicited a request and within hours of receiving it, faxed his approval for a commitment of almost US$900,000.

The lesson from BAIF's experience of government is more cautionary. BAIF worked through the 1960s and 1970s with the rural poor of Maharashtra, initiating a range of rural development projects, the core of which was the cross-breeding of cattle for improved milk production. Heavily dependent on state government funding, BAIF suddenly found itself stranded when government resources were terminated in the early 1980s. Faced with the closure of 250 branches, the organization spent the ensuing years developing a more balanced donor portfolio. International donors were sought, but, more importantly, the organization spread to six other states, developing long-term agreements of seven to ten years with their governments. It has allied itself with research institutions such as the Indian Council for Agricultural Research, and it has an active programme of inviting elected officials and civil servants to visit its programmes. While there may be antipathy from some officials at a working level, the organization is careful to maintain good ties and appropriate etiquette. An external study on government–NGO collaboration in Rajasthan found several reasons for BAIF's good working relationship.

> *First, this collaboration is a fairly straightforward one; it is measurable and it is time bound. Second, the relationship is guided by a written agreement which is binding on both partners. Third, there are clear and well established procedures for forwarding proposals, review of the programme and release of the funds. Fourth, BAIF is able to meet the requirements of detailed record keeping and reports meticulously to the government. Above all, BAIF has developed a strategy of working with patience to induce changes in the system that make sense for their activities, without challenging it radically.*[15]

BAIF's President, Narayan Hegde, puts it more simply, recalling the approach of the founder: 'With government, do not criticize. We were always told by Manibhai that government is only a bureaucratic frame. You can abuse the iron frame, but don't abuse the people who are working in it . . . Make sure you understand that it is the systems that are bad, not the people.' He is clear that BAIF must respond to government, not politicians. 'And another thing,' he says, 'do not go to the government unnecessarily. And don't go to the senior person if things can be done by a junior man.'[16]

Throughout South Asia, NGO–government relationships have been shaped by the political climate of the day, and by changing perceptions of NGOs – perceptions held by government as well as by NGOs themselves. NGOs that work on a relatively small scale to alleviate suffering are not likely to attract much government attention, positive or negative. While several of our case study organizations started with limited ambitions, all have grown in both size and vision, attracting attention of various sorts. Salehuddin Ahmed, Deputy Director of BRAC, identifies three broad phases in the organization's relationship with the Bangladesh government. He sees the 1970s as the 'decade of ignoring each other'. The 1980s, on the other hand, were years of 'arrogance and jealousy', when the rapid growth of NGOs bred hostility and suspicion on both sides. He sees the 1990s as a 'decade of rapprochement', with government accepted by NGOs as the logical supplier of many services, but recognizing that it needs the cooperation of NGOs as social mobilizers for the success of government programmes.[17]

The PROSHIKA experience has been similar: a relationship marked by antipathy and hostility in the 1970s and early 1980s, mellowed into an eventual rapprochement. For PROSHIKA the thaw came during the severe 1987 and 1988 floods when it was able to assist the government in moving relief supplies quickly and efficiently. In the ensuing years, a number of small joint projects were undertaken – livestock vaccination, strip plantations, nursery development and fisheries projects. Like the Indian case study NGOs, BRAC and PROSHIKA now sit on various government committees, and their directors have put considerable personal effort into building an NGO umbrella organization that can represent broader NGO interests to government.

While it may seem, overall, that our case study NGOs have developed positive working relationships with government and that this is the way of the future, such a conclusion would be premature and somewhat facile. What the studies demonstrate is that good NGO–government working relationships can develop over time, and that in South Asia, these have improved as the NGO phenomenon has evolved and become better understood. This suggests greater maturity and confidence on the part of governments, but it also reflects greater maturity and confidence on the part of NGOs.

NGOs still exist largely at the pleasure of government, however, and it remains unclear what the longer term relationship will be. Ironically, the greatest levels of antagonism and the greatest levels of mutual admiration are found in India. Our Indian case study NGOs are generously supported by government, and India is the only country in the region with a formalized NGO support fund, administered through the Council for Advancement of People's Action and Rural Technology (CAPART). India, however, has also been the setting for major government–NGO confrontations, culminating in court cases, NGO closure and general cooptation. What the case study NGOs demonstrate is that NGOs and governments *can* work effectively together at all levels, from relief programmes, to joint development projects, to policy-level interaction on issues as mundane as tree planting and as fundamental as a national conservation strategy. From an NGO perspective, however, the relationship must be managed with caution and dexterity. An old joke comes to mind: 'How do you sleep with an elephant?' The answer: 'Carefully'.

DONORS

General

With the possible exception of BAIF, which receives substantial government financial support, none of the NGOs in this study (and few anywhere else) would exist in anything like their present form without the support they have received, and continue to receive, from international donors. This is a broad statement and it is not to suggest that all would collapse without on-going donor support. Many have developed important additional sources of income over the years – from government, from the sale of goods and services, endowments and interest income on revolving loan funds. But international donor support at key points in their early years, and donor support for scaling up over time has been an important defining feature for all of them. Donor relationships are central to the lives of most NGOs. It is odd, therefore, that donors are usually little more than names on a list, or a footnote at the end of an NGO's annual report. Equally odd is the fact that in most studies of NGOs carried out on behalf of donor agencies, the donors themselves are seldom mentioned. While our case studies aimed to correct this lacuna and to explore the nature and quality of the donor relationship, few produced more than the bland statements common to NGO annual reports.

There are perhaps two reasons for this. The first is that the average NGO is unlikely to criticize a donor publicly, and even off the record many remain cautious. The second could be that NGO–donor relationships, however complex and difficult in their detail, have been, over the years, generally positive. Looking at the broad sweep of time and the generosity of international support, there might be little reason, therefore, to delve into prickly detail. There have been dramatic shifts in donor thinking and behaviour in recent years, however, and several of our case study NGOs have benefited or suffered from the changes. The most dramatic example of both was the generous USAID funding that gave life to SRSC, and its sudden withdrawal two years later over a political dispute between the governments of Pakistan and the United States. It is worth examining in greater detail, therefore, the evolution of the donor relationship and how South Asian NGOs have managed it over time.

In the Beginning

The first international donor for most Southern NGOs is usually a Northern NGO. The largest Northern NGOs today grew out of wars and emergencies – Save the Children was a product of World War I; Plan International grew out of the Spanish Civil War; Oxfam and CARE were products of World War II. World Vision emerged from the Korean War and Médecins sans Frontières began during the Biafran War. In time, most of them added a development component to their work, and in some cases this became their predominant activity. Until the mid-1970s, however, all of them designed and managed their own programmes in developing countries. They were directly operational and, beyond support to a handful of local church-run projects, most had little contact with domestic NGOs in countries like India and Pakistan. One reason for this was arrogance – a 'we know best' attitude. Another was that there were few apparent or appropriate domestic NGOs for them to work with. Many of the most prominent South Asian voluntary organizations in the 1950s and 1960s had a welfare rather than a development approach, and looked more like soup kitchens than progressive poverty reduction development operations.

This began to change in two ways during the early 1970s. The first change came when some Northern NGOs began to realize that they could not reach the poor as quickly or as efficiently as a local organization could. Responding to the desperate plight of war-torn Bangladesh in 1971, Oxfam was a newcomer to a country in turmoil. Where it could find willing and able local partners to assist in programming, this made eminent sense. One of the first was a tiny relief operation called the Bangladesh Rehabilitation Assistance Committee – BRAC. If giving money to a local NGO was new for Oxfam, it was also new for BRAC and other fledgling domestic operations. Eventually, just as Oxfam and other international NGOs had moved beyond their own relief origins, so did BRAC, changing its name within a couple of years to 'Bangladesh Rural Advancement Committee'.* The Oxfam support, however, continued and, within a few years, working with local NGOs became a global trend among Northern NGOs. PROSHIKA was a variation on this theme, created by Bangladeshi project officers in the mid-1970s working for the Canadian NGO,

---

* In 1998, BRAC abandoned the acronym and became simply 'Brac'. The upper case was, however, retained.

'CUSO'.** In fact, the basic CUSO operation was soon converted into a freestanding, locally registered NGO, and supporting PROSHIKA's early efforts became CUSO's main raison d'être in Bangladesh.

By the mid-1980s, organizations like BRAC and PROSHIKA in Bangladesh, and AKRSP in Pakistan, were outstripping the capacity of Northern NGOs to keep up with them financially. These organizations and others throughout the region were growing in both sophistication and size. And others like them were emerging every year, increasing the competition for resources. At the same time, some bilateral development agencies noticed the trend and began to explore ways in which they might add their support to that of Northern NGOs. Some did it directly – Sida, Danida and NORAD – while others did it indirectly through a Northern NGO. As PROSHIKA began to outpace CUSO's funding capacity, CUSO – already a recipient of matching grant CIDA funds – went to its benefactor for special assistance, and new bilateral funds were eventually made available, channelled to PROSHIKA through the Canadian NGO. This type of arrangement has continued for some of our case study NGOs. The Aga Khan Foundation, for example, acts as a channel for Dutch, British and European Union funding to the AKRSPs in India and Pakistan. The Aga Khan Foundation Canada acts as a conduit for CIDA funding to BRAC.

Multilateral agencies entered the picture in the 1990s, sometimes with grants – as with UNICEF's support to BRAC's non-formal primary education programme – and sometimes through a contractual arrangement. SRSC, for example, entered into contracts with the International Fund for Agricultural Development (IFAD) and the Asian Development Bank to undertake village mobilization and conscientization as part of larger projects that these agencies had developed with government. In a variation on this theme, CIDA signed a five-year contractual agreement with IUCN in 1995 in support of the National Conservation Strategy. Two government departments and a research institute were also involved, but IUCN Pakistan was the official implementing agency on behalf of CIDA, a role that in earlier years would normally have gone to a Canadian organization or private sector firm.

Projects and Programmes

The shift from relatively small partnerships with like-minded Northern NGOs to contractual arrangements with bilateral or multilateral agencies is, for most South Asian NGOs, a leap of quantum proportions. One

_____

** Until 1981 when it also abandoned the acronym, CUSO stood for Canadian University Service Overseas.

development that made the change workable was a gradual move on the part of some donor agencies away from projects to more holistic funding arrangements. Projects make sense up to a point. They describe a discrete set of activities, a clear budget and a specific time frame. They provide a framework for planning and they allow both donor and recipient to evaluate results against clear targets. The problem with projects, however, is that they tend to reflect donor priorities and time frames more than those of the recipient or the people that they work with. And they take certain activities out of the context in which they function. Farmers do not plant according to a donor funding cycle; a preventive health programme may not function unless it is combined with curative services. By the mid-1980s, many larger South Asian NGOs were balancing a large portfolio of projects, some well funded and some badly funded, while many necessary ancillary activities and support functions were not funded at all.

One way out of this dilemma was 'programme' funding. Rather than supporting a health project or a women's project, for example, the Department for International Development (DFID) supported all AKRSP's activities in the Chitral District of Pakistan's Northern Areas. The German development organization GTZ supported the overall programme in Astore. A variation on the geographic theme is a sectoral approach. Several donors, for example, support BRAC's non-formal primary education programme (NFPE). Although this may be described in project-like terms, it differs in two important ways. First, all the components required to make the programme function are included – teacher training, the publication of textbooks, salaries for teachers and so on. Second, the full cost of the programme is supported, providing for the appropriate professional and administrative back-up rather than an arbitrary administrative percentage for overheads. Under a 'project' regime, BRAC might have been obliged to go to one donor for school construction, to another for textbooks and to a third for a training budget. In addition to making for a lopsided programme in which one component is always out of balance and out of sequence with another, the overheads allowed by one donor might be far lower than those allowed by another, making for inadequate administrative support, corner-cutting and inappropriate transfers between project budgets.

Consortia

Another innovation in recent years has been the creation of donor consortia which take a programmatic approach to everything an organiz-ation does. Pioneered by Sarvodaya in Sri Lanka in the mid-1980s with CIDA, the Norwegian Agency for Development Cooperation (NORAD), DFID and the Netherlands Organization for International Development

Cooperation (NOVIB), the consortium approach has several advantages for both donors and recipients. As with the programme approach, everything is included. Unlike geographic or sectoral compartmentalization, however, 'everything' means everything. The NGO prepares a comprehensive plan and budget covering, say, three years. A group of donors meets, discusses it with the NGO, refines, adds or subtracts, and funding is provided according to a donor's level of interest or capacity. Because each donor supports a percentage of the overall programme, each donor has the advantage of seeing the overall programme and of knowing that the whole enterprise is being adequately supported. From the NGO's point of view, in addition to providing a holistic form of financial support, a consortium can reduce the amount of time required to service donors. In the donor consortia established for BRAC and PROSHIKA, there is one set of reports, one set of donor monitors and one set of evaluators.

At least that is the principle. Donors still require the occasional 'special' evaluation and there are still streams of visiting donor representatives. The establishment of a 'donor liaison office' (DLO) can help to keep this to manageable proportions. The BRAC and PROSHIKA DLOs act as a kind of buffer, in fact, arranging visitors, monitors and evaluators in ways that meet the optimum requirements of both donors and recipient. They can interpret one to the other, help to modify reporting requirements and provide an orientation function for visitors and new donor representatives.

Although AKRSP (P) has never had a consortium, by the early 1990s it was experiencing administrative difficulties with donors. The size, complexity, geographic spread and remoteness of the areas in which it worked meant that each of almost a dozen donors had either to mount costly review missions of their own or take AKRSP's reports at face value. In 1992, at AKRSP's suggestion, the main donors established what became known as a 'Joint Monitoring Mission' (JMM), comprising team members from CIDA, DFID, NORAD, AKF, the European Union and the Netherlands Government. Continuity in the core team and regular visits over the next few years allowed the JMM to focus on issues that were important to both donors and AKRSP, to reduce the reporting burden on AKRSP, and to provide insights that would have been costly or impossible had they been attempted on an individual donor basis. The weakness of the JMM was that it reported to a loose collection of donors with similar interests, but with very different funding arrangements for AKRSP. They were not a consortium, and by 1998, many were requiring their own monitoring and evaluation missions in addition to the JMM. Regardless of the quality of JMM reports, this defeated one of its main purposes, which was to reduce the evaluative burden on AKRSP. As a result, by 1999 the JMM had become peripheral rather than central to AKRSP's relationship with its donors.

In India, Sadgurgu has experimented with another mechanism to reduce the stream of visitors and to increase the confidence of its supporters – an 'Advisory Council' of donors and government officials. Initiated in 1991, the council had 26 members by 1999, meeting once a year to review strategies, programmes and funding, and to debate future directions.

Buffering Strategies

While donors often refer to their support for NGOs as 'building civil society', much of the relationship is contractual and output-oriented. An NGO is funded to do what the donor wants and some of its own priorities can easily go missing. From the donor point of view, consortia, joint monitoring missions, programme funding and advisory councils are all mechanisms that provide greater transparency and reduced levels of administration. From the NGO point of view, they are that and more. Essentially they are buffering strategies that help to protect core activities from undue outside interference and from the inherent instability of the funding regime.

Alnoor Ebrahim examines a number of other buffering techniques that he terms 'symbolism', 'selectivity' and 'professionalization'.[18] Symbolism refers to the formal gathering of the information – through monitoring, evaluation and research – that is necessary for building donor confidence, even if it is sometimes irrelevant to the way an NGO actually makes decisions. 'Self-criticism,' he says, 'when present at all, is minor, and there is a tendency to highlight success while downplaying negative events.' He quotes a senior evaluation officer in Sadguru: 'I don't write anything negative about the organization because it may put us at a disadvantage with funders'. While failures may be well known and incorporated into future planning, Ebrahim argues that these are seldom made public in the formal reporting systems established for donors.

Ebrahim's 'selectivity' refers to the donor desire for, and the NGO willingness to supply, 'product data' rather than 'process data'. Donors have a tendency to focus on the quantifiable: how many check dams, how many tubewells, how many children vaccinated. These may or may not be tied to a longer term result such as reduced poverty or reduced child mortality, but the process of getting to dams and tubewells and vaccinated children is usually missing from the data. This serves to entrench two problems, according to Ebrahim. The first is a reinforcement of on-going:

process-product tensions in which the rhetoric (especially of funders) emphasizes the importance of process issues in development, but standard reporting is biased towards products (ie physical and financial targets). And second, they produce insider-outsider tensions in which NGO members (the 'insiders') view funders (the 'outsiders') as being out of touch with ground realities.

The danger lies not so much in donor–recipient tensions, however, as in the possibility that product will overshadow process in reality. Ebrahim quotes a senior AKRSP (I) manager:

[In] the last three years I've had only one mission – it was like a bloody cricket match – and that was to reach 100 per cent target achievement . . . What you review determines very much what you do. If you review targets, you end up doing targets.[19]

To their credit, many donors have begun to move away from output targets, placing greater emphasis on 'results'. This too can be problematic, however, especially where the intended result – such as a demonstrable correlation between health or education and poverty reduction – falls outside the donor time frame. The heightening donor desire for concrete measurables may also serve to diminish some of the fundamental NGO hallmarks: innovation, experimentation, risk-taking. And it could move NGOs away from poorer people and communities where success is more difficult, more expensive and more time-consuming.

The 'logical framework analysis' (LFA), much beloved of donor agencies, reinforces the problem. Although it is supposed to be flexible and iterative, more often than not it becomes a blueprint against which activities and results will be measured, months and years after it is written. It describes the results to be achieved and the indicators against which these will be measured, but it rarely if ever discusses process. It assumes that all stakeholders – donors and recipients – understand what the process of development is, and it is almost always based on the assumptions of stability, predictability and controllability, leading to one result: success. There are two ways of dealing with the 'success problem' where product targets are concerned. The first is to underestimate achievements in advance so that success in reaching targets is more assured. The second is to exaggerate achievements after the fact and to downplay problems. Whatever method is used, because the LFA is a necessary part of most donor–recipient relationships, it becomes a ritualistic part of symbolism and selectivity.

According to Ebrahim, a third buffering strategy is professionalization – the hiring of engineers, social scientists, managers and computer experts. This is a universal trend among NGOs, required not so much by donors as by the needs that NGOs seek to address. It does, however, serve an additional purpose – to smooth communications between NGOs and funders:

These professionals share with funders a common development language – terms such as participation, sustainability, cost benefit analysis, impacts, indicators and so on. Thus, the professionals are able to communicate their activities in terms acceptable to funders. By justifying their work in terms of a dominant currency, the NGOs are able to deter probes into their work.[20]

If this sounds devious, it is no less so than the behaviour of donor agencies that permit few insights into their own management and inner workings; that provide few explanations for late funding, delayed decisions, policy and staffing discontinuity and a propensity for cherry-picking. IUCN's Aban Kabraji talks about the problem of balancing two sets of constituencies, one demand-based and the other supply-based:

The demand-based constituency is the one to whom we must deliver our services – government, NGOs, the people for whom we work; the supply side is the funding agency or donors. The real challenge is to try to balance these two, matching demand with supply and still maintaining the integrity of purpose in terms of one's own organization, mission and strategy . . . It was less of a challenge when funding flows were more flexible, but [today] it is much more difficult . . . especially when you realize that your financier has totally different agendas and objectives.[21]

In fairness, however, perhaps Kabraji's IUCN colleague, Stella Jafri, should have the last word on donor relations, which she believes can be constructive and mutually beneficial:

Some donors, usually from smaller countries, do work in a true partnership mode, helping to define and shape the conceptual design of programmes, and building in a degree of flexibility which allows for an interactive approach to the mutual satisfaction of both parties.[22]

THE BANGLADESH CONTEXT: SOMETHING DIFFERENT?

There is much speculation about why so many domestic NGOs have developed in Bangladesh, and why a handful have risen to such regional and international prominence. Where NGOs are concerned, Bangladesh left from the same starting gate as Pakistan, yet within ten years of its independence in 1971, the old-fashioned welfare organizations that characterized the pre-1970s Pakistani voluntary sector had been completely surpassed by a throng of vibrant young activist organizations. It took another two decades for a similar generation of Pakistani NGOs to emerge. In India, the NGO sector is huge and its roots are deeper than its counterparts in Pakistan and Bangladesh, but Indian NGOs have generally been overshadowed by the achievements and growth of their Bangladeshi counterparts, despite the fact that India has eight times the population.

A satisfactory answer is unlikely to be found in the national Bangladeshi character because Bangladeshis were there long before 1971. Nor is the answer likely to be cultural, as the 75 million Bengalis in India have not created anything like a BRAC or a PROSHIKA or a Grameen Bank. Nor is the answer to be found in religion, at least not in a comparison between Pakistan and Bangladesh. Most of the answers have to do with context. In the early 1970s and since, the needs in Bangladesh were great. It is too easy for outsiders to forget that as many as a million Bangladeshis died in the war that gave the country birth. Ten million became refugees and when they went home, they returned to lives that were already marked by destitution. Neither the new government, nor the myriad new aid agencies that arrived with unprecedented levels of funding, were even remotely able to meet the challenge. Not surprisingly, the independence movement spawned a cadre of young activists who wanted to help to rebuild their communities, or in some way to contribute to the creation of their new country. The drive and energy of the youth who formed the core of the first post-independence NGOs cannot be underestimated.

Donor funding was available of course, but to suggest that these early organizations, many of which are household names in today's NGO world, were only in it for the money is as invidious as it is erroneous. Nevertheless, without the unprecedented levels of donor money, none could have become as large and successful as is the case. The sheer volume of donor funding, therefore, sets Bangladesh apart from both India and Pakistan. There are obviously other factors, however. One is the unified nature of the Bangladesh Government. The federal structures in India and Pakistan add a layer of governmental bureaucracy and control that has undoubtedly been inhibiting to NGO growth. And, despite its efforts to control NGOs, the Bangladesh Government has never imposed the draconian constraints that have occasionally characterized state, provincial and national behaviour in India and Pakistan. The size of the country is also a factor: Bangladesh is relatively small and, despite serious communications problems, most areas are accessible from Dhaka in less than a day. Another more important factor relates to cultural and economic homogeneity. Over 90 per cent of the population shares the same language, the same religion, the same traditions. And while there are great economic disparities between the haves and the have-nots, these are nothing like the feudalism and the economic disparities inherent in Indian or Pakistani society. In Bangladesh, only 7 per cent of the population own more than 5 acres, and 10 acres defines a major landholder.

Finally, because poverty is so deep and so widespread, and because it is not greatly dissimilar from one part of the country to the next, it has been possible to replicate health or education or agricultural programmes from one village to the next without having to alter them dramatically for linguistic, cultural, religious or social considerations. The process of group mobilization can be similar throughout the country, an impossibility in either India or Pakistan.

NGO RELATIONSHIPS

NGOs throughout South Asia live with another problem: jealousy. Most successful NGO leaders receive poison pen letters and even death threats as a matter of course. They are frequently accused of religious heresy, of treason, of communism or capitalism, theft, corruption and sexual misconduct. In some cases, the trigger is a vested interest that has been challenged; in others it is a disgruntled employee. But often it is pure jealousy. Starting in the late1950s, Abdul Sattar Edhi began to provide assistance to the destitute of Karachi, eventually creating a large national foundation with a vast network of hospitals, ambulance services and rehabilitation centres. Throughout Pakistan his selflessness is widely known and respected. His 1996 autobiography catalogues a lifetime of achievement, but it is also a sad chronicle of attacks, vilification and abuse. 'Two out of three people were hostile to my accomplishment, always ready to oppose me,' he writes.[23] Barring the occasional letter to the editor, usually there is little an NGO can do about this, deriving strength from accomplishments and inner light rather than discouragement from detractors. Occasionally, however, animosity can get out of hand. Such was the case in Bangladesh during the mid-1990s when religious zealots smeared all NGOs with charges of heresy and launched physical as well as political attacks on their work. This story is told in greater detail in Chapter 5.

Relationships with Other NGOs: the Prisoner's Dilemma

In contrast with the 1970s, donors today often complain about the surfeit of South Asian NGOs, about their inability or unwillingness to cooperate with each other, and about the duplication of effort and the reinvention of wheels. From the NGO side, there is frustration as well. Aban Kabraji says that the most difficult alliances are not those with donors or government, but with other NGOs: 'Levels of competition, threat, fear, mistrust – it has always been the case; mostly it has been the big versus the small ones. We being a big one, are seen as the big fish against the smaller ones, but it is not only big versus small. I can't develop proper relations even with [my peers] . . .'[24]

Game theorists have found many ways to describe failure to cooperate for mutual benefit, a problem of varying degrees in all societies. In the tragedy of the commons, no herder can limit the grazing of others, but if he limits his own grazing, he alone loses. In public good theory, everyone benefits from, say, clean air, whether or not an individual contributes. Many, therefore, do not contribute, causing problems for all. However, it is the prisoner's dilemma which may best explain the hesitancy of NGOs to cooperate with their counterparts. As Robert Putnam describes it:

> *In the prisoner's dilemma, a pair of accomplices are held incommunicado, and each is told that if he alone implicates his partner, he will escape scot-free, but if he remains silent, while his partner confesses, he will be punished especially severely. If both remained silent, both would be let off lightly, but unable to coordinate their stories, each is better off squealing,* no matter what the other does.[25]

What this means in NGO terms is that most are caught in individual, competitive and proprietorial relationships with donors and governments, rarely sharing lessons and substantive intelligence with each other. The lack of cooperation between NGOs is not restricted to South Asia. The particular Asian problem, however, has to do in part with governments which, as shown above, have a history of unpredictability and instability throughout the region. Donors must also take a large measure of responsibility for creating and cultivating a 'silo' mentality among Asian NGOs because of the donors' own unwillingness to coordinate among themselves, and because of the competitive patron–client relationship they establish with their 'partners'. As the dominant relationships for these NGOs tend to be vertical – upward with donors and government, and downward with their beneficiaries – they are characterized, as Putnam puts it, 'by dependence instead of mutuality, [and where] opportunism is more likely on the part of both patron (exploitation) and client (shirking)'.[26] Putnam and others have argued that it is the horizontal networks of civic association that build social capital and a willingness to cooperate for mutual benefit. This is the essential meaning of civil society – not a collection of individualistic, stand-alone organizations, rather collaborative networks based on the norms of reciprocity and collective action.

Putnam explains that:

> *the strategy of 'never cooperate' is a stable equilibrium, for reasons that are well explicated in standard accounts of the prisoner's dilemma. Once trapped in this*

situation, no matter how exploitative and backward, it is irrational for any individual to seek a more collaborative alternative, except perhaps within the immediate family . . . Actors in this social equilibrium may well realize that they are worse off than they would be in a more cooperative equilibrium, but getting to that happier equilibrium is beyond the power of any individual.[27]

Of course NGOs are not prisoners, donors are not to blame for all their dilemmas, and game theory does not excuse their lack of cooperation. Besides, there is good evidence that it is possible to transform isolationist situations over time. In Bangladesh, the threat of new and draconian government regulation brought NGOs together in the early 1990s, turning a somewhat conventional NGO talk shop – the Association of Development Agencies of Bangladesh (ADAB) – into a more strategic alliance. In order to validate and protect its work on Pakistan's National Conservation Strategy, IUCN created a network of other NGOs and business leaders, in addition to its work with government agencies. While smaller 'fish' may still be suspicious of IUCN, environmental issues are much more prominent on the Pakistani NGO agenda than it is in India or Bangladesh, and informal networks now form and re-form to fight environmental threats posed by the private sector or by government-planned roads and dams. The youngest NGO in our study, Sungi, has perhaps been one of the most active in the use of networks. Saneeya Hussain observes that 'Sungi's role as an advocacy and development NGO has been largely defined by the relationships it has had with other key players in the NGO sector and civil society at large'.[28] It has done this in three ways: by creating networks for specific purposes around a particular environmental issue; by working with other organizations (including IUCN) on collaborative projects, and by mentoring smaller organizations.

Many of our case study NGOs have heard the frustration of smaller NGOs and have tried to find ways of working with them more actively. BRAC has assisted many in replicating its non-formal primary education project and has offered a programme to train the managers of smaller organizations in strategic planning. PROSHIKA also offers training programmes and secondments on women in management, and on their approach to sustainable development. Sadguru looks at growth in various ways. One is its own growth. But growth can also occur through the spread of its approach and technologies, and it works closely with smaller organizations on natural resources management, especially in tribal areas. In 1998, with Irish and Norwegian support, it began to work with Ethiopian professionals, training them in the Sadguru approach.

The Dutch NGO, NOVIB, supports an exchange visit programme, bringing people from NGOs in the Middle East, Latin America, the former Soviet Union, and other countries in Asia and elsewhere, to study and learn from both PROSHIKA and BRAC. In Pakistan, AKRSP was the model upon which SRSC was established. SRSC's first Executive Director understudied the AKRSP process for months, and several of the organization's key staff were seconded from AKRSP. AKRSP was also the model for a National Rural Support Programme (NRSP), founded by AKRSP's first Director, Shoaib Sultan Khan, after his retirement from AKRSP.

CONCLUSIONS

Suffice to say, the modern South Asian NGO movement came into being over three decades of dramatic social transformation, chronic political instability and at a time of considerable change in donor thinking. Where government is concerned, several of the case study NGOs began with a close relationship, two with an antipathetic if not hostile relationship, and one or two with no relationship whatsoever. Gradually, all have moved closer to government, partly as a defence mechanism, partly because cooperation has been more productive for their beneficiaries than competition, and partly because donors have encouraged it. 'Better' relationships, however, are not always the same as 'good' relationships. Improvements notwithstanding, most South Asian NGOs continue to exist at the pleasure of government, and even the largest and most successful suffer from governmental unpredictability. Relationships may be highly personalized, especially at a programming level, where a friendly and constructive government officer may be followed by the precise opposite. Relationships with the Ministry of Health may be excellent, while those with the Ministry of Agriculture may be dismal. Operations in one state or province or thana may be friendly and productive, while in another the NGO may be fighting with a local official for the very survival of its programmes.

One defence mechanism has been the creation of informal groupings on sectoral issues and more formal coalitions, such as ADAB in Bangladesh, or the Sarhad NGO Itehad in Pakistan's Northwest Frontier Province. Participation in national and international fora is another defence mechanism. In 1997, BAIF's President was serving on ten national and state technical committees. In 1998, Sadguru was represented on ten district government committees, nine state committees and five national committees. IUCN's Country Representative served for several years on the Board of the International Institute for Sustainable Development; BRAC's Executive Director has served on many boards and committees, including the World Bank's NGO Liaison Committee. As their organizations matured, all of the case study leaders travelled extensively, not just to 'service the donors' but to stay abreast of changes in the international development world, to 'see and be seen', and to build alliances that could prove helpful in the years ahead.

Donor support has been both advantageous and problematic in shaping NGO relationships with government. When assistance was provided mainly by Northern NGOs, government took little notice. As bilateral and multilateral agencies began to support South Asian NGOs in the mid-1980s, some governments viewed this as direct competition. In financial terms they were right – it *was* competition, although the amounts were rarely significant as far as either donor agencies or governments were concerned. Perceptions of competition aside, bilateral and multilateral agencies, on occasion, have been important allies for South Asian NGOs in other ways, especially when restrictive new legislation has been proposed. On at least one occasion in Pakistan and one in Bangladesh, bilateral donors stepped in, successfully persuading governments to modify their plans.

With the exception of BAIF, which expanded mainly with support from state governments, it was changes in the thinking of bilateral donors that led to the dramatic growth of all the case study NGOs. Most began with a handful of Northern NGO supporters. Apart from the Aga Khan Foundation and NOVIB, most of these had moved on to different pastures by the 1990s, and bilateral agencies had, for the most part, taken up the challenge. Bilateral donors have been generous, but not unproblematic. Frequent changes in personnel make for weaker relationships; formal contracts replace NGO-to-NGO partnerships; opaque decision-making and distant priority-setting mean that funding for the 'next phase' is almost always worrisome. Precipitous withdrawal, while not common, can be disastrous, or – as in the case of SRSC and USAID – near fatal. Our case study NGOs have sought to modify these problems in a variety of ways. All have attempted to diversify their donor portfolio, so that a single dramatic change will not be overwhelming. Some (BRAC, PROSHIKA, Sungi) have created donor consortia which help to build donor understanding and solidarity, and a more secure base for overall institutional support. Others have experimented with 'joint donor monitoring missions' (the two AKRSPs, Sadguru), and Sadguru has created a Donor Advisory Committee which includes government as well as international donor representatives. These 'buffering' techniques and others help to bridge the gaps in understanding, in priorities and in funding that inevitably exist between donor agencies and their recipients, each of which must balance a variety of competing (and sometimes irreconcilable) accountabilities and pressures. If there is a lesson for donors in this, it is that a reduced emphasis on formal systems, in favour of greater transparency, alacrity and coordination on their part, would go a long way to improve the chance that development objectives will be met.

There are two areas in which management of the external environment remains somewhat stunted, even among the oldest and largest of the case study NGOs. The first is their relationship with other NGOs.

Most have begun building bridges, mentoring smaller organizations, working in coalitions with their peers around issues of political or sectoral importance. But vertical relationships – upwards with donors and governments, and downwards with beneficiaries and village organizations – remain the norm. This may be inimical to the creation of more horizontal civic engagement and the building of stronger civil societies, but NGOs alone cannot be blamed for centuries of patron–client feudalism, nor for the asymmetric patron–client relationship of the international aid regime.

A second area of underdevelopment is the weakness of the NGOs' local donor base. This is a stick that Southern NGOs are often beaten with, somewhat unfairly. While there is a great deal of private wealth in South Asia, the rich did not get rich by giving their money away. What philanthropy there is tends to be heavily welfare oriented, aimed at the creation of hospitals and orphanages and at religious causes, rather than at longer term development. It is nevertheless true that many Pakistanis, Indians and Bangladeshis *do* give to hospitals and orphanages, demonstrating that local philanthropy exists. Sadguru was initiated by the Mafatlal Group of Industries, which continues to support BAIF. The multimillion dollar Edhi Foundation in Pakistan was created and is sustained to a large extent by private donations. As long as there are alternatives, however, such as international donors, the incentive for NGOs to build a local donor base remains weak. The effort required to persuade a NORAD or a NOVIB to support a million-dollar project is considerably less onerous than that required to generate the same level of support from local individuals.

To their credit, however, several of the case study NGOs have developed alternative sources of independent income. A few have created endowments, although these remain relatively small, victims of donor apathy and a preference for spending on needs *now*, rather than in the future. Some, over time, have built up a large asset base, including property, buildings and revolving loan funds that will provide longer term economic security and income. The microcredit operations of some, such as BRAC, PROSHIKA and SRSC, have become largely self-financing, reducing the need for donor support to core programmes. Some have experimented with efforts to earn income, although only BRAC has taken such efforts to scale. BRAC Cold Storage and BRAC Printers were established to support agricultural and educational programmes, but their services proved saleable beyond their own limited universe. Disappointed by the low volume taken up by alternative trading NGOs in Europe, BRAC created its own handicraft outlets in Bangladesh, and now supports over 30,000 rural artisans in a multimillion dollar domestic handicraft market. In 1998, a BRAC dairy was established, taking advantage of the withdrawal of milk subsidies in the European Union. The dairy provides new income for thousands of villagers, requiring little in the way of donor support because the economic basis was secured from the outset.

This chapter has shown that South Asian NGOs sail on a dangerous sea, one fraught with peril and unpredictability. It has also shown that successful NGOs have learned how to navigate the sea, taking a balanced approach to government, donors and critics. They spread their risks as widely as possible, rarely confronting a threat head-on. While they have developed a variety of navigational tools, perhaps their greatest asset in managing the external environment is time. Time is the enemy of politicians and the undoing of forgetful donor agencies. Governments change and donors depart, but NGOs, at least those in our case studies, have a lengthening perspective, and memories that serve them – and more importantly, their beneficiaries – well.

CHAPTER 3

SYMBOLS AND SYSTEMS: ELEMENTS OF ORGANIZATIONAL CULTURE

Come, ye comet,
Come to build a bridge of fire across the dark,
Hoist up on the castletop of evil days
Your flag of victory!
Let omens be carved on the forehead of the night,
Awaken, startle those that drowse.

Rabindranath Tagore

We now shift our attention from the external environment to the more intimate aspects of an organization's internal environment. We will approach this by starting with a question about whether NGOs are unique organizations. Some argue that they are unlike others because of their particular values and their distinctive mission. Yet they share behavioural characteristics that are common to all organizations, irrespective of motives or goals. NGOs, like any other type of organization, can be seen as an inclusive collection of human behaviours. They are certainly distinguished by their purpose, but they have established systems and structures, and they employ staff and resources to achieve their purpose. Their organizational behaviour is partly the product of the local environment, partly of mission and values. But they are also shaped by the way the people within them work and socialize together. This chapter explores the dynamics of this process in South Asian NGOs, and it also highlights the role of formal systems in facilitating and creating an effective and purposive organizational culture.

In subsequent chapters we will explore the issues of leadership, strategies, structures and governance. These are important, but our research has demonstrated how dependent well-managed NGOs are on the way that staff and volunteers interact and work together. Obviously mission, purpose and values are major determinants of this. But it is striking how formal human resource systems are used increasingly among our case study NGOs to promote a strong organizational culture and to influence individual performance. This in turn raises questions about the continuing usefulness of traditional NGO values and personal commitment in motivating staff and volunteers.

Evidence from our case studies raises a number of important questions. Can NGOs continue to rely on values and personal commitment to determine staff performance? If not, is this a function of size and complexity? Is belief in the cause, and concern about inequity and exploitation sufficient to motivate staff? To what extent are pay, promotion and training important determinants of individual performance and personal behaviour? In other words, are NGOs becoming more like other organizations in the way they use human resources to build a distinctive culture? And if so, is this a good thing or a bad thing in terms of overall organizational aims and objectives?

ORGANIZATIONAL CULTURE

In very simple terms, organizational culture is the glue that holds organizations together, often in the face of adversity. As with so many aspects of management, there is a diversity of definition. To some, organizational culture is about 'how things get done around here'. To others it is 'a shared sense of meaning, shared understanding, and shared sense-making', while to others it is merely 'a metaphor for organizational life'. Most NGOs have a distinct cultural identity; this chapter attempts to identify the key characteristics of this culture, and the common cultural attributes of successful South Asian NGOs.

Evidence from our participating organizations suggests that organizational culture is a product of the interaction of five distinct elements. First are personal values and the assumptions that lie behind them. Second are the symbolic properties of culture, in particular the formal language of mission statements. But important too are rituals, artefacts and stories associated with a particular organization. A third element is the maturity or age of the organization. Fourth is the way that groups and teams work together, both formally and informally. The fifth element is the collection of formal policies and practices articulated and used by an organization.

Anyone trying to understand the dynamics of an organization needs to appreciate the impact of all five elements. Organizational culture is the key to explaining how NGOs cope with change while continuing to grow. The public face of this culture can be found in organization charts, mission statements and policy documents. In our case study NGOs, many of these structures and systems, such as human resource policies, were not formalized until the mid-1990s. Until then, informal, ad hoc systems were the norm in many, and institutional culture was dependent on, and reflective of, the personal intervention or interest of the founder.

It is useful, perhaps, to ask whether these new policies and systems have added or detracted from the quality of organizational life. They may provide clarity, transparency and objectivity, but in doing so they can threaten the informality and flexibility of the old order. They may inhibit personal commitment, shift the balance of power and actually constrain organizational behaviour. Charles Handy argues that the way an organization is constructed, the systems it uses and the management style it adopts are crucial to an understanding of how it works.[1] Others believe that there are specific and tangible 'attributes of success' that are common to all successful organizations. In their study of the key cultural character-istics common to 'excellent' companies, Peters and Waterman highlighted a number of common attributes – for example, the ability to stay close to customers or to maintain focus by 'sticking to their knitting'.[2] One of the challenges in our study was to identify attributes that are common to the organizational culture of successful NGOs in South Asia. Some of these follow.

VALUES AND ASSUMPTIONS

Any analysis of an organization's culture needs to go beyond the 'espoused' views of staff and volunteers, and to dig into how culture is enacted in personal behaviour. It is clearly important to understand how shared values and shared assumptions influence the way that staff perform. Edgar Schein has raised awareness of the way that such values and assumptions impact on organizational culture. He highlights the role of the 'assump-tions that lie behind the values' of an organization, arguing that these assumptions are developed and shared over time. They determine the behavioural patterns and visible artefacts that are commonly shared within an organization.[3]

NGOs traditionally have attracted staff with deeply held values based on concerns about human rights, equity and justice. They also hold certain basic assumptions about the way that NGOs should work. These are commonly derived from notions of participation, empowerment and sustainability. In practical terms this is reflected in a preference for collective decision-making, consensus and a general suspicion of 'manage-ment', as manifested in controls and systems. Strongly held beliefs of individual staff members can result in personal values overriding the strategic intent of an NGO, and can place personal agendas at odds with wider organizational imperatives. This in turn can lead to the creation of informal groupings with their own informal power structures, coalitions and unwritten rules of operation.

What is striking from our case studies is the diversity of core values. While there is a common commitment to help the poor and disad-vantaged, the values that underpin NGO approaches to development vary. Some, such as Sadguru or the two AKRSPs, highlight professionalism and the quality of their work, as exemplified by a strong work ethic, discipline, accountability and the efficient use of resources. Staff of AKRSP Pakistan cite the first general manager, Shoaib Sultan Khan, as having created a culture that stressed honesty, hard work, discipline and commitment. Staff in AKRSP India refer to their culture as 'professional and caring'. Harnath Jagawat, Director of Sadguru, feels that such values are key to the identity of his NGO. He says that 'since we are an NGO, we should be above suspicion in our performance'. He believes strongly that NGOs should be fully accountable for every rupee they receive.[4]

In contrast, while remaining fully accountable for their spending, PROSHIKA and Sungi place greater emphasis on mutual trust, empowerment and participative interaction. Thus, Sungi staff identify core organizational values based on a participative philosophy that encourages openness, accountability and trust. PROSHIKA's values highlight empowerment, participation and faith in the abilities of the poor. Its President, Qazi Faruque Ahmed, says that these are based on a fundamental belief that the poor 'are able to maximise the most, with minimum opportunities, and that given the opportunity, not only will they improve their own situation, they will improve the situation of the entire country'.[5]

In some cases the cause can take on a political or even a spiritual character. For example, Gandhian principles are inherent in the way that BAIF works. Manibhai Desai, the founder, was a close disciple of Gandhi. But he firmly believed that faith and commitment were not enough, and that the poor would benefit as much from scientific advances as from good intentions. He was able to merge the scientific approaches needed for cattle breeding and horticulture with the spirit of Gandhian philosophy. Much of BAIF's success can be traced to Manibhai's capacity to maintain this strong philosophical strand, while at the same time introducing innovative technologies and science. In this regard, Manibhai was able to 'make Gandhi come alive', while still meeting the technical needs of the community.

Through the 1990s, there was a growing understanding of the importance of adaptation and change. One approach has been to emphasize the importance of learning as a core organizational value, as BRAC has done, devoting a considerable proportion of its budget to training and staff development. Other agencies have recognized that they too must develop a set of values that will help them to cope with change. Thus, AKRSP India has invested in efforts to reinforce an organization-wide understanding of its 'vision, ethos, values and mission'. This acculturation process depends on improved communications, rewards for quality work, increased investment in training and learning, and constant reinforcement of core values – hard work, honesty and a respect for the communities with which employees work.

ORGANIZATIONAL SYMBOLS: MISSION, RITUALS AND STORIES

There is a growing appreciation of the influence of the symbolic properties in organizational culture. Organizations are shaped by formal symbols and messages, but they are also shaped by informal rituals and stories that develop over time. Andrew Pettigrew has referred to these as the 'expressive social tissues' that give meaning to activity.[6] These are not incidental or trivial; they are powerful symbolic expressions of the core values and emotional drives that determine organizational cultures. They can be symbolic statements of purpose, such as mission statements, logos or public images; alternatively, they may take the form of rituals, stories or shared myths.

Take mission statements as one such formal symbol of purpose and direction: mission statements are now part of the NGO landscape and, over the last ten years, most in our study developed one (if not several). Good practice suggests that a mission statement should consist of two essential components. The first is a statement of common values held by people in the organization. The second is an explanation of why the organization exists and who benefits from it. Missions are, as Mike Hudson notes, 'concerned with both the hearts and the minds. The beliefs that comes from the heart, and the rationale that comes from the mind'.[7] All organizations have missions, even though they are often implicit and not written down. But how influential are such symbolic statements in influencing staff performance? Do they shape organizational culture, or are they merely reflective of it?

In some cases, mission statements are derived from a wider organization. IUCN Pakistan has a relatively focused mission statement as part of the global IUCN emphasis on environmental issues. In other cases, the wording of a mission statement may change over the years, but the inner essence remains the same. In the case of PROSHIKA, the core philosophy is based around the concept of empowerment through human development. The wording has been through a number of iterations, partly reflecting the increasing sophistication of PROSHIKA's work. But it also reflects the federal nature of the organization, with an emphasis on shared discussion, empowerment and collective decision-making.

There is much debate in the management literature (and some in the previous chapter) about the value and role of mission statements. Are they of any practical value? Are they merely a glib communication device or are they a symbolic statement of intent? We will return to this question in greater detail in Chapter 5. Whatever the strategy, however, communicating it clearly can be an important determinant of organizational success. Obviously one of the major challenges for an NGO is to ensure that staff are motivated and committed to both mission and strategy. This becomes all the more important as the organization grows, with more staff and a wider geographical spread of operation. Barry Underwood, Chief Executive of AKRSP, India, emphasizes the value of a clear, understandable and motivational mission statement. It should be visible, readable and memorable. He views the mission statement as 'something that we constantly go back to . . . I keep referring to it again and again, as do staff in the field. It has been a strong motivational force for the organization and a strong orientating force for people coming into the organization'.[8]

Theory suggests that the bigger the organization, the more important the mission statement as a mechanism for reinforcing staff awareness of the purpose and intent of the organization. It is also possible, however, that such statements could merely be symbolic utterances with little practical significance. As noted in the previous chapter, NGOs have developed a number of buffering strategies to protect them from outside interference. One could be the symbolic use of mission statements to placate donor demands for an overall statement of purpose, with little relevance to the everyday working reality of the organization. We will return to this issue in Chapter 5, which deals with strategy formulation.

Whatever their impact and relevance, it is clear that there are a variety of symbols, rituals and stories that have no formal role but are nevertheless embedded in the warp and the weft of an organization. Experience tells us that they have considerable significance in shaping staff perceptions and influencing behaviour. All organizations, for example, have a subculture of rituals, mythologies, stories, humour, even informal dress codes that impact on daily life. Rituals and stories reinforce shared values and can help to bond disparate elements together. For example, every morning all Sadguru staff gather together for a five-minute prayer meeting, reflecting on the message of 'the Sadguru', and praying for the strength and energy to carry on his work. In the same vein, images and stories about Manibhai are commonly heard in BAIF, acting as an ongoing reminder of his influence on the organization. His concern for discipline and time-keeping is legendary – for example:

> *If he was travelling with a group of staff, he would say the day before, 'Tomorrow we are going to start at five o'clock', but at four o'clock he would actually send somebody to make sure we were all awake, and we had to be by the vehicles at five o'clock precisely. He set an example. It was his behaviour, his simplicity, his working ability that set an example to the people.*[9]

Such stories are also powerful ways of communicating an organization's ethics. F H Abed tells of a field trip in the early days of BRAC. Returning to Dhaka from a BRAC fish project, he found two large fish in the trunk of the car. He sent a strong note back to the project, insisting on an invoice.* Similarly, a story about Gandhi insisting on paying for simple accommodation in the early days of BAIF sent a powerful and lasting message to staff about their own behaviour. Such stories become part of the folklore that shapes the culture of an organization. On a more prosaic level, many staff talk about the importance of informal discussions held during tea-breaks and how important these can be in shaping organizational thinking. Quite clearly such conversations are the foundation on which an organization's oral history is based. They are particularly important in the more personalized, informal culture that is common during the early stages of organizational growth. Individuals and their characters are still central to the organization. At this stage, small incidents have great impact, and stories about individuals and events can be both vivid and colourful. In time such stories become mythologized as people think nostalgically back to the early days, often forgetting the tensions, the long hours and the difficulties they faced. As organizations grow, however, communication systems change and the culture may be less conducive to the creation of shared myths and stories.

ORGANIZATIONAL AGE AND MATURITY

The culture of any organization is clearly shaped by a variety of influences, politics and personalities, by assumptions and ascribed values, by the legacy of history and by perceptions of future potential. Evidence from our case study NGOs suggests that management needs and organizational cultures differ according to age and maturity, or according to where an organization is in its life-cycle. Greiner first described the stages of growth experienced by most organizations, and identified the life-cycle crisis that they can expect to face.[10] Researchers have elaborated and refined this model, and some have applied it to NGOs. David Korten, for example, hypothesized that NGOs go through four generational stages, starting as welfare organizations and eventually – if they do the right thing – becoming 'social movements'.[11] Alan Kaplan has identified three stages of growth: the 'pioneer' stage; a phase of 'differentiation'; and a third

---

* There will undoubtedly be many stories about the day in March 2000 when US President Clinton did *not* visit the BRAC school at Joipura Village during his one-day state visit to Bangladesh. Although everything had been set up weeks in advance, including a military telecommunications control tower behind the school, US officials decided at the last minute that a helicopter trip across unsecured rice fields was too risky for the President. Instead, all the school children were hurriedly bussed to Dhaka, where they were able to sing a song for the visitor in the safety of the US embassy.

stage of 'integration'. The majority of the NGOs in our study are still going through a pioneer, or start-up phase, although clearly, a few, such as BRAC and BAIF, have moved on to the second or third phase of growth, becoming more systems-driven, decentralized organizations, with more collective leaderships.[12]

Evolution notwithstanding, evidence suggests that the impact of the founder is profound. In a seminal study on organization and leadership, Edgar Schein described how organizations tend to be moulded in the image of their founder.[13] The founder can, and does, determine the organization's mission, its culture and the type of staff employed. Our study suggests that such founder-leaders tend to have high levels of self-confidence and determination. They are usually quite comfortable in imposing their views on the rest of the organization, often unconsciously. Experience across South Asia suggests as well that leaders' successes are easily tested in the founder stage. If strategies fail, the organization rapidly disintegrates. If they succeed, the organization will grow, reinforcing the original assumptions.

It is therefore in the pioneer stage that the culture and strategies of many organizations are determined, with the influence of the initial leadership continuing to shape the organization over many years. In the early days, organizations may be run almost as a family unit – highly personalized and highly informal. Relationships are usually strong and there is a warm atmosphere. Leadership is held in respect and generally staff are content to follow. Decision-making is informal and intuitive. Systems are rudimentary and there are high levels of energy, motivation and commitment. Highly vulnerable to the often hostile environment in which they develop, organizations in the pioneer phase are often willingly and understandably dependent on the whim or the health of a few individuals. As the organization matures, however, the need for structures and procedures gradually eclipses informality. Staff become more confident in their own skills and abilities. They are no longer content to be mere followers; they want to be active participants. At this stage there may be a crisis of confidence in the founder-leadership.

In PROSHIKA, organizational culture has evolved over 25 years from a small, rural action research 'ad hocracy', to that of a large organization with formal structures, a complex set of programmes, a widely dispersed field staff and strong international linkages. Growth led to two particular types of change within PROSHIKA. First, there was much greater formalization in structures, systems and relationships. Second, there was at least a partial absorption of features common to the culture of other large organizations in Bangladesh: deference to seniors; a tendency to talk of policy as though it is actual practice, and a somewhat top-down approach to training. It is important to emphasize, however, that PROSHIKA's origins still exert an important influence over its culture and actions. It retains a highly personalized management style, an operational orientation, a genuine concern to help the less advantaged, and it uses ad hoc teams for problem-solving. It is still marked by a degree of ad hocracy, collegial leadership, and an emphasis on 'co-ordination' rather than management. Even though PROSHIKA is today one of the largest NGOs in the world, its culture remains rooted in the early stages of maturity, bearing out the thesis that the management of change is at least partially determined by the style and attitudes of the founders.

Similarly, with rapid growth there has been a marked change in the culture of IUCN Pakistan. Among its staff there is nostalgia for the early days, and the more intimate, informal culture – one in which talented, if sometimes idiosyncratic, staff could flourish. As the organization grew, however, there was increased investment in new management systems and the creation of new layers of authority. As a result, some staff feel that the organization has become increasingly bureaucratic and top-heavy, and that senior management has become isolated from the rest of the organization. This complaint is common among organizations experiencing rapid growth. The friction in IUCN between those who are nostalgic for the early days and those promoting today's new systems-driven, expansionist culture, is played out in many NGOs around the world. The tension between the 'old guard' and 'young turks' is a common feature of NGOs faced with the challenge of growth.

And it does not always work out well. GSS was a successful Bangladeshi organization that grew very rapidly during the 1990s on the basis of a highly regarded approach to non-formal primary education. It grew too rapidly, however, tripling in size in as many years. There was none of the time taken by others in our study to acculturate new staff, to build the necessary teams, or to develop systems that could withstand public scrutiny. When factions developed among the staff, they quickly boiled over into the public arena. Donor confidence faltered, the board wavered and a government inquiry found fault. A court case ensued and, by the time the verdict was handed down in 2000, GSS had all but disappeared.

TEAMS AND TEAMWORKING

As organizations grow, there is greater emphasis on delegation, self-empowerment and teamwork. Such teams are found at all levels and are tied together by different tasks or responsibilities. BRAC's Executive Director, F H Abed, sees them as small learning sets, bound together by their 'devotion to service'. In the case of Sadguru, teams set targets, allocate work and define roles or responsibilities at a departmental level. In Sungi, management actively engenders a sense of competition between teams working in different zonal offices, regularly monitoring their performance. Such self-motivated teamworking satisfies basic psychological needs, and it helps individuals to engage constructively with others, both inside and outside the organization. Alan Fowler regards participative teamworking as a core NGO characteristic, one that is essential for developing partnerships and external relationships.[14]

Many NGOs in our study consider teamworking essential to the type of work they do. Senior staff of AKRSP Pakistan recognize that their integrated rural development work depends on interactive teamwork. The holistic nature of their efforts and the importance of community collaboration requires multisectoral teams with a variety of specialists. The importance of such team-based activity was apparent from the early days of AKRSP's work in the Northern Areas. Shoaib Sultan Khan insisted on taking the entire management team with him on visits to community leaders. An informal code of conduct was soon established. Team members were discouraged from sitting on chairs during meetings in villages. They were not to accept food. They were never to miss an appointment with village officials, and the doors of the AKRSP offices were always to remain open to villagers. Team effectiveness was measured by its degree of participation with the local community and by the way they prioritized their work. Thus, respect for the local community became integral to teamwork.

Sungi too sees teamwork as essential to its integrated community approach, and BRAC views it as central to the way it works in the field, where teams are motivated by a 'passion for development work'.[15] Commitment is important to understanding what inspires teams to work long, arduous hours. Many senior executives comment on the commitment and the hard work of their staff. While this is a strength, however, it can also be a potential weakness. Organizations value the energy that comes with commitment, but, as noted above, personal agendas, under the guise of commitment, can deflect individuals from strategic organizational priorities.

For an NGO like BAIF, long hours and teamwork are regarded as part of the value set that binds the organization together. In BAIF, teams work across the organization, at field level and in regional offices. The senior management team based in Pune provides collective leadership at the head of the organization. Below this are state teams, regional teams and district teams. Running alongside these are specific project teams or specialist task forces, brought together to achieve particular purposes. Although these teams have clearly defined responsibilities, they are not rigid and can act in a relatively informal manner, cutting across hierarchies and sectoral specializations.

Based on over 30 years of experience, BAIF managers suggest that there are two major barriers to successful teamwork: the first is a sense of hierarchy, by which they mean 'bossism'. The second arises from the division of the organization into sectoral specialization. Consequently, even though BAIF has more levels of hierarchy than many organizations, it tries to create a culture where hierarchical issues are minimized. In an effort to encourage better teamworking, staff are rotated through different jobs; they are encouraged to take on new roles; junior field staff are encouraged to articulate views during meetings. Behind this is the sense of 'family' that was fostered by the founder, Manibhai, and his own vision of BAIF as a family rooted in shared values and a common philosophy.

Despite all the conscious strategies to promote teamwork, however, our case studies actually show that the most effective team-building is unplanned, informal and highly personalized. Staff gathering for a regular morning cup of tea or an informal after-work chat can be as important to team-building as any planned strategy. Many staff comment on the importance of travel as a great team-building occasion. Conversations during long car drives, or discussions on endless bus or train journeys are an excellent opportunity for senior and junior staff, or head office and project staff to share experiences and concerns. Informal meetings are clearly an essential part of communication flow, but they are also an effective way of building bonds between senior and junior staff.

The picture, of course, is not all about successful teams. Quite clearly there are conflicts and frustration. Teams can work against each other. They can engage in turf-wars and departmental squabbles. They can be actively dysfunctional and, when this happens, there is a need for mechanisms to resolve conflict. In Sungi, there is an unofficial under-standing that conflicts are to be resolved at a programme level, with the head of programmes acting as arbitrator. As organizations grow, as staff become more distanced from the leadership and as more formal systems are introduced, staff frustration levels can grow. There may be disputes over pay and conditions, redundancies or new appointments. Many of our case study NGOs have faced mini protests or the threat of strike action. While these may be symptomatic of a simple communication breakdown or of disenchantment with new management systems, they may also reflect a breakdown in teamworking. Such breakdowns can destroy teams that have taken years to build.

There is much to suggest, in fact, that teamworking is not about value statements and formal team-building exercises. It is about the ability to resolve conflicts and to allow people to work together in their own way, operating much of the time according to their own unofficial rules, forming their own coalitions and perhaps sometimes working counter to what senior management deems appropriate. Teams take on a life of their own, a small price that organizations pay for the benefits that accrue from the overall success of teamwork.

HUMAN RESOURCE DEVELOPMENT

NGOs are people-intensive. Staff are a key resource to be marshalled, developed and nurtured on a formal basis. Michael Beer, a Harvard human resource strategist, reflects a strong body of specialist opinion when he identifies employees as a measurable human 'asset' or as 'social capital'.[16] Because of the limited resource base of many NGOs, the skills and knowledge of individual staff are their only real asset. Human capital, rather than technology, economic influence or economic clout, is their defining asset. One consequence is that organizations are expected increasingly to have policies to ensure that these 'assets' are suitably productive. Such policies should promote teamwork, create a conducive work culture and ensure that personnel systems, such as recruitment, training and appraisal, are properly implemented.

Human resource policies, therefore, are as much about introducing effective systems as about inculcating shared values. They are concerned with the tangible, structural elements of people management, rather than the intangible and contingent. Mike Hudson suggests that such policies are particularly important in the non-profit sector because there is a supposition that 'people development' is something that will happen automatically.[17] He argues that proactive human resource strategies are needed to develop staff.

Most of our sample NGOs, however, have only introduced such policies on a systematic basis in the past few years. Failure to do so earlier has created in some a legacy of weak management skills and an ad hoc approach to staffing issues. As our case study NGOs grew during the late 1980s and early 1990s, there were increased levels of staff frustration with the unsophisticated, personalized nature of personnel arrangements. In some, tensions and frustrations manifested themselves in the form of high staff turnover, low morale, accusations of favouritism, informal unionism and anonymous complaints to trustees.

This led most to implement formal human resource policies, recruiting specialist personnel managers and producing detailed manuals. Some agencies favoured organization-wide policies, while others delegated the personnel function to the programme level. BAIF, with 1700 staff in seven states, has decentralized its structure and now each state is registered as a separate society, with its own board of trustees and its own human resource policy. There is one vice-president, however, who has overall responsibility for personnel issues throughout the organization. AKRSP, India commissioned a major human resource review in 1994. This resulted in the creation of a human resource department and the introduction of a formal organizational manual. An innovative mentoring system was introduced, job descriptions were written for all staff and an organization-wide appraisal system was introduced. The formal purpose of the new policy was 'to develop required competencies in employees to carry out various tasks, developing a healthy organizational climate, and motivating employees for better performance.'[18] But there was concern that such policy statements were insufficient on their own to create the sort of culture and the level of social interaction required. So informal initiatives such as daily prayers, picnics and festival celebrations were also introduced to complement the formal policies, encouraging people to share time together and to build stronger personal bonds. This balance between the formal and the informal is common to many of the NGOs in our study.

Recruitment

There is a strong recognition that the recruitment of staff with the potential to develop the right skill sets, along with the appropriate attitudes and values, is crucial to organizational success. AKRSP in Pakistan actively seeks to recruit a diverse cadre of managers in an effort to achieve improved gender balance as well as a balance in religious affiliation. It recognizes the difficulty in recruiting good staff through traditional means, and has therefore used headhunters, or has taken fresh recruits as interns and trained them for specific jobs. PROSHIKA continues to recruit through traditional means, advertising in newspapers and using written examinations. Because of its size, PROSHIKA interviews applicants every month, and, for every 100 applicants, about 25 to 30 will get to the interview stage. Of these, 60 per cent will pass, with an approximate 1-to-5 ratio of all applicants being hired.

Like all the NGOs in our sample, Sadguru receives a number of applications each month. Because of the organization's reputation, some applications are from development professionals. Sadguru has close relations with a number of academic institutions, and these send a steady stream of applicants as well. In reality, however, over 80 per cent of Sadguru's staff are locals, and the majority hear about vacancies from friends working in the organization. Similarly, BAIF relies heavily on local recruitment. It perceives recruitment and staff selection as the key to its success. Manibhai devoted much of his time to the recruitment process, and many of the current senior staff were hired by Manibhai himself. This ethos continues, with an intensive selection process supported by a bank of staff training opportunities and career development initiatives. These include on-the-job training, job rotation, alternative work experience and distance learning.

Induction and Training

All the senior NGO managers interviewed for this study commented on the importance of investing in effective and appropriate staff training. They appreciate especially the importance of induction programmes in raising the level of staff understanding of organizational values, mission and culture. The length and sophistication of these induction programmes vary considerably. All new staff recruited by Sadguru, for example, go through a one-month induction period, spending a few days in each department and a week in the department that they are going to join. They also spend some days with senior managers, learning about the history of the organization and the philosophy of their guru.

New employees at PROSHIKA undergo a 13-day foundation course within three months of recruitment. This course explains PROSHIKA's vision, mission, strategy, goals and objectives. The purpose of the AKRSP (I) induction programme is to help new staff to appreciate the varied dimensions of the organization's culture. There is a week-long orientation programme which includes sessions on the history, mission and values of the organization, as well as operational details. More importantly, each inductee is assigned a mentor. Mentors – role models for new entrants – are expected to act as teacher, philosopher and guide. BAIF has also introduced a mentoring system, supported by a range of formal staff counselling opportunities.

With its strong emphasis on shared learning, BRAC has in many ways been a role model for several of the organizations in our study. BRAC has focused on learning and on creating a stimulating environment in which people can work. F H Abed likens the organization to a university, with continuous learning, interesting discussion and respect for research. He also regards training as an inherent part of the work of BRAC managers.[19] They are expected to play a facilitative role, encouraging learning, acting as philosopher, guide and mentor. Deputy Executive Director, Salehuddin Ahmed, suggests that in BRAC a manager needs to be 'a super-person' with many qualities: 'a psychologist, a communicator, a negotiator, a motivator, a conductor, a leader and a listener'.[20] BRAC recognizes that shared learning and staff development is a serious pursuit and it invests considerable resources – 7 per cent of the total salary budget – in staff development.

Pay, Promotion and Appraisal

There is an ongoing debate about the extent to which NGOs are motivated by values and commitment, and whether increased professionalism saps dedication. Our evidence suggests that commitment is important, but as an organization grows, staff become increasingly concerned about salary scales and the quality of benefits. Most large South Asian NGOs now offer a comprehensive range of benefits which, although not comparable with international NGOs or donor agencies, are comparable with government service. PROSHIKA's package includes gratuities, access to a provident fund, health support, housing loan funds and a credit union. There are also special facilities for insurance and pensions. In the case of an untimely death, the family of a staff member will receive a pension for 15 years. Sadguru's benefits package includes a rent allowance, annual bonus, a provident fund, a superannuation scheme, medical and accident insurance, and allowances for lunch, transport and vacation travel. There is a recognition in many NGOs that more competitive reward structures are needed, and a variety of special merit awards, prizes, citations and certificates have been introduced. At AKRSP (I), these rewards emphasize group achievements, and there are annual awards for the best-performing teams – 'the best cluster award' or the 'best spearhead team award'. Winning teams receive a trophy and a cash award.

For most individuals, however, a more critical question than trophies has to do with levels of pay and promotion. To deal with this, most of our case study NGOs have introduced formal staff appraisal systems. This reflects an increasing acceptance of structured management tools that were alien to the culture of many NGOs only 10 or 20 years ago. BAIF, for example, has a well-established organization-wide performance appraisal system akin to that found in the private sector. Employees are appraised by supervisors and the system is directly linked to monetary incentives. Increments are not standardized – they are based on performance and target achievement. Promotion is based on knowledge and expertise, a willingness to take additional responsibility, initiative in learning and trying out new ideas, and an ability to take decisions and solve problems. Because of the inherent tensions that such a system can create, there is an extensive appeal and review system. In PROSHIKA, the informal appraisal system used for many years was found wanting as the organization grew. In 1994, therefore, a formal performance appraisal system was introduced, based on each person's individual action plan and targets. Assessments are undertaken by the immediate supervisor and tabulated at head office, with an assessment sheet going back to each staff member.

Sadguru, however, whose Executive Director was once a private sector personnel manager, believes that appraisal systems which reward individual effort are divisive. Sadguru has no formal system for rewarding or praising individuals for upholding organizational values; nor is there a formal mechanism for criticizing them if they fail to do so. Directors and many staff feel that a structured, incentive-based appraisal system would lead to divisive competition and interpersonal conflict. Harnath Jagawat recognizes the positive aspects of appraisal systems, but he is concerned that they are neither foolproof nor unbiased, and that instead of acting as an incentive, they make those who fail to benefit increasingly annoyed and unhappy. He feels that Sadguru's time-based incremental system is, in reality, more equitable, reflecting consistent quality and good work throughout the organization. He prefers to put greater emphasis on training and staff development for those who fall short, rather than emphasizing promotion and higher salaries. In general, therefore, Sadguru's staff are paid on the basis of educational qualification, work experience and job designation. Promotions are time-bound and occur every three to five years. Once staff reach the ceiling in their respective grades, they are entitled to the benefits of the next grade up without being actually promoted to the next category.

While the jury may be out on how best to do it, it can be said that over time, all the case study NGOs have introduced increasingly formal human resource policies and systems aimed at motivating, improving and managing staff. Personal values and shared commitment are no longer seen as sufficient arbiters of the 'NGO way', and formal policies and systems have become necessary to supplement them. Taking the most extreme view, these systems are actually a form of social engineering designed to change attitudes or to reinforce appropriate behaviour. This is especially true where organizations have tackled attitudes about, and taken on programmes relating to, the role of women.

GENDER POLICIES

Many of our case study NGOs have focused squarely on the advancement of women in society. Chapter 5 will discuss the evolution of gender strategies in some of them, but gender strategies in programming have actually been easier for some to adopt than gender strategies within their own management structures and systems.

Gender is a cross-cutting issue that brings together many different strands of an organization's human resource policy. While the majority of our case study NGO staff are still men, there are considerable efforts made to encourage the recruitment and promotion of women within most of them. This is a strategic priority with which all have struggled: gender sensitivity may be a priority, but it has not come easily or naturally. Most organizations, in fact, have had to impose gender policies, introducing new structures and investing in specialist training. While this demonstrates the powerful role of formal systems and procedures and the limitations of the informal, it does not alter the fact that in other circumstances, informal processes can effect real change. It also demonstrates the dichotomy between strategic rhetoric and operational reality.

Although it is relatively easy to articulate a strategy, it is much harder to implement it across the organization.

A range of policy initiatives have been introduced to sensitize NGO staff to gender issues. In the early 1980s, BRAC – an organization whose primary target group is poor rural women – realized that it needed to address its staff gender imbalance. It was not until the 1990s, however, that BRAC management actually took concerted action to promote women within the organization. In 1991, a Women's Advisory Committee was established to deal with women's issues among staff. In 1993 the first gender training programme was run, and in 1994 a gender team was established with the intention of linking gender to wider organizational change issues. In 1995, a Gender Resource Centre was established to act as a catalyst in sensitizing staff to gender issues. This Centre and a 'Gender Quality Action Learning' programme have grown in size and have successfully raised the profile of gender issues throughout the organization. Perhaps as important, the initiatives have given women the confidence to believe that they can achieve senior positions within the organization.

The larger challenge facing BRAC and other NGOs is how to change deeply held attitudes to the role of women in society, and how to convey the message that gender is not about women, but about relationships between men and women. In BAIF this became an issue of some importance as the focus of work shifted away from male-dominated technology-based development projects to more women-sensitive, community-based programmes. The traditional male culture within the organization has changed, but there remain pockets of resistance. Some unreconstructed older staff still see gender as a 'donor thing', imposed by outsiders and derived from Western ideas of feminization.

Much of this is a leadership issue. NGOs have demonstrated that they *can* lead in overcoming resistance, both internally and externally, to new practices and innovative ways of working. The issue of women NGO staff riding bicycles and motorbikes arose during the 1980s in Bangladesh. As long as female managers had to be driven about in jeeps, they could never be taken seriously as rural development workers, or as managers. NGOs like BRAC persevered with bike-riding experiments and, through a process of dialogue, persuasion and example, persuaded communities, staff and even religious leaders that the world would not end if a woman rode a bicycle. This is not merely a question of changing attitudes on a particular issue. It is about introducing genuine social innovation and, as such, promoting a fundamental shift in attitudes about the role and behaviour of women.

PROSHIKA has also had to face resistance to the changing role and status of women. A 1997 midterm review referred to what it called a 'sometimes hostile or teasing environment' within the organization. The report also noted several constraints that limited the recruitment of female staff. These included the lower educational level of women, the reluctance of women to leave established homes or husbands to live in remote areas, and the difficulty of travelling at night to or from work. In reality, many of these constraints are diminishing with the rapid pace of social change for women in Bangladesh. But PROSHIKA has tried to make staff understand that this is a strategic priority for the organization as a whole. Increasing the number of female staff is about improving the quality of development work. As a response to the critique, PROSHIKA introduced a clear gender policy, a code of conduct concerning ethics and sexual harassment, and workshops on gender and development. More recently a Women's Co-ordinating Unit was established to review the congeniality of the working environment for women and to facilitate the development of women's careers in the organization. A Gender Resource and Co-ordination Cell (GRCC) was established to monitor progress.

On International Women's Day in 2000, BRAC felt confident enough to organize a parade in Dhaka of almost 200 of its female staff riding bicycles and motorcycles. While the fundamentalist threat had perhaps not passed, the greatest danger for the women that day was from exhaust fumes and television cameramen dodging the traffic.

PROSHIKA has also introduced a fast-track programme designed to enable new female employees to achieve senior positions. They undertake an 18-month period of training and are then rapidly promoted to middle-management positions throughout the organization. PROSHIKA's Executive Director, Faruque Ahmed, believes that the success of this fast-track programme will mainstream women's issues across the organization.[21] A number of other affirmative action policies have been instituted among case study NGOs. Sadguru has several programmes that are managed exclusively by women: forestry, horticulture, income generation. More recently, women have begun to manage technical work on the construction of lift irrigation projects and check dams. In Pakistan, AKRSP has allocated special funds to support a similar accelerated professional development programme for women. However, because of local differences, each region has opted for its own gender strategy. At one level this has caused confusion, but it reflects the difficulty in trying to promote undifferentiated gender issues in communities where change actively threatens religious and political sensitivities.

As an organizational issue, gender is a microcosm of all the debates about how best to facilitate and manage change. It highlights the value and importance of formal human resource systems, and the limitations of informal processes and piecemeal solutions. But it also highlights the constraints. Resistance can be deeply entrenched, and the evidence from our case studies suggests that individual attitudes and behaviour will not be changed by superficial manipulation of organizational cultures or by vague hopes that reason and rational debate will make a difference. In such cases, change is more likely to result from comprehensive long-term strategies that have the active support of the leadership, strategies that are integrated across the organization and embedded in its values.

CONCLUSIONS

What are the key attributes of organizational culture in the successful NGO? They clearly extend beyond espoused values and personal commitment. NGO culture is as much a product of history, stories and symbols, structures and systems as it is a product of participation, team-work and shared values. The attributes of this culture are multifold. But if one had to identify key elements, the following would stand out:

- shared commitment to a cause and a common mission;
- the development and preservation of key symbols, stories and organizational rituals, whether through informal discussions over a cup of tea, or in more formal gatherings such as morning prayers;
- the creation and sustenance of formal teams and teamwork;
- informal teamworking and accidental meetings that contribute to a common understanding and build coalitions; and
- the development and application of effective, formal human resource policies and systems that provide a level of consistent and transparent support to all staff in order to implement and support the organiz-ation's mission.

If there is a further lesson for outsiders, it is that levels of (and the need for) formality and informality will vary, according to the age and maturity of an organization. The informality that is appropriate to a small, youthful NGO will not be appropriate in a larger, multifaceted organization. Similarly, the formal systems expected of a mature organization could stifle a smaller one. The major varying factors in organizational culture, therefore, appear to centre around time and organizational size, rather than around shared values. While the need for commitment and values remains constant, these are not enough to carry an organization into larger and more effective programming. Formal human resource systems have a crucial role in shaping and preserving organizational culture, and in helping an institution to work effectively with local communities. These systems ensure that suitable staff are recruited and that they have the values, as well as the skills and understanding, to work with local people.

The role of formal systems, therefore, cannot be underestimated in defining a healthy NGO organizational culture. This does raise a question, however, about whether such systems and procedures threaten personal freedom and innovation. Our analysis suggests that the effective application of such systems does the opposite – it creates a firm foundation in which innovation can flourish. Where some types of change are concerned, as with gender policies, formality is not just appropriate, it is necessary. Systems, especially human resource systems, are the framework that shapes an organization's culture; they ensure that strategies *are* aligned with values; they promote teamworking and team learning – which will be discussed in the next chapter – and, in the end, they allow informal processes to flourish.

CHAPTER 4

LEARNING FOR CHANGE

O! This learning. What a thing it is!

Shakespeare, *The Taming of the Shrew*

Learning and knowledge management are crucial capacities for any NGO expecting to survive and thrive in the uncertain development environment of the new century. NGOs claim to be 'learning organizations', but how most promote shared learning and how they engage their staff in new learning remains something of a mystery. The evidence from the NGOs in our study confirms the important role of organizational learning in building capacity and facilitating change. The study does raise – and answer – an important question about whether the willingness and the ability to learn is inherent in the values and culture of NGOs. Our study suggests that it is not: effective learning is a hard-won goal that depends on both informal, participative processes, and on meaningful investments in formal training and research. This chapter examines the operational implications of this finding, and reviews the effectiveness of the systems used by nine South Asian NGOs to communicate information, to create knowledge and to share learning.

First, however, in an era cluttered with hype about 'learning organizations', it might be worth asking the question, 'learning for what?'. Most organizations, whether non-profit or otherwise, presumably want to 'learn' in order to improve effectiveness and efficiency. Further up the learning chain, however, serious development organizations will seek to improve the effectiveness and efficiency of their technical delivery, of their interaction with outsiders, of specific institutional capacities such as their advocacy, or their understanding of social engagement. Learning may be related to very small improvements such as BAIF's experiments to preserve and transport frozen cattle semen. Or it may be more fundamental, as with the gradual evolution of SRSC's mission statement, discussed in Chapter 5. Good learning will test an organization's management, its strategies and its values. It may be unwritten, or it may be found written down in unlikely places. The best book we have read on the subject of diarrhoea – in fact, the *only* book we have read on diarrhoea, *A Simple Solution*[1] – tells the story of BRAC's work on the development of oral rehydration therapy. But it is more important than that because it is also a story about how people in BRAC learn and how they impart that learning to others.

THE LEARNING NGO

The importance of learning as a key organizational capacity became increasingly apparent in the changing, unpredictable economic and political environment of the 1990s. Learning allows organizations to adapt continuously to an unpredictable future. The survival and success of any organization operating in a turbulent environment is dependent, as one of the early pioneers of action learning, Reg Revens, notes, on its rate of learning being 'equal to or greater than the rate of change in its external environment'.[2]

The reality for most NGOs is that the economic and political environment in which they operate is increasingly complex and unpredictable. Consequently, building NGO capacity to manage knowledge, promote learning and become a 'learning organization' must be a priority. As Alan Fowler comments, unless NGOs learn, 'they are destined for insignificance'.[3] Michael Edwards highlights the need for NGOs to introduce fluid, 'open' systems in which continuous learning is the sine qua non of being able to respond and intervene effectively.[4] We go further: development is in essence a knowledge-based process. Knowing what works and why is essential to the success of NGOs, and knowing what does not work is equally as important.

Knowledge involves awareness, memory and familiarity that develops with experience and learning.[5] Knowledge is the product of information, experience and judgement. It is of little use, however, if it is not disseminated, applied, and above all, used for learning. Knowledge and learning are therefore inextricably linked. Management writers such as Charles Handy[6] and Peter Drucker[7] argue that knowledge is *the* key resource, one that all leading organizations, in both the private and non-profit sectors, must manage and exploit if they are to maintain their position. Consequently, the role of 'knowledge workers' becomes important in explaining corporate success. Similarly, there is a growing recognition that the effective use of knowledge is a key component in the development process. The World Bank's 1998 *World Development Report*, 'Knowledge for Development'[8] emphasizes the unalloyed importance of acquiring, absorbing and communicating knowledge, if the gap between developed and developing countries is to be narrowed.

Learning and knowledge are the product of creative interaction between complex and critical processes that operate in an uncertain external environment. For the staff of NGOs, working with limited resources in difficult and unstable contexts, this has particular resonance.

As far back as 1980, David Korten argued that the success of many Southern development organizations depended on their ability to learn from both the local communities and the beneficiaries with whom they worked.[9] His explanation for success was that many had a 'well-developed capacity for responsive and anticipatory adaptation' and were prepared to involve local people in the planning process. They also embraced error as part of the learning process, and they actively linked knowledge with action.

There is evidence, however, that many NGOs fail to learn. Fowler suggests that a universal weakness of development NGOs is actually a 'limited capacity to learn, adapt, and continuously improve the quality of what they do'.[10] He observes that few senior staff can 'relate to failure in a positive way', failing to see error as a source of learning. Far from being an exclusive weakness of NGOs, the inability to learn and remember is a widespread failing of the development community as a whole. This is partly because there are few incentives to disseminate positive development lessons, and because there are many more powerful reasons to conceal and forget the negative ones.

The increasingly competitive aid environment, and the onerous nature of conditions imposed by donors, means that NGOs are disinclined to publicize mistakes. This may protect them from adverse comment and embarrassment, but it also reduces shared learning and threatens innovation. An NGO cannot become an effective learning organization unless it can embrace error, becoming more open and self-critical. This is an elusive trait which only a few NGOs have the courage to demonstrate.

Organizational learning is a precursor to change. If one accepts this conclusion, organizational learning should be seen as a process of active reflection, curiosity and dialogue. It is an informal, creative and interactive process that involves dialogue between staff, beneficiaries and other stakeholders so that they engage in 'real' or 'higher order' learning. Learning organizations are able to perform more successfully in turbulent environments and can introduce the structural changes that are necessary to cope with new conditions. In summary, most contemporary commentators argue that an organization's ability to learn from experience, from formal training, evaluation and research, are all key to its effectiveness.

It may be argued, therefore, that informal learning processes alone are not enough. Some elements of learning must be built on a firmer foundation. Good research will inform training, effective evaluations will help to shape strategy, and good publications will influence policy and practice. The picture of the 'learning NGO', therefore, is one that relies on both formal and informal processes to generate new learning, to reflect on past experience and to experiment with new approaches. The 'learning NGO' is marked by a curiosity and by an excitement with innovation.

Staff demonstrate a willingness to reflect, experiment and embrace new thinking. They are involved in a constant round of refining and fine tuning. Our case studies suggest that the key learning competencies needed by growing NGOs are the ability to filter data and information, the analytical capacity to reflect on past experience, a hunger to learn and the insight actually to remember lessons.

Many of the NGOs represented in this study demonstrate such competencies. BRAC is the one most commonly cited in this regard. Korten first referred to BRAC as a learning organization in 1980, when it was barely eight years old. He argued that its success stemmed from its ability to operationalize learning on and off the field, and its ability to balance its organizational capacity with beneficiary needs.[11] Lovell suggests that learning was always one of BRAC's guiding principles: that it had a 'learning atmosphere in which a spiral of programmes flourished'. In BRAC there was also an acceptance of error as part of the learning process, as well as an understanding of how their own actions shape the reality in which they operate.[12] A 25th anniversary review of BRAC provides extensive evidence of how trial and error, experimentation and learning have all marked the organization's approach to development since it was established in 1972.[13]

THE PROCESS OF ORGANIZATIONAL LEARNING

The 1990s were sometimes called the decade of the learning organization. The most articulate advocate of learning, Peter Senge, added systems thinking to already familiar learning disciplines of personal mastery, mental models, shared vision and team learning. His book, *The Fifth Discipline*,[14] has been important in shaping understanding of the concept of the 'learning organization'. In particular, he argues that learning commonly results in a creative process of change that can transform an organization. Senge defines the learning organization as one which is 'continuously expanding its capacity to create its future'. In a similar vein, Pedler suggests that a learning organization is one 'which facilitates the learning of all its members and continuously transforms itself'.[15]

The learning organization can therefore be seen as at least partially synonymous with the ongoing processes of individual learning, capacity building and organization development. The term 'learning organization' has arguably become a metaphor for managing change. Consequently, as Pedler points out, a learning organization is not one that merely invests in training, but is one that sees learning as a core value which is central to its effectiveness.[16] Roger Harrison, a pre-eminent organization development commentator, goes further, arguing that before real change can take place, both individuals and organizations must 'learn how to learn'. He also emphasizes the importance of 'higher order learning' in this process. He sees this as a complex process which questions basic assumptions and commonly held mental models, and he extends the focus of enquiry outside the current paradigm.[17]

Alan Fowler takes this yet another stage further by suggesting that critical questioning of assumptions within the organization is not enough. He argues that development agencies and NGOs should adopt a 'learning for leverage' strategy, drawing on their own experience and research (rather than their traditional focus on the task at hand), in order to apply leverage to other institutions.[18] This would typically involve local NGOs using their 'learning' and 'knowledge' to inform an advocacy campaign they may have initiated. This is an issue of growing importance, as advocacy is increasingly viewed as one of the core activities for NGOs in the years ahead. This implies that the 'learning NGO' should use learning to improve its own performance, but it should also use learning and knowledge as a lever to effect political change and to influence civil society.

All this depends, however, on the willingness and ability of individuals within an organization to engage in processes of collective learning that will result in tangible change. Thus, as Swieringa and Wierdsma argue, 'without individual learning there can be no question of organizational learning'. They point out that 'individual learning is a necessary, but not a sufficient condition for organizational learning'.[19] They conclude that organizations will not automatically learn merely because the staff themselves have learned.

Thus, both mainstream organizational theorists and the evidence from the NGOs in our study, suggests that individual learning and institutional learning are both the key and distinct organizational competencies in times of uncertainty and rapid change. This, however, begs larger questions: how do NGOs develop the capacity to learn, and how do they promote and encourage such learning among their staff?

One way of answering this is to examine the extent to which organizational learning is a product of informal, participative processes, and to what extent it flows from formal training, research and evaluation. Such an approach echoes a much wider discussion in management literature about whether organizations are more effectively managed, and whether productivity increases through formal management systems and controls, or through informal, consensual processes that motivate staff, improve performance and effect change. The latter approach is at the centre of most NGO management literature. And in broader management discourse, Peter Senge argues strongly that consensual, participative processes – personal mastery, creativity, openness, shared decision-making, and team learning – are the key to enhanced productivity and increased motivation. Crudely put, the debate can be reduced to an argument over the merits of control versus consent as the most efficacious approach to organizational learning and change.

CONSENSUAL LEARNING

Our research highlights the importance of both learning by doing, and the role of personal engagement, dialogue and consensus in helping NGOs to learn from a variety of different sources. These informal, participative processes lie at the heart of the way that many NGOs learn. The ethos of learning by doing and action learning has been central to shaping the way they work and learn.

Dialogue and Process

The process of listening and learning has been central to the way that many of our case study NGOs work. In India, for example, Sadguru has worked with tribal communities in Eastern Gujarat since 1974. Its founders, Harnath and Sharmistha Jagawat, spent the first year of the organization's existence walking up to 30 kilometres a day in order to meet with local people, listening to their concerns and discussing how best to meet their needs. Twenty-five years later, Harnath Jagawat feels that the only major difference in how they work is that Sadguru can now call on a much wider pool of expertise (and, of course, they travel mostly by car). The organization still depends on feedback and input from the local community to develop its programmes. Jagawat claims that their success comes from 'learning from our experiences, from feedback from the communities, and from continuous appraisals by external consultants and academics'.[20] In another example from Gujarat, AKRSP(I) believes so strongly in the philosophy of 'learning by doing' and 'action learning' that the approach has fundamentally shaped the way it works and trains its staff. Most training now consists of a mix of practical briefings as well as field attachments.

Virtually all the NGOs in our study rely on similar village-based processes to assist internal learning and to develop their understanding of the needs of local communities. In Pakistan, the staff of Sungi understood very early that their most valuable learning experiences came through regular interaction with local communities – 'village or cluster-based dialogues' and other participatory processes. In AKRSP (P), most early staff training took place through village dialogues between a team of AKRSP staff and local people. The dialogues were held outdoors and were open to everyone, not just village elders and other notables. Although purdah prevented women from attending in a formal sense, many could hear the discussion at a distance and this helped to lay the foundation for women's programming as the relationship between AKRSP and the village matured. The original discussions were recorded and studied, and they became the basis for future interventions. As AKRSP grew, and as training needs became more sophisticated and specialized, the organization gradually became more reliant on formal courses and structured training processes. Nevertheless, staff still look back on the village dialogues as the most effective training they received. Not only did it give them practical insights, it led to the creation of shared understanding, a strong team spirit and a more integrated approach to their work.[21]

Similarly, rapid growth has had an impact on BRAC's ability to learn in close partnership with local communities. For example, in an effort to expand the scope and impact of its health programmes, staff were 'mobilized with motorbikes'. They became so focused on meeting quantitative project objectives, completing tasks quickly and dashing around the countryside on their new motorbikes, that they had little time to sit and talk with local people. It was soon apparent that 'when we walked and went by bicycle, we did much better'. So BRAC reintroduced slower, more time-consuming ways of working with local communities.[22]

BRAC's Executive Director, F H Abed, has commented on how such learning is a two-way process. From the outset, he saw himself acting as teacher to his staff, while in turn learning from both his colleagues and the communities with whom they worked:

> *I made a point to go to the field, at least for four to seven days, live there, and talk with BRAC staff. The staff would congregate in one place, and we would then discuss and analyze strategies and problems, and take vital decisions on the spot. This is how we learned . . . in fact BRAC started learning while doing things, and the excitement was that everybody was learning too. It was like a 'little university'.*[23]

The informal learning process includes other techniques. Staff from all our Pakistani case study NGOs have visited BRAC and PROSHIKA in Bangladesh. In turn, BRAC and PROSHIKA watch each other closely, as well as other Bangladeshi organizations, such as Grameen Bank. F H Abed frankly admits that he is an 'unashamed replicator' of other people's good work, and that much of BRAC's success comes from its ability to learn from other organizations.

There is clear evidence that in their early years many of these NGOs were keen to use external sources of expertise and outside consultants to effect change. For example, the major organizational and operational changes at IUCN Pakistan in the last five years have been the product of two major management reviews conducted by external consultants. More established NGOs – say, BRAC or BAIF – while happy to use external consultants, are likely to do so in a more selective manner. This may be because the pace of expansion in newer NGOs allows little time for internal reflection, while older, more established organizations are naturally more reflective and are more willing to invest in research. It is noteworthy that in comparison with their Northern counterparts, the Southern NGOs in our study seem more willing to hire external advisers and management consultants in order to promote and facilitate organizational development and change. Donors in turn are willing to underwrite the cost of such consultancies, something they occasionally find hard to justify for themselves.

External inputs aside, there is a keen awareness among the case study NGOs of a need to learn from themselves, and above all, to learn from past mistakes. Barry Underwood, Chief Executive of AKRSP (I), talks of the importance of 'embracing one's mistakes, and learning from them', creating in the process a culture that accepts criticism.[24] In the same vein a senior AKRSP (P) manager comments that 'if an organization can't experiment and innovate, the spirit of change finishes'.[25] Abed sees mistakes as an inherent part of the learning process, and suggests that BRAC had many failures from which it had to learn:

> You go to a woman's house and find that the loan you have given her is taken away by her husband. Or a child comes to your school and suddenly has to drop out because the parents have moved away, and the child doesn't learn anymore. These are all failures . . . little failures are, of course, inherent in any successful program. You must accept that, for they are part of the learning process.[26]

While it is apparent that NGOs will admit to 'little failures', or will even publicize major mistakes from the distant past, they may not actually be as welcoming of the learning that comes from mistakes as they seem. BRAC was particularly embarrassed when a donor pointed out serious weaknesses in a deep tubewell project, not so much because of the failure, but because insiders had not recognized the failure before outsiders had. Some experienced NGO-watchers are sceptical about whether mistakes are actually 'embraced', and to what extent they are disguised or merely overlooked. Where the latter is true, the reputation of NGOs as learning organizations is protected and enhanced at the level of myth rather than fact.

Such reservations notwithstanding, one of the most distinctive characteristics of our case study NGOs has been their willingness to promote and invest in learning, almost from their start-up days. There is a clear culture of 'learning by doing' and 'active reflection', where dialogue complements formal training, and the poor are seen as a primary source of organizational learning. The challenge is how to ensure that learning is shared and that different perspectives are accepted within the institution.

Institutional Learning

One of the major challenges for large NGOs, such as AKRSP, BAIF, BRAC and PROSHIKA, which recruit large numbers of new staff each year, is the issue of 'unlearning' and 'relearning'. This is particularly true for new specialists or management staff coming from the educated middle class, people who may carry inappropriate attitudinal baggage, or who see issues through the lens of a privileged university background rather than the perspective of a villager. For example, BRAC has had to rethink its whole approach to educating children, accepting that full-time education may not always be appropriate. Its educational professionals have had to learn to respect the priorities of poor rural families and to accept that children will not be at school during harvest time.

This process of relearning is an essential part of the orientation process for new staff. BRAC's Director of Training, Dr Samdani, believes that the immersion process for new recruits should be a time of 'unlearning and relearning'. He talks about 'creating a new kind of learning environment, and new ways of information sharing' which, in turn, will help to 'develop new knowledge, new skills, attitudes, and behaviour'.[27] The challenge for trainers and managers alike is to find effective ways to help staff to unlearn and relearn. This is not just about changing attitudes or skills; it is as much about subtracting from what is known as adding to it.

BAIF has approached this by consciously moving staff around the organization in order to encourage cross-functional learning. Their policy of transferring staff from research posts to field positions, from single programmes to multiple programmes, from specialist to management positions has generated greater awareness across sectors, and, in their view, has enhanced learning throughout the organization. This approach is reinforced by BAIF's highly decentralized organizational structure, and has created a perception that head office staff in Pune are external resource persons with whom field staff can share ideas and experiences, relying on them for professional, external comment.

For many NGOs learning is a product of internal processes, and institutional memory is a function of participation. As Faruque Ahmed, President of PROSHIKA, notes, 'If I, as the head of the organization, had to remember everything, then probably there wouldn't be much remembered. But if you use participation in the decision-making process, then there is much more chance of institutional memory.'.[28] PROSHIKA uses a variety of participative tools and participatory rural appraisal (PRA) techniques to get feedback from the groups and communities with whom it works, and it has established internal processes to generate feedback and dialogue. It holds quarterly meetings where 200 senior staff and group representatives meet together to review performance and discuss change.

Most NGOs use a mix of regular meetings, retreats, workshops and seminars to promote shared learning and to disseminate new ideas. Sungi, for example, has used retreats as an opportunity to analyse current problems and to propose new strategies. One retreat helped the organization to rethink its approach to advocacy in the light of tensions that had developed in a particular village project. Similarly, a sudden cut in funding in 1995 became the driving force behind a strategic planning workshop that enabled senior management to take a critical look at itself, review past practice, and make some fundamental changes to both the organization and its programmes.

At an institutional level, Sadguru holds regular meetings on the last Saturday of the month, allowing staff to share experiences and insights, and to give feedback from other meetings or courses they have attended. Such meetings are attended by everyone, from drivers and office assistants to the senior management team. By 1998, however, Harnath Jagawat felt that these meetings were becoming something of a ritual. Few questions were asked, junior staff were not really involved, and there was little time to stand back and reflect on the issues raised.[29] The meetings had been reduced to a litany of reports, with little time for critical questioning, reflection or learning.

Sadguru is not alone in this sort of problem. It is axiomatic of the NGO sector that there is a premium on time for thought and critical reflection. As NGOs become increasingly target-driven and workloads increase, staff have less time to critique their work and analyse problems. Moreover, it is clear from our case studies that creativity and innovation are rarely generated in formal, organized meetings or strategy workshops. The creative process takes place mainly outside official forums, commonly during informal sessions in the office or the field. A considerable amount of staff learning and innovation result less from formal meetings than from creative and informal processes in which they can reflect actively on shared experience.

We can safely conclude from our case studies that NGOs learn through a variety of informal processes: through village dialogues, mistakes, experimentation, staff discussions, and through the work of other NGOs. There is a constant process of questioning, reviewing, fixing and refining. Learning by doing is a well-tuned NGO mantra, but it is also a fact of life for those we examined.

A question arises, however: are informal participatory learning processes sufficient for an organization that is undergoing rapid growth in diverse projects and different regions? Regardless of their value and success, informal processes do not work in a vacuum. Is there a role for more formal, structured mechanisms in promoting quality and consistency of learning across an organization? To what extent do scheduled training courses, financial incentives, performance appraisal techniques, research and commissioned evaluations play a role in the learning process of successful South Asian NGOs? One of the most important findings of the overall research programme is that informal processes require the support of more formal, structured efforts, if learning is to be genuinely embedded at an organizational level,

FORMAL LEARNING PROCESSES

Virtually all of our participating NGOs dramatically increased their investment in formal training and research during the 1990s. And AKRSP, BAIF, BRAC and PROSHIKA all expanded their specialist research departments. Both Sadguru and BAIF opened large purpose-built training centres in the second half of the 1990s, while together, BRAC and PROSHIKA increased their training capacities to handle almost a million people a year. Clearly these NGOs see formal processes of training and analysis as an essential and major part of their learning toolkit. This realization can be traced back to the 1970s when their first training and research centres were started.

What is even more striking is the comparison with Northern NGOs, where such investments have been limited or non-existent. Most Northern NGOs have surprisingly small research departments (or none at all), with relatively limited opportunities for staff training. This failure to invest in their own learning and self-reflection stands in marked and odd contrast with their willingness to build the same capacities in their Southern counterparts.

IUCN's Stella Jafri notes that NGOs are often forced to recruit for 'potential' and for 'openness in learning' rather than for present competency. Ambitious NGOs wanting to maintain the quality and integrity of their work have to invest in staff development, partly because of the relatively small pool of competent people available to them in their inevitable competition with the private and public sectors. In addition, many staff have to be re-educated in order to adjust to the multidiscipl-inary demands of development work. In the process, they must unlearn much of the compartmentalized, fact-based education which is common to the colonial inheritance. Training and staff development are a strategic response to a recruitment dilemma and the limitations of the education system.

Training: a Strategic Instrument

BRAC's preoccupation with staff development and training, as discussed in the previous chapter, has been central to the way that it has operated since the mid-1970s. Part of the remit of its Training Division is to ensure that a lack of skills and weak management competencies do not constrain efforts to grow. Indeed, training is seen as a strategic instrument to facilitate programme development. BRAC has long acknowledged the importance of formal training in its success and sets aside 7 per cent of its overall salary budget for staff development. This is a remarkable figure when one considers that in 1999 BRAC employed 24,700 full-time staff and 34,000 part-time staff. In physical terms this has resulted in the creation of 12 Training and Resource Centres (TARCs) in different locations throughout Bangladesh. These employ 150 trainers, offering management, human resource development and skills-based training courses to BRAC employees, villagers and the staff of other NGOs.[30]

In 1998, TARCs ran courses that were attended by 45,000 participants, the majority of whom were BRAC staff. But nearly 3000 were from other NGOs or government departments.[31] BRAC was conscious, however, that such courses did not fully meet the needs of senior staff, and consequently it established its own Centre for Management Development in 1991. By 1997, the Centre had developed sufficiently that it was offering post-graduate diplomas and masters degrees in NGO management through its 'Global Partnership for NGOs' studies programme, operated in collaboration with the Organization for Rural Associations for Progress (ORAP) in Zimbabwe and the School for International Training in Vermont. BRAC now has plans to establish its own university – what Abed calls 'an institution of excellence, not just any other ordinary university'. Among other things, the university will aim to help to develop 'ethical leadership' in Bangladesh.[32]

In PROSHIKA, 'development education' is regarded as key to its success because it links all its activities together and makes them an integrated whole. The fact that in one year, nearly half a million people attended PROSHIKA training programmes reflects not only the scale of these activities, but also the importance that the organization places on learning. PROSHIKA separates its formal training into Human Development Training (HDT) and Practical Skills Development Training (PSDT), both types attended by staff and beneficiaries in the organization's different Rural and Urban Training Centres. PROSHIKA describes the HDT courses, that were attended by more than 694,000 participants in 1998–99, as a systematic process of conscientization – by which it means that they help to situate people's development efforts in a larger social context, in order to help them to understand the social processes that affect their behaviour. In comparison, the purpose of PSDT is to provide participants (totalling over137,000 in 1998–99) with specific knowledge and skills so that they can make informed decisions to identify and carry out various economic activities.[33]

As noted in Chapter 3, larger NGOs are also placing greater emphasis on orientation and induction training for new staff. This is particularly important in an environment of rapid growth, decentralization and organizational restructuring. BAIF's orientation programme is designed to offer new staff insights into the organization's ethos and history, and is followed by a process in which all new staff meet with, and work alongside, a senior staff member. SRSC has tried to increase staff understanding of the broader personal and social issues they may face through a series of staff workshops on 'humaneering'. AKRSP (P) has expanded its international profile through an internship programme for young graduates. This training innovation attracts people from all over the world, giving them an opportunity to work at a grassroots level, to gain new skills and to benefit from different perspectives on their work.

Staff Development: Benefits, Incentives and Follow-up

Despite its obvious importance, there are concerns about the cost-effectiveness of formal training. BAIF estimates that most of its staff go on at least two or three training courses or exposure visits each year. Although they accept that this as an essential investment, it consumes a considerable amount of staff time. Sungi also had to ensure a balance between training courses and work output following a donor evaluation which revealed that a whole year's worth of person-days had been devoted to staff training courses, study trips and seminars.[34] One response was to have managers quantify the value of training through cost-benefit analysis. Others have come to understand that staff development is not merely an expensive overhead, but, like learning, it is a core value that must be espoused throughout the organization, and actively supported by the Board and senior management team.

A further challenge for several of our case study NGOs is the development of systems to reinforce learning and ensure that training actually does result in increased productivity and improved performance. Practical examples include the use of annual appraisal schemes to analyse training needs, systems of planned career development, and the introduction of 'high-flyer' programmes that are linked to overseas training and post-graduate opportunities. More specific techniques include the introduction of financial incentives and the rigorous monitoring of post-training performance. An example of the former was exemplified in BRAC's oral rehydration therapy programme (ORT) that was designed to spread new approaches to treating diarrhoea in villages. BRAC had been at the forefront of developing a simple, effective and user-friendly oral rehydration therapy that can be used by poor families to treat the diarrhoea that is often fatal for young children. Oral Rehydration Workers (ORWs) were recruited to train village women in how to prepare and use a salt-gur solution. Success depended in part on the ability of the

ORWs to do this training well. In an effort to motivate the ORWs and to ensure effective learning, a financial incentive scheme was introduced. The calculation of an ORW's salary was based on the response of a sample of those trained to ten standard questions. The more questions a mother could answer correctly, the higher the incentive payment to the ORW.

As the programme evolved, one of the main concerns was that a third of those trained failed to remember accurately the details of the mix. BRAC addressed the problem with more systematic follow-up and further refresher training for the ORWs. The additional effort paid dividends, and within two years, 90 per cent of those evaluated a year after their training could properly prepare the salt-gur solution.[35] The introduction of incentives and follow-up monitoring are good examples of human resource management systems being used to ensure that effective learning actually takes place. The lesson here is that reliance on open-ended training is inadequate, especially where the investment is high and the results are important. Objective measures with identifiable time-scales can reinforce an effective skill transfer.

GENERATING INFORMATION AND KNOWLEDGE FOR LEARNING

Knowledge and learning are inextricably linked. Knowledge is as much the product of information, feedback and analysis, as it is of experience and process. Consequently, most of our successful case study NGOs have made a conscious decision to invest in research as a key learning resource, and they see evaluation as part of the ongoing feedback process.

Research for Effective Development

One of the clearest statements on the importance of research comes from BAIF, that 'development without research is outdated, and research without development is irrelevant'. Consequently, BAIF's leadership has placed great emphasis on high-quality technical research. The organization invested heavily in the establishment of a Central Research Station outside Pune, now recognized as one of the leading livestock research centres in India. BAIF staff are actively encouraged to publish their research findings in academic journals, and to give papers at national conferences. The 1996–97 Annual Report provides detailed abstracts of 20 publications and academic papers produced by BAIF staff over the year, and it identifies nearly 60 publications and videos. In Pakistan, research stations sponsored by AKRSP have developed a similar national profile in the area of crop development and reforestation.

In Bangladesh, both PROSHIKA and BRAC also invest heavily in research. PROSHIKA's approach has been to marry research with training and to explore synergies between the two. As a result it has attached its Research and Demonstration Project to its Central Training Centre at Koitta to help to ensure that research findings are incorporated into training programmes. PROSHIKA's Institute for Development Policy Analysis and Advocacy makes direct links between its grassroots programmes and macroeconomic social and development policies. With the Royal Tropical Institute of the Netherlands, for example, it has taken part in an international study of the religious and cultural beliefs of Muslim women and how these influence their reproductive choices and education.[36] While learning by doing is the hallmark of BRAC's target group approach, it does not underestimate the importance of research, and has correspondingly expanded the size of its Research and Evaluation Department. In 1990 they employed 16 researchers, and by 1997 this number had quadrupled to 52 full-time researchers, 10 of them with doctoral degrees.

Monitoring and Evaluation

The benefit of formal evaluations is that they can provide feedback and alternative insights into quality, performance, impact and long-term sustainability. Some NGOs also see external evaluations as an incentive to undertake advance internal assessments in order to ensure that records and documentation are up to date before the outsiders arrive. Prior to a 1997 evaluation by NOVIB, Sungi, for example, undertook its own self-evaluation exercise which partly pre-empted the conclusions of the external evaluation and contributed to a new four-year plan.

Most of our case study NGOs, in fact, have developed over time sophisticated internal management information and monitoring systems. Sadguru gathers monthly reports from its projects and conducts regular impact studies that include feedback from the communities with which it works. PROSHIKA uses an Impact Monitoring and Evaluation Cell (IMEC) to monitor the work of its Area Development Centres (ADCs). Increasingly this process is being computerized and the findings are shared at quarterly coordination meetings with all ADC coordinators. Similarly, BAIF accepts that much new learning emerges from formal review processes, leading to changes in both routine procedures and project work. It has established an integrated review system across the organization at both district and state levels, incorporating input from its own researchers and outside specialists. For example, an evaluation of the cattle-breeding programme encouraged BAIF to introduce a more comprehensive package, integrating the provision of vaccines, fertilizers, cement and other building materials with the existing cattle-breeding programme.

BRAC's Research and Evaluation Division (RED) is based on the idea that evaluation is meant to improve, not punish. The fact that this division was set up in 1975, when the organization was only three years old, reflects the importance that BRAC has placed from the beginning on monitoring performance and quality. The division's work ranges from the identification of potentially viable economic opportunities to rigorous in-house evaluations. These studies are not merely for internal consumption; dozens of RED's studies have been published in national and international journals. RED also publishes its own research journal in Bengali, *Nirjash*, sharing its findings with staff at all levels.

AKRSP (I) established a Research and Monitoring Team in 1994 to undertake in-house research and policy development. One of its innovations has been the introduction of 'Significant Change Documentation', a process which enables individuals to reflect on and analyse their experiences by identifying and recording major changes and events in their work. This process helps the organization to assess the impact of qualitative issues that are not normally covered by formal measures and indicators. NGOs are investing increasingly in innovative approaches such as these to help monitor performance and evaluate programmes. The point to be made about the different approaches is that they are all attempts to systematize the documentation and put it to effective use.

There is a debate as to whether donor-led monitoring and evaluation is a genuine attempt to promote learning and to reflect on practical experience, or whether it is merely an attempt to police performance, to ensure accountability and value for money, and to shape future productivity and behaviour. If this were true, it could well drive weaknesses and failures underground, negating useful lessons that might be learned from them. The picture is unclear, and there are differing donor and NGO perspectives. It does appear, however, that older, more established organizations treat external evaluation as a positive process that can be useful for monitoring performance, and for generating useful insights and learning. Newer, and possibly more financially vulnerable NGOs, on the other hand, may not always see external, donor-led evaluations in such a positive light. They may view them more as a judgmental process, at the end of which a donor will make an important decision about further funding. In such a situation, evaluation becomes a threat rather than a positive good. This is why some internal monitoring and evaluation systems were initiated originally as a defence mechanism, established to discover and correct shortcomings before donors found them.

DISSEMINATING INFORMATION AND KNOWLEDGE FOR LEARNING

The ability to generate new information and research is of little value unless there are effective dissemination systems for sharing and for ensuring that lessons really are learned. However, evidence suggests that formal documentation systems are of little value unless staff become actively engaged with the information and are involved in its analysis. A BAIF staff member, commenting on the organization's elaborate financial and physical monitoring systems, observes that the organization has 'lots of information but is poor at analysis'.[37]

Documentation: a Surfeit of Information

There is evidence in many of the case studies that there is a counter-productive surfeit of information that is of little real value in promoting learning. This is exemplified in AKRSP (P), which in its early years developed a broad range of documentation that was specifically intended to provide feedback from the field and to assist in the planning process. In particular, its 'Note for Records' (NFRs) and the daily diaries of Social Organizers provided invaluable feedback, and were discussed and debated at monthly regional review workshops. As the organization and the demands upon it grew, however, there came a point when few staff had time to read or collate the findings from the thousands of dairies that had been written. Consequently, the motivation to prepare NFRs flagged and the quality of documentation from the field became increasingly weak. Moreover, there was growing evidence that mid-level staff were unaware of new strategic plans, partly because they had not read the minutes of strategy meetings and partly because no one had thought to discuss the key issues with them.[38]

Thus, while there is a general recognition that information is the hallmark of a learning organization, its usefulness depends on the ability of staff at all levels to access and become engaged with it. Mere delivery of information is clearly not an indicator of a learning organization. This example also highlights the importance of tailoring information to the needs of specific groups or project teams and tracking what these needs are – in the case of AKRSP the needs changed but the process stayed the same.

Our case studies also identified a concern among many NGO staff that official documents and reports often dwell on 'targets' achieved, rather than on the processes used or the lessons learned. This can be explained at least partially by the ubiquitous donor demand for standard indicators of performance and quantifiable measures of achievement. For example, SRSC developed a sophisticated six-monthly reporting system that was able to measure progress and performance levels, but that had little value as a vehicle for sharing lessons with staff. What was considerably more useful was a series of short, quick case studies that SRSC field staff prepared to highlight lessons and the urgent corrective action that was required. These case studies, based on personal observation and interpretation, are actively used in the planning process, helping to ensure that similar mistakes are avoided. To give an example, one study explored staff concerns that training was too theoretical and unreflective of practical reality. As a result, training now incorporates field visits and exposure tours.[39]

Another example can be found in Sadguru, which is often described, even among its well-wishers (and maddeningly to its leadership), as an organization which is 'very good at hardware, but not good on software'. This partly reflects its emphasis on technical infrastructure, such as lift irrigation schemes and other tangible natural resource projects. It also reflects Sadguru's conscious choice not to invest significant amounts of staff time in writing reports and preparing documentation. While eminently understandable, such an approach can have negative repercussions. A European Union evaluation team, while generally very positive about the work of Sadguru, was critical of its failure to document its development methodologies and replication techniques. In response, Harnath Jagawat said, 'We are implementors, not researchers – I don't have funds and time for process documentation.'.[40] He also argues that 'hardware and software are two sides of the same coin', and neither can succeed in isolation. Local development agencies need good process skills to ensure that the technical aspects work successfully and vice versa. Jagawat questions the value and cost-effectiveness of investing in documentation, given the diversity of their activities and the potential unwieldiness of what might result: 'If we get into the documentation business, it consumes a lot of time, at least 30 per cent of the time we could very well spend in four or five more villages.'.[41]

Publications

While there may be doubts as to the value of producing large quantities of internal documentation that will be of limited value to staff, there is a growing recognition that publications for external consumption are a key implement in the NGO toolchest. Publications do share learning and good news. They shape attitudes, influence thinking about issues and build reputations. Most of the NGOs in our study work actively with the media, and most have produced books, journals and videos for public consumption. Some have relied heavily on traditional publishing channels. BAIF produces a quarterly journal which publishes case studies and shares field experiences across the various states in which it operates. BRAC established its own printing house in 1977 to meet the in-house need for books and other materials. This is now a high-quality, profitable commercial operation, providing printing services to various organizations and businesses.

PROSHIKA has begun to publish a development journal, *Discourse*, and its Development Support Communication Programme has pioneered the use of video and television to help communicate its work and share learning. In the late 1990s, the unit was producing a television programme on development issues – *Diganta* – which was shown periodically on national television. As of 1999, the unit had also produced 90 different videos on different topics to disseminate skills and ideas to its village organizations. PROSHIKA also sponsors a Participatory Video Programme (PVP) in different Area Development Centres. This programme encourages local groups in the use of videos which capture and present their own problems, sentiments and solutions on tape.

Several organizations in the study have taken advantage of newer dissemination technologies, establishing their own Internet websites with details of their objectives, programmes and staff. BAIF, IUCN (P), PROSHIKA and BRAC can all be 'dialled up' from anywhere in the world in a matter of seconds. IUCN worked with UNDP in establishing a quasi-commercial e-mail facility known as the Sustainable Development Network. PROSHIKA and BRAC have both gone one step further, actually setting up their own commercial Internet service providers as income generating initiatives. Why pay outsiders for the service, when outsiders will pay you?

THE REALITY OF LEARNING

The learning NGO is marked by curiosity and by an excitement with new ideas. Its staff demonstrate a willingness to reflect, experiment and embrace new thinking. Successful NGOs also accept that there needs to be a process of 'unlearning' and 'relearning', emphasizing the importance of action learning and learning by doing. Learning is a constant process of refining and fine tuning.

However, it is also clear that there are powerful blocks to learning in some of the NGOs we have studied. One of the most formidable barriers to learning is anxiety among key managers about possible loss of income, status or power as a result of change. To some senior staff, knowledge is power, and attempts to promote learning or to disseminate knowledge can be a threat. Consequently, key individuals may attempt to contain learning within specific groups or teams, or may even thwart the spread of important information through the organization.

Another powerful block is a consequence of the 'action culture' that is common to many NGOs and the fact that this is closely associated with the personal drive and work ethic of the leader. A focus on action and rapid decision-making does little to encourage critical reflection or open self-assessment. Linked to this is a concern that time spent analysing and understanding the causes of failure may be seen as a diversion of resources and staff away from the organization's core purpose of helping the poor, and as such is an unjustifiable cost with few tangible benefits. Another barrier to learning is an unwillingness to admit to or analyse mistakes for fear that 'washing dirty linen in public' will attract criticism and provoke a backlash from donors and government. Operational barriers can include the sheer quantity of documentation; the weight of moribund lines of communication; personal fiefdoms which work against shared learning; and the loss of key staff along with their experience, learning and insight.

One solution is the introduction of specialist systems that are designed to overcome resistance and to promote new learning. In Britain, for example, Oxfam has invested in a range of systems and processes to encourage the free flow of critical analysis and cross-project learning, including bilateral exchanges, workshops, networks, publications, videos and e-mail conferencing.[42] The findings of our case studies suggest that NGOs can make more effective use of human resource management systems, including staff appraisals, mentoring and targeted training, and staff incentives that reward experimentation and enquiry. For these systems to work there must be indicators that demonstrate effective organizational learning. These might include the extent to which staff are actively engaged in the process of fixing and adapting; how often there are changes in a programme; the degree of internal criticism; the amount of research commissioned, or the number of reflective documents produced. Such indicators are a prerequisite for any process of assessing effective learning.

An important finding of our study is that most of the organizations – all of which have enjoyed significant growth and praise for their achievements – invested heavily in formal training and dedicated research early in their existence. Among many, there have been two key pay-offs: NGOs with a solid capacity to learn are intellectually fit enough to handle change, and they are agile enough to drive change forward. Early in their lives, all the NGOs in our sample inculcated their basic values and vision throughout their organizations, incorporating them into all their training. These values include a strong work ethic and an emphasis on efficiency; a strong vision of what the organization was trying to achieve; and a commitment to developing the skill-base and core competencies of all the staff. Finally, they gave staff the freedom to perform, encouraging them to act on their own initiative.

CONCLUSIONS

This study highlights the all-important role of learning in the success and growth of NGOs. But it questions the idea – a myth, perhaps – that learning is inherent in the values of NGOs. In reality, NGOs must work hard to promote learning, and they must invest considerable time and money to make learning happen at an organizational level. This does not come naturally or easily to NGOs, or to any other type of organization. Nor is it a formulaic process, readily available from blueprints and manuals. Rather it is an ongoing informal process of action learning supported by formal training, research and other management systems.

Organizational learning is a dynamic process that integrates informal processes with formal structures and systems. The informal processes are those associated with dialogue, reflection and learning by doing. The more formal, structured inputs are those associated with training courses, seminars, commissioned research, evaluations, documentation and reporting systems, as well as such management tools as performance appraisal and the creation of incentives. Whatever the mix of the processes involved, it is apparent from our study that the hallmark of a successful learning NGO is a constant process of refining, fixing and improving – doing things cheaper, faster, better. Learning is both an incremental and an experimental process.

Successful NGOs are not merely replicators of successful programmes, they are relentless innovators, looking for new challenges and working to make existing efforts better. Three features of organizational architecture stand out. First, shared vision – the guiding ideas that shape values, goals and objectives. Second, there is a solid infrastructure for learning – management support, networks, facilities, time and management information systems. Third, there are tools and methods that promote learning – financial rewards, training opportunities, appraisal schemes, internal evaluation techniques with solid indicators of productivity and quality; publications and newsletters. All three are essential features of the 'learning NGO'; they are fundamental aspects of an organization's ability to manage change, to mobilize resources and to meet the needs of the communities with which they work.

CHAPTER 5

STRATEGY: FADS AND FANCIES

A cardinal problem of strategy, whether in war, or in football or in chess, is the question as to which objectives one's strength should be directed against, and in which order.

Martin Van Crevald, *The Transformation of War*

Much has been written about strategic planning, strategic management and strategic choice in non-profit organizations. It is said that if development is to be sustainable, managers must give added prominence to strategy. This requires a change of focus away from individual projects towards an 'external boundary management' that includes influencing the national and international policies of donors and governments. According to Brinkerhoff, strategy 'can be thought of as the way a nation, sector or organization relates to its environment to accomplish its intended goals'.[1] Writing about NGOs, David Korten suggests that they must go beyond short-term considerations in an effort to create desired and desirable opportunities that do not exist.[2] Peter Drucker puts it this way: 'There is an old saying that good intentions don't move mountains; bulldozers do. In non-profit management, the mission and plan are the good intentions. Strategies are the bulldozers. They convert what you want to do into accomplishment'.[3]

The strategic management approach is said to be long-range and process-driven. It should take into account components of the external environment such as technology, politics, economics and social dimensions in order to determine how each of these will inhibit or facilitate development. Key steps in strategic management include a review of mission and current strategies; identification of weaknesses; assessments of threats and opportunities; determination of stakeholder expectations; identification of key strategic issues; design and selection of options; implementation and monitoring, review and adjustment.

According to one definition:

Strategy is the basic how, *the principal method of accomplishing the mission. It embeds the fundamental choices made to govern the use of resources and day-to-day actions. Strategy embodies the notion of positioning and perspective. Position refers to the service or expertise your organization has to offer. Perspective involves values and ways of operating which come from experience, knowledge and dialogue.*[4]

Another writer suggests that in large non-profit organizations, strategies exist at three levels:

- overall strategy for the organization;
- divisional strategy (eg for the rural development or the health programme); and
- service-level strategy (eg for the credit part of the rural development programme or the mother and child health care part of the health programme).[5]

Like other management ideas that have worked their way through the private sector and government to the non-profit sector, strategy has its origins in the military. The word strategy, in fact, comes from the Greek *stratos*, which means army. By the mid-18th century, strategy was a word used by military officers to make a distinction between tactics – the conduct of battle – and all the preparations that took place before it. There is something else about strategy: writing about warfare, Martin Van Crevald says that not long after its birth, the concept of strategy:

> *began to acquire an aura of mystery that has lasted to the present day. Directed from the office with impressive looking desks, maps, coloured pencils and (later) telephones and computers, it supposedly required mental faculties different from, and higher than, those needed in the hurly-burly of battle.*[6]

OUR APPROACH

When we began our study, we took no position on strategy, heeding a warning offered by Australian writers Frederick Hilmer and Lex Donaldson about 'false trails . . . built on poor language and loosely defined terms'.[7] They use strategy as a key example of this problem, offering seven different definitions from management literature.

> *Strategy is one of the most common terms in management-speak, but how does a person know which of the seven another person means? If there were only four possible meanings, there would still be only a 1 in 16 chance that both people would mean the same thing!*

In their 'guided tour through the wilds of strategic management', Mintzberg, Ahlstrand and Lampel describe ten schools of strategic management that have ebbed and flowed across management theory over the past 40 years.[8] Three of the schools – the design school, the planning school and the positioning school – saw strategy formation, respectively, as a process of conception, a formal process and an analytical process.

These approaches were prescriptive in nature, and although they were somewhat marginalized in business theory by the 1980s, they have remained very much alive and well among government departments, donor agencies and, by association, NGOs.

Six additional schools have enjoyed varying degrees of favour more recently. These include the entrepreneurial school, which views strategy formation as a visionary process, and the cognitive school which sees it as a mental process. The learning school emphasizes emergent strategies, and the power school views strategy in terms of negotiation among conflicting groups within an organization. An eighth school sees strategy as something rooted in the culture of an organization, while the environmental school sees strategy formation as a reactive process, with initiative lying outside the organization. Mintzberg and his colleagues define a tenth, configurative school which essentially combines the others into distinct stages and episodes at different periods in the life of an organization.

Where NGOs in general are concerned, both the literature and the practice are somewhat confused. For some NGOs, strategy may relate to growth in size or quality; for others it may relate to the maintenance of the status quo or, as one observer has put it, simply 'survival'. For most organizations, however, strategy lies somewhere on the continuum between work planning and vision. Between these lie the organization's definition of its position and purpose in relation to other organizations and the external environment. Although many NGOs equate strategy with workplan, the middle ground between workplanning and vision was of greatest interest as we began our study, and it turned out to be the most critical aspect of strategic management in the day-to-day lives of our nine organizations.

'Strategic planning' came into vogue for NGOs in the late 1980s, in large part because donor agencies, having picked it up themselves from the private sector, wanted their partners and grantees to benefit from (or conform to) what they had learned themselves. The same was true of management by objectives (MBO) and zero-based budgeting in the 1970s, total quality management (TQM) in the 1980s and results-based management (RBM) a decade later. Interestingly, a search for the expressions 'strategic planning', 'strategic management' and 'strategic choice' in a large 1977 compendium entitled *Managing Non-Profit Organizations* turns up absolutely zero references, including none in a chapter written by American management guru Peter Drucker.[9] By the mid-1990s, however, 'strategy' occupied at least one good-sized chapter in almost every book about non-profit management. It takes up almost a third of Drucker's own 1992 offering, *Managing the Non-profit Organization*. By then, an NGO bereft of strategic management was seen, at least by the writers of books on non-profit management, to be retrograde, old-fashioned and definitely unstrategic.

Are strategic planning and strategic management fads? Although the terminology may be relatively new and the prescriptions as changeable as the seasons, non-profit organizations certainly have strategies, and they always did. These may have been informally agreed among senior managers, they may have been written down, or they may have resided solely in the mind of the organization's founder. Our study sought to answer a basic question: How important, relevant and useful are formalized strategies in actual practice? Case study researchers were asked to address the following questions in each organization:

- Does the organization have a formalized strategy for its short- and long-term future? If so, how does it define strategy? (eg is there a mission statement or the equivalent? Is it alive? If yes, how has it been used, monitored and adapted over time). Are there formal substrategies (on gender, health or education)? When, why and how did formal strategy-making develop?
- Before the evolution of a formal strategy, was there a more flexible, ad hoc approach to strategy? Did it serve the organization well or did it cause aimlessness? Was the formalization of strategy a helpful thing?
- Organizations are often caught in a struggle between development objectives and organizational objectives. They may have programming strategies aimed at beneficiaries or participants, but they also have institutional strategies that may relate to donors, government and others in the external environment. How does the organization balance strategies that may be at odds with one another?

We also asked the case study writers to think of innovative ways of addressing the issue, possibly through the following additional questions:

- Are there broad formal strategies that the organization developed and/or abandoned over its history?
- Has a key strategy changed quickly? If so, why and how?
- Where does strategy come from (eg senior managers, other staff, board, communities, government, donors)?
- Is 'participation' an important component of the organization's strategy? If so, how is it managed in practice?
- Are strategies generally understood and accepted at different levels of management?
- How does the organization view its strategic challenges today?

STRATEGY: A ROADMAP

Just as in the literature, it turns out that there is considerable confusion among South Asian NGOs about what strategy actually is. Sometimes it is a plan, sometimes a policy, sometimes a vision. There is also confusion about where and how it originates. The following sections describe a continuum of strategy wellsprings, starting with a basic evolutionary incremental process at one end and running through selective opportunism to crisis and finally to institutional catharsis.

Incremental Strategies

At the more prosaic end of strategy development among our sample NGOs, there are many examples of service-level strategies developing incrementally, often on an ad hoc basis. F H Abed describes the evolution of BRAC's health strategy:

> *We wanted people to be healthy, but we didn't know how to get to that in terms of what interventions would make people healthy. So we started with doctors in the field; then you find they don't stay, and they are very expensive. So you start training paramedics to be present in the village so they can provide the basic services; then public health consciousness and water and sanitation which can improve health as a whole, rather than responding to an illness. So gradually you evolve certain kinds of work that seem effective in getting to your objective of better health. As you go on doing things, you also learn to isolate things that are not essential and things that are essential, and then you try to replicate these in other areas. So in a way it is learning by doing and isolating the non-essential aspects and discarding them.*[10]

Similarly, BAIF, which for many years focused solely on cattle development, began to widen its focus in 1979 when it went into tribal areas to work with other NGOs on an emergency relief programme. Following the emergency, BAIF attempted to introduce its cattle programmes but found that they didn't work because so much of the area consisted of wasteland. Gradually they introduced fodder crops and then trees that would eventually produce timber and help to rehabilitate the soil. This in turn led to new opportunities for donor funding.

Sadguru's forestry programming began with a community approach and gradually shifted to farm-based forestry and the household level. It then moved to joint forest management with communities and the state forestry department. Because of a changing economic context, it also moved into horticulture which provided greater scope for fruit trees and fruit processing. In addition, it began to play an advocacy role, especially where women were concerned, to ensure equal access to afforestation programmes and outputs. What started as a tree-planting programme with ambitious quantitative targets was gradually converted into a multifaceted social forestry programme that brought the interests of villagers and government together in a comprehensive programme where trees were more a by-product than a purpose.

In management literature, this might be described as the emergence of a 'complex adaptive system', and it might even find a home in the growing body of more current writing about chaos theory, which aims to provide a better understanding of non-linear, complex and dynamic systems, and of managing growth in times of dramatic change.[11]

Strategy and Selective Opportunism

'Opportunism' is not a flattering term, but for several of our NGOs it has been a key element in the way they have evolved. A more flattering term might be 'entrepreneurial', but this does not quite capture the way in which NGOs are sometimes able to match needs with opportunities which may appear only briefly. Saneeya Hussain describes Sungi's work with flood victims in 1992 as 'an opportunistic moment' which led the organization into much broader awareness of rural needs and a correspondingly much broader set of programming activities. IUCN, reflecting on its first decade, was not shy about using the 'o' word:

> *In some ten years, IUCN (P) has developed from scratch into what it is today. To get there it had to be opportunistic, and above all, entrepreneurial. But its rapid growth has also depended on its endeavours to maintain a high standard of work. This has, in turn, led to high expectations from donors and partners.*[12]

The rapid conversion of IUCN (P) from a small office into one of Pakistan's largest NGOs was the result of many things: energetic and purposeful leadership, dedicated staff and the support provided by donors. But without opportunity, and without the ability to recognize and take advantage of the opportunity, these would have been insufficient to make IUCN (P) what it became. The key was a desire by the Government of Pakistan to develop a National Conservation Strategy (NCS), an opportunity that IUCN(P) seized and ran with through the late 1980s and early 1990s, a time when the environment was high on the international donor agenda as well. That IUCN (P) has continued to grow, working on the implementation of the NCS and on the development of provincial conservation strategies, is an example of how opportunity can be converted into action that is consistent with the aims and objectives of the organization.

BRAC works with some 67,000 women livestock rearers, and 23,000 BRAC participants borrowed money for cattle between 1993 and 1995. Their income, however, was stunted by competition from cheap imported milk powder and by their inability to market milk beyond their own village.

In recent years, the European Community has reduced subsidies on milk and milk products, bringing an end to unfair competition with the developing world. Better prices offered more scope in the average Bangladesh village, but ultimately the local market would be quickly saturated. Seeing a golden opportunity, BRAC began to investigate the possibility of creating its own dairy. Opened in 1998 near Dhaka, the new milk processing plant eventually will have a capacity of 50,000 litres a day, and will expand into butter, cheese, powdered milk, ghee and other dairy products. Backed by five regional chilling centres and a modest transportation system, it is envisaged that the effort initially will involve about 35,000 farmers. Realizing, however, that there is still much to learn, BRAC has made an arrangement with BAIF in India to help train its staff and improve the standards of its cattle-breeding efforts.

Strategy, Mission and Catharsis

There are perhaps two broad categories of NGO start-up 'mission' and the strategies chosen to implement them. The first is essentially technocratic and service-oriented. Alnoor Ebrahim suggests that the early thinking of Sadguru and AKRSP (I) was not unlike bilateral and multilateral agency thinking about development, in which economic problems are seen as the result of the'natural' limits of geography and demography – shortages of land, perhaps, and food, combined with over-population – problems to be 'solved' with technological and managerial approaches, rather than by tackling the political economy of poverty.[13] The second type of strategic genesis uses Freirian conscientization as the organizing principle. Writing about the origins of several Bangladeshi organizations, including BRAC, Hashemi and Hassan describe:

> *the essential analytical premise underlying such a strategy [which] suggests that poverty is sustained by the prevailing inequality in the structure of power and access to resources, and this can be rectified only through effective challenges to the system.*[14]

Analysts in search of a problem, however, can be (and sometimes want to be) misled by NGO advertising; especially by very early advertising, when ambitions – whether technocratic, managerial or 'system-challenging' – are expressed in the brightly coloured exuberance of youthful mission statements and emotive project proposals. The reality for most NGOs is usually less clear-cut and considerably less dramatic.

In their early years, the aims and objectives set by many of the NGOs in our survey were expressed in somewhat technocratic terms, seeking answers to development in new approaches to health, education or management. Many, including BRAC, began with a community-based approach which assumed that the poor and other disadvantaged groups would benefit from a general community uplift. A rising tide would float all boats. This approach was not surprising, as the founders of South Asia's earliest development NGOs took their initial cue from international agencies for which 'community development' – combined with tractors, tubewells and high-yielding varieties of seed – had been the basis for most spending since the 1950s. It was only when NGOs saw that the smallest, most numerous and poorest boats were being submerged that the concept and the strategies underlying community development were questioned. For BRAC, the strategic change came in 1975, in its fourth year of operation, when it moved to a 'target group' approach. BRAC's Executive Director, F H Abed recalls the discovery that:

> *Communities are in conflict too. There are the rich and the poor, and their interests are in conflict. Ultimately the benefits of community development accrued to the very rich and the well to do. So we began what we called a target group orientation, and focussed our attention on the poor. Obviously this change in emphasis meant that our staff now had to work with the poorest, and this made the rural elite unhappy. They were suspicious of our motives and our staff had to cope with a lot of opposition.*[15]

The change was something of a strategic catharsis for BRAC and is still remembered as a major turning point in the life of the organization. Several other NGOs in our study underwent a similar strategic catharsis. PROSHIKA, formed in 1975, had a pro-poor bias from the outset. Faruque Ahmed, PROSHIKA's President, recalls that:

> *Before PROSHIKA, nobody had heard of organizing the poor separately. The previous paradigm was to organize everybody in the community. But the concept that the poor need to be organized separately in order to channel resources to them better and to build institutions among the poor, that is something I introduced in Bangladesh, and it caught on. Many others have now taken this as the basic foundation of NGO work in Bangladesh.*[16]

That may well be true, but it did not protect PROSHIKA from a debate on strategic direction which culminated in a division of the organization into two separate entities in its sixth year of operation. One faction believed that the poor should be mobilized solely to struggle against the tyranny of landlords and other vested interests in the rural areas. The faction led by Faruque believed that savings, credit and other economic programmes were essential to the development process. He did not agree that conscientization and credit, for example, were mutually exclusive. Rather he believed that 'without economic empowerment, it is not possible to have total empowerment'.[17]

Not all NGOs go through as profound a catharsis as BRAC's or one as bitter as PROSHIKA's, but additional examples are worth mentioning. The first is BAIF, the oldest of our participating NGOs, and the second is Sungi, the youngest. BAIF began its work in the state of Maharashtra and, for its first two decades, much of its funding was provided by the state government. In 1985, government funding was stopped and 250 BAIF branches had to be closed. While this might have killed a weaker organization, it taught BAIF a strategic lesson about dependency on a single source of income. Instead of winding down, BAIF expanded to other states, making agreements with other departments of animal husbandry. Such has been the quality of BAIF's work, that today some 90 per cent of its income is derived from state governments, making it unique within the Indian NGO scene.[18]

Sungi, founded in 1989, began as an activist, advocacy organization, with the objective of 'bringing about institutional and policy changes so as to create an enabling environment for integrated community development aimed at improving the quality of life of poor communities'.[19] Saneeya Hussain characterizes the first years as 'an exploratory period for Sungi, cutting its milk teeth on advocacy, and developing relations with potential donors for what was till then an initial dabbling in development work'.[20] Several things happened in short order, however, to alter Sungi's strategic approach. The first was a devastating flood in 1992, which Sungi, along with other Pakistani NGOs, addressed through relief and rehabilitation efforts. But, according to Hussain, it was clear that temporary relief was not enough: 'The root causes of poverty would need to be tackled through more permanent institution-building mechanisms ... With social mobilization as its core approach, Sungi took the plunge into integrated rural development work.'[21] The second element in Sungi's catharsis was the sudden withdrawal of funding only a year after its main rural development project had started. The key donor – the only significant donor, in fact – changed its priorities and simply cancelled its support. This forced a ruthless self-re-examination, a reorganization of management style and structure, and the eventual creation of a donor consortium to strengthen and spread the support base. Saneeya Hussain says that 'Sungi started out with a particular vision that defined the focus of its work in its early days, a vision that placed heavy emphasis on bringing awareness of social change through advocacy and through collective action.'. The floods demonstrated another kind of need and another kind of opportunity to Sungi, while the donor débâcle forced a re-examination of the financial bottom line:

The strategic consensus was that advocacy and social mobilization would have to be applied in an integrated fashion and not as two separate streams. This approach of combining advocacy with development gave Sungi its specialist niche, differentiating its work from the work of other rural support programmes in Pakistan, and providing the overall framework for its current and future programme and institutional strategies.[22]

For other organizations, the change was perhaps less dramatic, but in some ways no less profound. Stella Jafri describes IUCN's decision to make the National Conservation Strategy the framework for its programming in Pakistan. With hindsight it looks like the logical course of action, but it was the subject of much soul-searching at the time:

A second crossroads was the decision that, in addition to policy work, we should undertake large field projects. And this despite all advice to the contrary from consultants, and some internal trepidation as to whether we had the capacity to manage it all. Several imperatives factored into this decision: the need for IUCN to demonstrate to itself and others that the NCS was not just a document and could be implemented; the need for someone to test and demonstrate new approaches and to ensure that IUCN (P) policy remained grounded in reality; the need for growth in the size of the organization if it was to make an impact.[23]

The consequent upheaval was dramatic: 'The growth in size and complexity brought a sharpened focus on the development of stronger systems for a different level of financial management, human resources and administration.'. Management structures had to be adjusted and all thematic departments were forced to deal with changes in the size and status.

AKRSP India began in 1984 with an approach that stressed a technical, rather than a social approach to development, aiming to serve as a model 'for a private, non-profit company to catalyse rural development and, where appropriate, to complement and supplement government efforts; and for the sustainable development of fragile ecosystems in drought-prone areas'.[24] This would be done, inter alia, by promoting the evolution of local institutions, testing new technological and management approaches, and working 'with rural people to identify and implement opportunities to promote income and employment generation, with particular emphasis on the weaker sections of rural society'.[25] 'Equity' was part of the mix, but this took something of a back seat to the technical side of the programme, which emphasized water conservation, watershed management and social forestry. By 1994, the mission statement had changed considerably:

AKRSP (India) exists to enable the empowerment of rural communities and groups, particularly the underprivileged and women, to take control over their own lives and manage their environment, to create a better and more equitable society.[26]

SRSC went through a similar change. Its 1992 'purpose statement' said that:

> *The long-term objective of SRSC is to facilitate rural economic growth by supporting the evolution of organized rural communities capable of carrying out their socio-economic development with improved managerial abilities and financial means. SRSC is thus an institutional capacity-building, rather than a service delivery organization.*

By 1995, however, its purpose statement had become a 'mission statement' that was much more explicit about the organization's social goals and its concern for the poor:

> *To build the capacity of local communities through participatory community-based organizations for sustainable social and economic development, with a primary focus on the rural poor and disadvantaged.*[27]

Regardless of refinement, it may well be impossible for an organization to cram all its goals – some of them perhaps at odds with others – into a single statement of objectives. Similarly, the strategy for one organization at one point in time will not be right for another. It is interesting to see, however, how most of the NGOs in our study have moved, over time, from a technocratic, community-based approach to one that more explicitly targets the poor, the landless or women, combining some form of social mobilization and advocacy with the delivery of training, health, education or natural resource management services on the ground. More interesting from the point of view of this study is the fact that whether it was formal or not, from the outset each NGO had a reasonably clear understanding of its mission and the strategies that would be entailed, but each went through a gradual and incremental change, influenced in some cases by a cathartic event, in developing the mission and the underlying strategies that are used today.

INFLUENCES ON STRATEGY DEVELOPMENT

Strategy and Ambition

Individuals can have a strong influence on strategy development. In virtually all our case studies, for example, the founders and chief executive officers have been ambitious. Ambition of two sorts, in fact, plays a key role in the evolution of their strategies. The first has to do with quality and the second with quantity.

An insistence on high quality in programming is a fundamental underpinning for the feasibility and success of any strategy. An organization will not grow and will not be meaningful to its intended beneficiaries or its donors if quality is poor. Technical excellence and adaptive learning were high on the agenda of AKRSP (I) from the outset, but the process of development was equally important. Robert Chambers paid several visits to the organization in its early years, helping to improve its organizational processes and culture, while at the same time developing his own ideas about rapid and participatory rural appraisal.[28] Careful attention to the process used in establishing village organizations was also a hallmark of AKRSP (P). There was a high degree of effort placed on innovation and incremental learning in the development of field crops and orchards, livestock and forestry – all keys to improving the lives and incomes of people in the remote Northern Areas. Not only did the organization employ some of Pakistan's most knowledgeable professionals in these areas, it brought in Pakistani and international consultants to advise on how programmes could be improved. AKRSP (P) also took the unusual step of inviting and paying for the World Bank's Operations Evaluation Department to conduct three evaluations of its work, in 1987, 1990 and 1996. The Bank's advice was, no doubt, useful, but its evaluations served another strategic purpose – building external credibility and support among donor agencies (of which the Bank was not one).

BAIF represents perhaps the most impressive combination of high technical competence and high ethical purpose. As already noted, the organization was founded by a young man – Shri Manibhai Desai – who had become a disciple of Mahatma Gandhi in 1946, working on cattle breeding for over 20 years as part of a Gandhian order. Although the organization he subsequently founded in 1967 never veered from its Gandhian roots, Manibhai put a high premium on scientific excellence, bringing in experienced technicians and ensuring that lessons were learned and remembered. Working closely with government and farmers, one of BAIF's achievements was a high-quality artificial insemination service, delivered at lower cost than government, combined with an extensive programme of progeny testing, research into semen quality and on-farm services. BAIF pioneered frozen semen technology in India and is today estimated to have been responsible for producing as much as 10 per cent of the entire Indian cross-bred dairy herd.[29]

Where quantity is concerned, growth strategies are also in clear evidence throughout our case studies. A long-time BRAC official makes the case:

If you want to make an impact here, you have to be big. If you are small, you can't really make an impact. It is partly because of the size of the population . . . The other kind of impact is that unless you are big, you are not taken seriously.

For example our Nonformal Primary Education Project – if we had only a few schools, nobody would have paid any attention to us. But now that we are big [with 34,000 schools in 1999], the policy makers take us seriously. Also the donors and the intellectual community. If you want to make an impact, size is very important.[30]

In real terms, with a 1998 turnover of more than 13 billion taka (US$262 million), BRAC is nothing, if not big. Where size is concerned, PROSHIKA's President agrees:

There is Schumacher's idea that small is beautiful. For technology maybe, but when you are attacking poverty, which is big, which is massive, which is deep rooted, you cannot expect to be small and make a big dent on it. Many NGOs mistakenly think that they have to remain small in order to be pure and pristine and non bureaucratic and all these things. So they don't think big . . . I felt from the very beginning that we had to go big, but through a process of trial and error. If things worked, we should be willing to replicate, not hand it over to someone else . . . Small is beautiful, but big is better – I subscribe to that.[31]

In Bangladesh, growth is in some ways more possible than it is in India or Pakistan because the country is smaller, the population is culturally and linguistically more homogenous, and the development challenges are not vastly different from one part of the country to another. Growth, nevertheless, creates a wide range of management challenges, and for some there are limits that pose different kinds of strategic challenge. A senior programme officer in Sadguru says, 'We have already expanded and covered a 70–80 kilometre radius; we cannot expand further. We could expand, but to manage our work beyond a certain point and maintain quality may be difficult.'.[32] The strategic choice for Sadguru, rather than expansion, has been to work through other NGOs in order to continue the spread.

IUCN (P) faced a similar dilemma in the early 1990s. It had grown from a single staff member in 1985 to an organization with 53 staff and a project portfolio of almost $3 million by 1992. Its biggest concerns as it reorganized the way that it worked were to retain the professional staff and the innovative spirit that had been the key to its success:

Innovation does not flourish if an organization becomes too bureaucratic, yet some level of management is needed if the focus and cohesion of the programme, and the accountability of its units are to be maintained. A lack of focus often degenerates into over-extension . . . and a falling off in quality as the attention to detail is lost . . . Maintaining quality in a larger, more devolved structure will [also] depend on the ability to attract and keep high quality staff.[33]

Donors and Strategy Development

Can donors play a constructive role in the strategy development of Southern NGOs? Often they cannot, and mostly they should not, but there are exceptions. The evolution of AKRSP India's gender strategy is worth considering. According to AKRSP's first General Manager, 'In 1984 gender was not on our agenda. And [I was told] you better include it, or CIDA money won't come to you, [although] I was not opposed to it.'.[34] This gradually resulted in the creation of women's programmes, gender-related consultancies, further donor pressure and the eventual formation of a Women in Development (WID) unit in the early 1990s. During this period, 36 women's groups were formed, although the approach was still somewhat ad hoc, and something less than a strategic shift in either programming or thinking. It was not until 1993 that a gender strategy actually emerged. AKRSP's 1993 Annual Report explained the change in thinking:

> *Though the number of* Mahila Vikas Mandals *(Women's Development Organizations) remained the same as in the previous year (36), our emphasis in 1993 was to strengthen these, and to work on conscientizing men, making our approach a truly gender approach, rather than a women's focus [approach] . . . Though in the past women have been involved increasingly in our different programmes, too often we have not been able to give women real ownership and control over programmes.*[35]

A similar transformation occurred in SRSC, despite its geographic base in traditional and conservative Muslim communities. It started its women's programme in 1990 with the vague objectives of 'making women aware of their potential and to enhance their capacity by encouraging their participation in the development process of their family and community'.[36] Within a few years it had become clear that a WID unit and parallel programmes for women were not really going to 'enhance capacities' or 'encourage participation in the community'. On the contrary, the approach was creating divisions in families, in communities and within SRSC itself. This recognition, plus pressure from its primary funding agency, NOVIB, led to a complete overhaul in 1996. Under the new approach:

> *SRSC aims to empower women by reducing the inequities they face and increasing their role in the decision-making process within the household and the community. To achieve this, programme interventions strive to be responsive to practical needs identified by women and incorporate means of addressing their strategic interests.*[37]

This meant more concretely that the WID unit was abolished and gender was 'mainstreamed' throughout the organization. Easier said than done, it required changes at three levels for SRSC: within the organization, in field programmes and in its relationship with other development agencies. At the field level, greater emphasis was placed on education opportunities for girls and improved health programming for women. But 'more' does not necessarily mean 'better', and considerable emphasis was also placed on an internal understanding of gender-related issues, including the development of a sexual harassment policy. Where field programmes were concerned, SRSC began to examine the assumptions behind its various 'packages' for women, finding, for example, that a gender analysis of its livestock programme could significantly improve access, control and income for women in a programme that was already aimed at women.[38]

Strategies have to be simple and clear, they have to respond to real needs, and there has to be organizational commitment to them. In the case of AKRSP (I) and SRSC, the early approach to gender was vague, and was more a response to donor pressure than to the needs expressed by the intended beneficiaries, or to anything that was internally driven. Gender-related activities were simply that – activities, without a clear sense of purpose, and without the commitment needed to make them an intrinsic part of the organizational mandate. The articulation of a clear purpose, the development of an action-oriented strategy, and the fostering of an internal commitment to it was needed in order to begin making programmes more effective.

Donor pressures on NGOs are not always constructive, and coercion is understandably resented. Donor-hired consultants, evaluators and inspectors will invariably be treated politely, but they are often ignored. One NGO in our study has so far resisted donor pressures to establish a WID programme, saying that long ago it internalized the gender issue. Its work is largely oriented towards women, one-third of its board are women and half its department heads are women. 'What do the funders want?' asks a frustrated senior manager. In this case it may not be clear what donors want, although it could be something along the lines of the transformation experienced by SRSC – from a set of activities aimed at helping individual women, to a longer-term strategy that attempts to improve their opportunities and their place in the home and in society. Where gender is concerned, donor pressures have not always been misplaced, especially in helping organizations to confront some of the societal demons they fear.

A Strategy Too Far?

That said, societal demons can be very real, and organizations everywhere have to be careful in how they attempt to implement a strategy that is aimed at societal change. In the 1970s, Gonoshasthaya Kendra, a Bangladeshi NGO, trained young women as paramedics, sending them from village to village to work in a public health programme. Travelling on foot was both tiring and time-consuming, but motorized transportation was economically out of the question. A strategy was needed if the programme was to expand on a cost-effective basis. Gonoshasthaya Kendra gave the women bicycles, an idea so outlandish that its radicalism at the time can hardly be exaggerated. Yet within a few months they had overcome the idea – widely held by society in general and by the paramedics themselves – that women could not, and should not ride bicycles. A decade later, BRAC started providing its female field workers with motorcycles, an equally radical idea that in fact met with little public resistance. Over three decades, Bangladeshi NGOs did considerably more than provide their female employees with transportation. They pioneered a wide variety of effective strategies for improving the lives and the status of women – health, education, microcredit and income-earning opportunities. They broke new ground and pushed the boundaries for women far beyond the limited horizons that had prevailed in the early 1970s.

But then something went wrong. In 1994, the fundamentalist Jamaat Party began to attack NGOs. There had been a prelude to this in 1991 and 1992 when the first democratically elected government in more than a decade came to power. Ostensibly concerned about the vastly increased foreign funding of NGOs and a growing number of newspaper articles about alleged 'anti-state' and 'anti-Islamic' activities of NGOs, the government instituted stiff new NGO regulations and attempted to shut down the NGO umbrella organization, ADAB. Following a brief respite, in 1994 there was a renewed flare-up, with street demonstrations against NGOs and the creation of something called 'The Society Against Atheists and NGOs'.[39] Hashemi and Hassan suggest that NGOs had run afoul of both right and left: 'Parties of the left accused NGOs of receiving donor patronage, of being agents of international capital, of stopping the revolution . . . [while] the right saw in NGO actions, especially in their work amongst women, an intrusion of Western modernity, a Christian attack on Islamic values.'.[40] At the village level, this manifested itself in PROSHIKA plant nurseries being uprooted and BRAC primary schools for girls being burned to the ground.

The lesson that many NGOs took from this was not that they had gone too far or moved too quickly, but that there had been gaps in their strategies. For PROSHIKA it meant the development of a more overt stance on the need for a properly functioning democratic system at the national level. For BRAC, the gap had been an assumption that conservative elements were irrelevant and that communities were fully supportive of their work. While the NGOs mounted individual and joint public awareness campaigns among journalists, academics, students and mainstream politicians, some, like BRAC, also reassessed their role in the village and sought new ways to make moderate leaders more aware of, and more involved in, their programmes.

A further flare-up in 1998 and a PROSHIKA-led confrontation between fundamentalists and NGOs over women's participation in development demonstrated that the issue had not died. Because of the violence that ensued, the Brammanbaria incident drove wedges into the NGO community over questions of both tactics and strategies.

Strategy and the Board of Directors

The case study of AKRSP (P) describes a period of strategic uncertainty during the first half of the 1990s, quoting a 1994 strategy document:

> *A vigorous debate surrounds the present situation and future direction of AKRSP. It is said by some that AKRSP has entered* terra incognita. *It is felt by many that it stands at the cross-roads . . . It is a situation that raises fundamental questions regarding the reality on the ground and the way it is perceived. One wonders for example, what is needed to chart and traverse the* terra incognita. *Why is the past no guarantor of the future? Why is available strategy not a signpost to the future? Why are notions of achievement being debated in a successful organization?* [41]

This sounds as though there was wilful confusion and time-wasting, failing to take into account major recommendations in the 1990 World Bank Evaluation for strategic change. Three things led to these concerns, however, apparently shared at the time by many of the organization's staff. The first was the issue of institutional sustainability, a preoccupation of AKRSP's founding donor, the Aga Khan Foundation. The second was the retirement of the first General Manager in 1992 after a period of rapid organizational growth and considerable success in achieving over one decade what other organizations had struggled with for two. And the third was the role – the 'interference' as some saw it – of the AKRSP Board of Directors.

The final question in the quotation above, 'Why was achievement being debated in a successful organization?', relates to the first issue and partly to the second. In the view of the Board, the time had come by the early 1990s to review the aims and objectives of AKRSP. The need to do this had been made clear in a 1989 review carried out by the World Bank at AKRSP's request. Rather than a permanent multi-function NGO, some saw the possibility and the potential desirability of creating a number of independent, stand-alone organizations: a development finance institution, a human resource development institute, an enterprise support corporation and others. This idea of 'successor organizations' had been there for several years, and some believed that geographic spread now had to be curtailed in favour of deepening and sustaining the roots of what had been accomplished. A change in leadership provided the opportunity to think this through, and in 1992 a 'Strategic Development Committee' (SDC) was appointed by the Board to help with the process of charting the future.

The SDC included Board members and outside consultants, but for some staff it seemed that the deliberations over a two-year period were symptomatic of a 'kitchen cabinet gone wild', of a takeover by an external 'development mafia' led by scores of consultants.[42] It was as though an organization that staff had created from nothing had been wrenched from their hands: 'Nobody knew what was happening to AKRSP. Most of us believed it was going to be finished off.'.[43]

While the Board of Directors might be faulted for participatory lacunae, the real 'problem' at this point in AKRSP's development was a rather standard tug-of-war between staff and board. Confusion over strategic direction is certainly not unknown among South Asian NGOs. The 1981 division of PROSHIKA into two separate organizations (described earlier) was the result of an inability to reconcile different strategic visions. In that case, however, the struggle and its resolution was largely staff-driven. What makes the AKRSP case interesting is that the 'standard' confusion between board and staff roles is mainly standard among Northern non-profit organizations. In the South the rarity of such conflict has to do with the fact that many NGO boards act more as rubber-stamps than as the policy formulation bodies so beloved of non-profit management literature.

The 'rubber-stamp board' is not unusual, either in the North or the South. It is most common – and most understandable – in young organizations that are the product of the founders' zeal and ambition. Having considered the more mature Northern 'model', it is not surprising that some in the South have protected their organizations from a higher and more autonomous authority. Writing about non-profit boards in the United States, John Carver says, for example, that they 'stumble regularly and visibly... They rarely say so, however, for the charade has a commanding history, eliciting the most conspiratorial agreement not to notice organizational fatuousness.'.[44] Robert Gale, president of the Association of Governing Boards of Universities and Colleges, observes that 'of some 35 non-profit boards I have served on, only one was truly effective'.[45]

Weaknesses notwithstanding, a board of directors is legally and morally accountable for the organization it serves, and has a mandate, if not an obligation, to act as guardian for what is, whether in the North or the South, a public trust. NGOs cannot be owned by their staff, no matter how difficult and painful this realization – whenever it happens – may be. The realization came earlier for AKRSP than for others in our sample, probably because AKRSP was founded by an institution – the Aga Khan Foundation – that itself worked under the auspices of a proactive Board of Directors. Their sail, in other words, was cut from the same cloth.

By 1996, the AKRSP staff were pulling themselves out of their introspective slump, and the organization was moving forward into the *terra incognita* that always exists for dynamic organizations. The lesson about the Board and the SDC, then, is not whether the Board made the right decisions or the wrong decisions, but whether it was out of line in examining the long-range strategic vision of the organization. In some ways, they operated in an appropriate and textbook-like fashion:

- they and SDC focused essentially on long-range vision;
- they forced an external focus, shifting attention away from internal organizational mechanics;
- they raised questions about longer-term results and forced forward thinking; and
- they encouraged diversity in thinking about organizational options.

If there are lessons to be learned about the process, however, they might include the following:

- the staff that will eventually have to implement any new strategy or vision have to be heard in the process, and have to feel they have been heard;
- other members of the constituency also need to be listened to: beneficiaries, government, donors; and
- the longer the process takes, the greater the likelihood of slippage in staff commitment and organizational effectiveness.

Conclusions

Reporting on a wide-ranging study of strategy development in the private and non-profit sectors, Henry Mintzberg says:

We found strategy making to be a complex, interactive and evolutionary process, best described as one of adaptive learning. Strategic change was found to be uneven and unpredictable, with major strategies often remaining relatively stable for long periods of time, sometimes decades, then suddenly undergoing massive change. The process was significantly emergent, especially when the organization faced unpredicted shifts in the environment, and all kinds of people could be significantly involved in the creation of new strategies.[46]

If this sounds familiar, it should, because it describes virtually everything our case studies have demonstrated about South Asian NGOs. Strategy can develop in a variety of ways. Broad strategies evolve over time, but they can take a sharp turn in direction as the result of a catharsis within the organization, or one created by an external force, such as government, a donor or a political event. Strategies, even fundamental strategies, may also develop in an opportunistic or an entrepreneurial manner. Institutional strategies are clearly influenced by changes in development thinking at large, as happened in the shift from community-based development to approaches that targeted the poor. A general evolution in the thinking about women and development has influenced the strategies of all the organizations in our study. At a programmatic level, microcredit, pioneered by BRAC five years before the foundation of Grameen Bank, has washed dramatically over the development world. It has become in fact, more than a poverty reduction strategy: because of its great attraction for donors, it has helped many NGOs to build a financially sustainable pool of independent working capital.

Formal strategy development is not the magic bullet that many have made it out to be. This is not to suggest, however, that it serves no purpose. Charles Handy warns of 'strategic delinquency' which can beguile an NGO into thinking that the cause is more important than the results, avoiding definitions of success and therefore measurement or evaluation. This can lead to 'strategic seduction' – the acceptance of money from any source as long as it serves 'the cause'.[47] Good strategies, on the other hand, are likely to make specific plans more achievable and the future more predictable. They can reduce uncertainty. They can encourage exploration and they can generate and maintain loyalty and commitment. A by-product is (the appearance, at least, of) coherence – a good selling point with donors. The workability of any strategy, however, will depend on whether assumptions made about resources, capacities and the external environment are correct. In a volatile political setting, with uncertain resources, the most successful formal NGO strategies are likely to be the broad institutional ones that serve to keep the organization as a whole on course.

The emergent, adaptive reality of strategy-making notwithstanding, NGOs everywhere are pressed, especially by donors, for explicit, prescriptive, long-range strategic plans, a throwback to a rationalist school of planning that has now fallen from favour in the business sector. There are perhaps three reasons for this. The first is that donors may believe that it is possible. The second may have to do with their desire for 'sustainability' – itself a confused subject, underpinned by the widespread and usually unrealistic desire for an early, money-related 'exit strategy'. This, of course, must be planned from the outset, realistically or not. A third reason, provided by John Kay, is because managers want to know what to do:

To observe that organizations are complex, that change is inevitably incremental, and that strategy is necessarily adaptive, however true, helps very little in deciding what to do. Managers wish to be told of a process which they can at least partially control and, whatever its weaknesses, that is what rationalist strategy appears to offer.[48]

Interestingly, despite this almost universal emphasis placed by donors on Grand Guignol rationalistic strategic planning, at least five of our nine organizations managed to get through their first decade without such an effort, and two of the oldest organizations in the sample waited more than 20 years before engaging in a formal strategic planning process. This is not to suggest that they were strategy-free, rather that formal mechanistic strategies are less important than donors and much of the management literature on non-profit organizations make them out to be.

There are some obvious reasons for this. One worth repeating is that NGOs work in a highly volatile environment. With the stroke of a pen, governments can take away the financial basis for their existence, as happened with BAIF in the mid-1980s. Governments can impose sudden and draconian new regulations that can punch holes in the most resilient of strategies. This has happened at least once in India, Pakistan and Bangladesh over the past decade. Or a donor may withdraw, sending the best laid strategies into free-fall, as happened with SRSC when USAID suddenly withdrew in 1992, or when Sungi suddenly lost its largest donor in 1995. A change in leadership may also herald changes in strategy. Despite the outside perception that South Asian NGOs are 'one-man shows', six of the nine organizations in our study have gone through at least one leadership change, with concomitant changes in style, if not strategy. All have survived the ordeal.

There is a second reason why formal strategies can be problematic. Rob Paton observes that:

Organizations, like people, espouse many values and pursue multiple goals, which may be more or less ambiguous, and between which all sorts of tensions and inconsistencies inevitably arise ... [S]ome inconsistency between values and action is inevitable – indeed it may even be desirable in maintaining the aspirations of the organization.[49]

'The ecology of values being enacted in any lively organization', Paton suggests, 'will always, and rightly, be subtler and richer than those magnificent specimens captured and mounted in the display cases of mission and value statements.'[50] Although most South Asian NGOs would probably deny it, given the environment in which they work, it is possible that some have gone into strategic planning exercises mainly because important outsiders think formal strategies are important.

A third factor diminishing the importance of formal strategy development relates to the trade-offs that exist between processes and individuals, between participation and the nature of the chief executive officer. In our case studies, there are many descriptions of how strategy develops in a participatory manner, involving staff and beneficiaries in lengthy consultative processes. PROSHIKA, for example, has a five-year plan, as well as annual plans that are developed at field level and then brought forward each July to what is known as the 'PROSHIKA Parliament' for debate and refinement. In addition, there are quarterly meetings that bring together about 200 field coordinators to debate key issues for two or three days at a stretch. Among NGOs, admission of anything *un*participatory would be met with widespread derision, if not condemnation.

Agreeing on the importance of informal strategy-making, IUCN's Stella Jafri goes further:

> *I would go so far as to add an 'unconscious' element to the non-formal . . . The non-formal strategy is never articulated in its entirety, nor are the same bits necessarily articulated to the same groups of staff. It is constantly and incrementally changing to take into account new perceptions and paradigm shifts, as well as to meet the challenges of a constantly changing environment. The imperative for articulation itself may bring about a refinement, or a change in nuance, or even a new dimension.*[51]

But if our case studies demonstrate anything about the origins of NGO strategy, it is that the role of the chief executive officers cannot be underestimated. They are all 'ideas people', not systems people or number crunchers and all have demonstrated great skill as organizational strategists. They have created and/or led organizations that have developed highly successful strategies for village-level development and poverty reduction. They have developed successful strategies for influencing governments and donors. All have developed successful strategies for growth and survival in a difficult and volatile climate. They are, as Alan Fowler puts it, people who manage with a strategic perspective: 'Managers must have an ability to judge the long-term implications of short-term events, in relation to the strategic direction, and respond accordingly.'.[52]

It is fair to say that all have also demonstrated high levels of ambition – not so much for themselves, as for their organizations and the purposes they serve. Learning and high-quality programming have been a part of this ambition. As Chapter 4 has shown, all NGOs in the study have placed a high premium on learning, and their strategies have undoubtedly been informed by empirical evidence of what works and by a clear understanding of their own capabilities. Most leaders realized at some point, usually in their first decade, that their organization had to become relatively large in order to enjoy the economies of scale, and in order to be noticed above the development fray that is so distracting for governments and donors. When it comes to strategy and leadership, however, most are modest, even shy in describing their role. Barry Underwood, General Manager of AKRSP, India, believes that 'most situations in organizational life can be dealt with in a participatory manner and the whole organization will go with you. You don't have to lead them.'. But when pushed on a definition of 'participation', he says, 'It is not democracy. In my organization it is not democracy. . . Ideally it is consensus.'.[53] Even PROSHIKA's President, who believes firmly that the role of the manager is to create the kind of climate 'where people *can* participate and become part of the decision-making process', admits that 'it is difficult to have a participatory discussion with 200 people.'.[54] It may well be that participation is not so much a part of the strategy-*making* process as part of the strategy-*affirmation* process. In other words, no matter where a strategy originates – with the chief executive, a donor or in the suggestion of a field worker – participatory processes are needed, and are widely used in order to build consensus and institutional support.

CHAPTER 6

THE ACCIDENTAL NGO: GOVERNANCE, STRUCTURES AND PARTICIPATION

The root of wealth or poverty lies in the ends we have in mind, not in the means to those ends. If the hand is ready, then finding the instrument of action should not be difficult.

Rabindranath Tagore

Among non-profit organizations, certain words carry great meaning, but over time these meanings can diverge dramatically from dictionary definitions. 'Hierarchy' is one such word. Although technically it means little more than 'a system of persons or things arranged in a graded order', it does suggest – in the grading of the order – that certain 'persons or things' will be of a higher order than others. In organizations where participation, sharing and democratic principles are valued, the concept of hierarchical management structures is problematic. It is so problematic, in fact, that the word 'hierarchy' did not appear once in any of our case studies, and it is used sparingly or not at all in management books on non-profit organizations. 'Structure' is a more value-free word, but this word and the concept of structure also fall victim to lengthy and defensive discussions about participatory management, decentralization, staff empowerment and the like.

Neuroses about structure and hierarchy are most prominent among Northern NGOs, but the transfer of these neuroses from North to South has been reasonably effective. This chapter will examine the evolution of thinking about governance, organization and structures in our nine case study NGOs, examining the formal arrangements as well as the sometimes more important informal arrangements that have allowed them to adapt and grow.

GOVERNANCE

In most countries, including Bangladesh, India and Pakistan, registered non-profit organizations are required to have a general membership and a board of directors. The membership may be as broad as the hundreds of thousands of individuals who join a Greenpeace or an Amnesty International, or it may be as small as the handful of individuals who sign an organization's application for legal incorporation. The membership may be comprised of individuals or of organizations. Most of the organizations in our study, and indeed most NGOs worldwide, have a small membership base.

Only one of the case study organizations – IUCN – has institutional members. More than a dozen NGOs and government departments make up the organization's Pakistani membership, meeting twice a year or as required to discuss policy and programming issues. Ultimate authority, however, rests with the management and governance structures of the parent body, based in Switzerland. The Pakistani institutions are also members of this larger body, but obviously they have a relatively small role in the global institution. While the Pakistani members of IUCN meet regularly in Pakistan to discuss the organization's local policy and programmes, their authority over the local body is thus more informal than formal.

For most of our case study NGOs, it is the Board of Directors (or 'trustees' or 'governors') that constitutes the formal governance structure. In most cases, the board membership is self-selected. In other words, it is the board itself that decides how and who to appoint as a new member when a vacancy arises. Members may be drawn from an inner circle of friends and acquaintances, or there may be a more formal search process aimed at attracting individuals with special skills, connections or experience.

Much of the literature on non-profit governance discusses what boards should be and do, and what can go wrong with them. It is not unusual, for example, for boards to spend too much time on the trivial, at the expense of the important. Boards can be reactive rather than proactive; they can become overly involved in day-to-day management issues that should be left to staff. They can become fixated on short-term problems, rehashing issues that the staff have already studied at length. Or they can be apathetic, acting as little more than a rubber-stamp approval mechanism for senior management. There are many prescriptions available for remedying these ills, although it is always easier to prescribe – for example, a board should focus on vision, fundamental values and policy – than it is to make it actually happen.

Our study suggests that how a board functions in a South Asian NGO has less to do with prescriptions and understanding of roles than it does with its origins and its age. Some of the NGOs in our study – BAIF, BRAC, PROSHIKA, Sungi – were founded by a very small group of dedicated and idealistic individuals. They had an idea of what they wanted to do, but they had very limited funding, few role models and little idea where their experiment might take them. They were, in a sense, 'accidental

NGOs'. In these cases, trustees were mostly friends and acquaintances whose primary function was to encourage the founders and offer what little assistance they could.

Other organizations in the study – AKRSP (I), AKRSP (P), Sadguru, SRSC – were more clearly premeditated. The first Executive Director was appointed by a sponsoring group that formed the core of a Board of Directors. Sizeable initial funding was secured before the ship set sail; there were role models (including some of the organizations in the first group); and there was a relatively clear idea of what would be accomplished in the first year or so. Among 'accidental NGOs', the chief executive officer (CEO) and a handful of key staff were the founders. In the 'premeditated NGOs' it was key members of the founding board, along with the donor agencies that backed them, who were in essence the founders. This is an important distinction. In each of these latter cases the CEO played a pivotal role, but he was not the *founder* of the organization. In each case, he was recruited from outside the NGO sector (in part, of course, because the 'NGO sector' at the time was miniscule).[1] In these organizations, the Board has played a much more proactive role in the development of both policy and programming than in the former. In three of the four cases – the two AKRSPs and SRSC – the Board has also presided over a change in CEO, acting in much the same way as the board of an established Northern NGO might. This is not to suggest that the Boards of these organizations have not occasionally fallen prey to the generic weaknesses of boards elsewhere. It is to suggest, however, that where the founding group becomes Board members rather than full-time staff, the Board is much more likely to be proactive from the outset than in cases where the founders of the NGO are also its senior managers.

The second issue has to do with time. Mike Hudson describes five phases in the 'life cycle of boards'.[2] For our purposes these can be compressed into three: a 'founding phase', a 'youthful phase' and 'adulthood'. In the founding phase, a charismatic leader with 'the vision and personality to define a social, cultural or environmental problem . . . creates an organization to address it', gathering people together who share the same ideals. The Board may be little more than a group of friends and supporters who endorse (or 'rubber stamp') whatever the leadership proposes. In the youthful phase, the Board becomes more active, often after founding staff members leave. The Board begins to set objectives, discusses the budget and, because there are new trustees, they require more details of what the organization is doing. As Hudson describes it, the Board 'meets more often and establishes subcommittees. Board papers become thicker, and before long, it is accused by staff of meddling in detail.'. As Boards mature into 'adulthood', they often adopt a hands-off approach, sometimes attracting prominent individuals because of their name and reputation. There may be an unwillingness to challenge accepted policies and programmes, and meetings may become ritualized. If and when a crisis erupts, it is not unusual for some members to leave and for the rest once again to become more involved in detail.

Where their Boards are concerned, two of our 'accidental NGOs' – BRAC and PROSHIKA – fall clearly into the founding phase, even though at 30 years of age BRAC is elderly by South Asian NGO standards. PROSHIKA too, founded in 1976, is a mature organization. In both cases, however, the Board has remained small, very close to the founder-leaders and it remains very much in the background. The fact that these Boards have remained quiet and supportive rather than proactive begs the questions: Does it matter whether an NGO has a proactive Board or not? Is the fact of a Board's existence actually a reason for any organization's success? One possible lesson is that it is not always necessary to have a Western-style board of trustees. While such a body may be important to the provision of continuity, legitimacy, image and protection from 'the environment', it may actually have very little to do with accountability or good management. In her 1992 book on BRAC, Catherine Lovell devoted only a single paragraph to governance, describing the nine-member General Body, from which seven were elected to form a governing body or board. In recent years efforts have been made to change and expand BRAC's governance structure, with particular reference to the question of succession at the Executive Director level. But for most of its life, the BRAC Board has exhibited most of the features of Hudson's 'founding phase'.

While more broadly based than BRAC in some respects, in others the governance structure of PROSHIKA is even tighter. Its 31-member General Body changed very little in more than two decades. The nine-member Governing Body or Board is drawn from this group of 31, and of the nine, three are actually founding staff members – the President/CEO and two Vice-Presidents. Efforts in Sungi to expand the membership base were initiated by senior staff rather than by the Board, in an effort to build a broader and more democratic constituency. Taking a leaf from the PROSHIKA book after a staff visit to Bangladesh, Sungi created a 'panel' of 20 members in 1996, 9 of whom are always on the Board. Six of the panel are founder-members, and two of them are always on the Board. Here is an example of a deliberate effort to move beyond the founding stage (but not too far), despite reservations from some of the original Board members who felt that they were being used as a 'rubber stamp' to approve this change and others.[3] Sungi has an idea that eventually its village-level organizations will act as an 'electoral college', electing community activists to an expanded panel, with some of them eventually making it to the Board.

The founding stage in Board behaviour was skipped almost completely in the premeditated NGOs. The Boards of the two AKRSPs, and SRSC in particular, were highly proactive from the outset, not just in policy development, but in the design of programmes, donor relations, staffing, and sometimes in what might be termed micro-management. While they may well have done all the things that boards are supposed to do, they also did many of the things that boards are not supposed to do. The reason is not that all boards must go through a 'youthful' stage of wilful meddling. The Boards of these NGOs included individuals who in one way or another took direct personal responsibility for the success of the organization. The Board of the two AKRSPs, for example, included staff members of the sponsoring Aga Khan Foundation. Through its first 15 years, the Board of AKRSP (I) handled most donor relations – an odd arrangement by any standard. The Board of AKRSP (P) drew the resentment of staff for its handling of a strategic planning review (described in Chapter 5). SRSC, which was an effort to replicate AKRSP (P) in Pakistan's Northwest Frontier Province, had the Executive Director of AKRSP on its Board from the outset, along with the Chief Secretary of the Province. Both of these men had a strong desire to see the organization succeed, and both played a prominent role in day-to-day programming and management issues in the early years. Advantageous and welcome at times, their involvement also transcended the normal Board mandate, becoming on other occasions intrusive and counterproductive. A 1996 evaluation of SRSC noted that the Board had understandably stepped into a management role because of a number of personnel and funding crises. It also noted that there had been several instances where:

> *The Board and its Executive Committee superseded their own procedures in order to facilitate decision-making. These decisions relate mostly to the hiring and firing of senior staff, and to the filling of senior positions without adequate advertising . . . Much of the Board's interest in detail would disappear if the Management Group had greater capacity, or took more responsibility in dealing with the myriad personnel issues now handled by the Executive Committee [of the board] when it sits as a recruitment and selection committee. Issues of personnel policy should be addressed at a much lower organizational level (e.g. in a personnel department) with an appeal process to the CEO, rather than to the Board of Directors.*[4]

Of all the organizations in our study, the one that best exemplifies the 'adulthood' governance phase is BAIF. This may be because it is the only one of the group that was founded by a charismatic and visionary leader who left the scene more than a few years ago. Enough time passed, both before and after the death of Manibhai Desai in 1993, for the Board to develop its own personality and to figure out an appropriate role for itself. Much in the way that Hudson describes the generic board, BAIF's includes scientists, industrialists and retired civil servants. The chairman has been associated with the organization for 20 years, and, according to the case study, trustees have played a supportive and non-interfering role. This is partly because, as the Chairman puts it, they share 'a common wave length on major issues ... a scientific approach [and a belief] that professionals should be used for development work'.

In fact, the real coming of age of boards in accidental NGOs probably has more to do with the aging or passing of the founder than anything else. As F H Abed began to contemplate his retirement at the end of the 1990s, he talked more and more about the Board of BRAC, understanding that the Board would have to take considerable responsibility for what (and who) might follow. When Omar Asghar Khan was unexpectedly offered a cabinet position in 1999, the Board of Sungi suddenly and necessarily loomed large in his thinking about how a transition could be arranged. The question, therefore, is not *whether* Western-style boards are important to NGOs, but *when*. How a board functions in a South Asian NGO has less to do with prescriptions and the understanding of roles than it does with the organization's origins and age, and perhaps with whether or not it has had to face a succession challenge at the top.

CULTURE AND HIERARCHY

All organizations are formed by and within the context of a country's history, culture and religion. Drawing on work done by Geert Hofstede and others, Alan Fowler provides a framework for explaining cultural differences in people's understanding of management and leadership. In one society there may be a high acceptance of the unequal distribution of power. In another, it may be very low. In one country, there may be a high emphasis on individual rights and responsibility, while in another, value will be placed on collective responsibility. In one society there may be a dominance of 'masculine' principles such as competitiveness, assertiveness and possessiveness, while in another, 'feminine' values such as creativity, caring, negotiation and persuasion may predominate. Similar differences can be found in attitudes towards risk, uncertainty, individual judgement and orientation towards time-bound values, such as thrift versus spending, reciprocity versus probity, saving face versus perseverance.[5]

Becoming more specific, and writing about the relationship between identity, Islam and human development in rural Bangladesh, David Abecassis says that fatalism, hierarchy and the subservient role of women are prominent characteristics of the culture. Fatalism is a mechanism for coping with deprivation and the realities of poverty and powerlessness. 'It is then a very short step to believing that one cannot do anything to change the situation', so there is a widespread belief among the poor that they will always be poor. Hierarchies dominate society and determine status. 'The more status one has, the more respect one is given and the fewer demeaning incidents occur in one's social life; and the more opportunities to gain power and resources.'[6] Property, education and money beget rank and power, creating in turn client–patron relationships. Hierarchical relationships are therefore a fact of life – in government, in commerce and in social intercourse. To the extent that these generalizations are correct, time will be an important factor in the creation of effective institutional alternatives.

In trying to explain the different evolutionary paths of voluntary organizations in the South, Salamon and Anheier have examined a variety of factors in 13 countries: colonialism, authoritarianism, religion. Islam, they found, was not especially conducive to the creation of voluntary organizations, 'stressing the integration of the individual into a larger social and religious order, rather than the existence of a separate social space for the exercise of individual initiative'.[7] 'The role of Hinduism in the development of the non-profit sector in India was more complex . . . Hinduism places great emphasis on individualism and individual initiative in its stress on personal spiritual devotion as a path towards inner peace.' Hinduism 'has therefore done little to foster formal organizational networks through which individuals could act'.[8] Following this logic, one might expect to find fewer NGOs, especially fewer large NGOs in countries like India, Pakistan and Bangladesh. The opposite, however, is true. There are both more NGOs and more CBOs in these three countries than in other parts of the world (absolutely and on a per capita basis), and there are more large and well-established modern NGOs as well.

Looking for profound meaning and serviceable generalizations among a few tea leaves can lead to curious explanations for regimented behaviour in organizations that extol the virtues of participation and decentralization. For example, Grameen Bank requires its members to shout slogans, salute and sit in straight lines at meetings. This is justified on the grounds that Grameen clients come from a strata of society that lacks confidence in its ability to change. Becoming a Grameen borrower does not automatically give them confidence or change their status in society. 'In the intervention model of Grameen Bank,' writes Susan Holcombe, 'discipline is manifested by regular attendance, vigorous participation in exercises and slogan shouting, ability to talk to a male Bank staff member, and growing self confidence . . . In this way discipline also supports the viability of the loan decision process.'[9]

History, religion and culture may well explain some aspects of organizational evolution and manners. If anything, however, it would appear that South Asian NGOs have emerged and succeeded almost *despite* history, religion and culture. Or it could be that these factors have played a much less prominent role than is sometimes imagined, and that other aspects of the external environment, as discussed in Chapter 2, have played a more important role.

There is another set of cultures – or another way of looking at culture – that may be equally as important in understanding the structure and management of South Asian NGOs. The first 'culture' is the personal: the culture of family, friends, status, education, religion, caste – not unlike what has been described above. The second is an associational culture – not just within a specific organization, but within a community of like-minded organizations. As late as the mid-1980s, Pakistani NGOs were mostly very small and they were virtually unknown among the public. An individual who worked for an NGO at that time was generally regarded by friends and family as either crazy or unemployable elsewhere. Within a decade that view had changed dramatically because a community of organizations had emerged, staffed by professionals and funded generously by donor agencies. New norms, derived in part within the community and in part from interaction with international agencies, were developed. New ways of working, thinking and organizing were not far behind. A subset of this associational culture, of course, is the culture that develops within each NGO, as discussed in Chapter 3.

The third 'culture' is the bureaucratic canvas on which the management structures of government and the private sector are painted. Based on clear systems of accountability and authority, bureaucratic systems of government and business are unequivocally hierarchical. In their dealings with government and official donor agencies, in the recruitment of new staff members, and in their reading of management literature, Southern NGOs are undoubtedly influenced by this third culture.[10]

The 'bureaucratic culture' is likely to be most evident in the organization charts, job descriptions and publications of an NGO, and might actually be mistaken by the casual observer for the dominant South Asian NGO operating mode. The personal and associational cultures, however, that are less formal but in some ways more profound, account for the apparent mismatches in definitions of words like 'hierarchy' and 'decentralization'. They account also for the occasional dichotomy between words and practice, as with Grameen Bank's participatory, decentralized approach to development, and its members sitting in straight lines at meetings, saluting and shouting slogans. Perhaps it is worth highlighting the fact, therefore, that hierarchy and participatory management are no more incompatible than decentralization and *dirigisme*. An organization with clear management hierarchies can also be participatory in style. A decentralized organization, on the other hand, may have no use whatsoever for participatory management techniques.

This leads logically, then, to a discussion of structure, which Brinkerhoff describes as 'the way a purposive entity . . . is set up to accomplish its mission and goals' – the choices made in dividing tasks between work groups and specifying how the work is to be coordinated. Brinkerhoff divides structure into categories – authority, hierarchy, decentralization, formality and complexity – which will serve as a template for the following discussion on South Asian NGOs.

Authority (and Power)

In her book on BRAC, Catherine Lovell juxtaposes the issues of hierarchy and participation, control and empowerment. She points out that in Bangladesh, hierarchy is a fundamental part of family, village and political life. While F H Abed says 'there are so many things in our culture that are bad for running an efficient organization', Lovell suggests that:

> *Hierarchical values also play an important role in BRAC. They reinforce stability by enhancing respect for leadership and by providing the basis for acceptance of structure and rules. An organization as large as BRAC, operating in a turbulent and often corrupt environment, requires a clearly delineating controlling structure and firm rules for some aspects of its work.*[11]

Authority is undoubtedly important, but in most of our case study NGOs, it rests not so much on cultural tradition as on respect for what the leadership has accomplished. The question of leadership is addressed in greater detail in Chapter 7. It is worth noting here, however, that while the basis for the leader's authority is probably similar in all our case study organizations, it is exercised differently from one organization to another. In some, the founder may mature from leader into manager, in other cases – as with Manibhai Desai – he may turn from teacher into guru. Some leaders have remained cool and aloof from their staff – or have seemed to, depending on one's vantage point – while others have seen their role as 'man of the people'. Some leaders are addressed as *sahib*, while others are called *bhai* (brother). In truth, however, most of our case study organizations exhibit more collegial relationships – vertical as well as horizontal – than authoritarian.

Much has been written in recent years about power relations and organizational politics.[12] All organizations are made up of groups, tiers and coalitions of individuals who inevitably form power blocks of one sort or another. These power blocks – rival camps, young turks, the old guard – can be a force for change, or they can become a barrier. While the organizational politics that they exemplify can be divisive, they can also ensure that issues are aired and debated before decisions are made.

Hierarchy

Most NGOs are organized as hierarchies; certainly those in our study are, and have been from the outset. One of the first questions about their use of hierarchy is the number of management levels: the more levels, the steeper the hierarchical pyramid. In NGO management studies, as in much current business writing, there is an idea that the flatter the structure, the better. Flat structures allow managers to be more closely in touch with other levels of staff; they minimize overheads and permit maximum levels of decentralization – or so the literature says.

In fact, the opposite can be true. When organizations begin, they are inevitably small, and they are flat simply because the number of people involved would make for a rather dysfunctional hierarchy. As they grow, however, there is a tendency for NGOs to remain flat, in part because flatness does allow senior management to stay in touch with field operations and staff at all levels. A 1986 evaluation of AKRSP (P), when the organization had already established 526 village organizations and had 191 staff, praised the three-tier management structure, saying that 'AKRSP's flat management structure contributes to open communication . . . [including] well documented and understood procedures'.[13] It also served to reduce management concern about details of implementation. In fact, as the programme grew, however, it became more and more difficult for nine managers, each with large programmes, to report directly to the General Manager. Weekly management group meetings became lengthier and less functional as senior staff grappled collectively with both important issues and minutiae. Although described as 'decentralized' because its structure was so flat, in managerial terms, AKRSP was, in fact, a highly centralized operation. Once the organization had grown to a certain size, flatter was not better, and the management pyramid had eventually and inevitably to be raised, with the insertion of new and more genuinely decentralized levels of management.

A 1997 evaluation of PROSHIKA found that its origins as a small collective still exerted 'an important influence over its organizational culture and actions. It retains a personalized senior management style [with] . . . limited accountability for senior staff, high levels of motivation and an emphasis on "coordination rather than management".'.[14] While this had some management benefits, the evaluators found that structures and systems were showing increasing strain in an organization that had over 50,000 active village groups and 3000 staff members – more than double the number only three years earlier. They recommended that the Executive Director decrease the span of his management responsibilities through the creation of new directorships and deputy directorships. In PROSHIKA – as in AKRSP (P) – flatter was no longer seen to be better.

Hilmer and Donaldson argue that:

> *The belief that flatter is better is a strong one. The idea that middle management is inherently destructive, or at least unnecessary, has enormous popular appeal . . . The flatten-the-structure theme is reflected in a number of fads including*

delayering, downsizing, rightsizing, inverting the pyramid, and replacing managers with communication and computing technologies.

These are false trails, they argue:

> *Large organizations exist because they can provide services by coordinating the actions of thousands of people. Hierarchy is one powerful way this is done, though not an easy organizational structure to make work. But throwing hierarchy and structure away is hardly a sensible response.*[15]

BRAC's Executive Director, F H Abed, says 'we have a normal hierarchy. We have a Programme Organizer, and one Area Manager, then a Regional Manager, and on top of them we have Programme Managers and a Director of the Programme. So we have hierarchies, but basically, BRAC is fairly flat.'. Even though BRAC has 'a normal hierarchy', Abed too is beguiled by notions of flat. He recalls British rule in India, when each Deputy Commissioner in a province reported directly to the Chief Secretary, a very flat system that worked well because of the communication system that was used – detailed monthly reports read and commented upon by the Chief Secretary.* 'Supposing we [in Bangladesh] had a very good communications system – phone or fax,' Abed says, 'then maybe we could do away with regional managers, but communications would have to improve a lot.' Abed also inclines towards Peter Drucker's analogy of the orchestra as a flat organization:

> *An orchestra is a very flat organization in the sense that the conductor handles it all. The first violinist does not report to the second violinist. They have the score in front of them, so you don't have to have bosses because everyone knows exactly what they have to do. So if you can transmit to your staff the knowledge and skills of what they are supposed to do effectively, then you can cut down on one or two layers.*[16]

Hilmer and Donaldson understand the seductivity for managers of the 'improved communications' idea and 'the orchestra myth', but they point out that few businesses, much less NGOs, operate in a world according to plans where every note is predetermined in tone, loudness and tempo. The orchestra works only when everyone plays exactly what was written by the composer – an individual who is not usually available to the average

---

* This, incidentally, is precisely how Shoaib Sultan Khan kept track of things in the early years of AKRSP (P): field staff kept copious logs that were submitted to him for comment.

NGO, notwithstanding the skill of their senior managers.** They also debunk the 'technology myth', arguing that 'real managers are neither calculating machines nor nodes in electronic networks that automatically summarize, reroute and highlight information'.[17] Our study demonstrates that the problem for NGOs is not hierarchies, but – as with teamwork, learning and decentralization – how the hierarchy functions. Hierarchies are not inimical to decentralization, nor are they at odds with a participatory management style.

Decentralization and Participation

Decentralization describes the degree to which authority and responsibility are spread down and outwards within an organization. Decentralization can be manifested in different ways. Deconcentration, such as the establishment of field offices under central authority, is the most elementary. Delegation – the allocation of authority to field offices – is a second level of decentralization. Devolution – the transferring of authority to individuals or groups that are independent of the organization – represents the most far-reaching level of decentralization.[18]

Most of the organizations in our study have struggled to find the appropriate mix of deconcentration, delegation and devolution. As they grew, there was no argument about the need for deconcentration, and, from their earliest experience of growth, all saw the need for, and the benefits of, deconcentration to regional or field offices. When AKRSP (P) made its organization structure steeper by introducing new layers of management, it also shifted responsibility downward, allocating greater responsibility to the regional and social organization level. Thus while the organization was less flat (ie more hierarchical), it had become more decentralized.

The delegation of responsibility is one thing; the delegation of authority is more complex. The first issue is the willingness of senior management to delegate authority in a cultural climate where this is far from the norm. The second is the ability of junior managers to accept the delegation of authority and to handle it responsibly. A former manager

---

** A refinement on the orchestra-as-management analogy is the jazz combo, where there is no conductor and no score, but where teamwork, knowledge and trust are essential. The jazz-combo-as-management analogy makes sense when there are three or four musicians, but a 50- or a 500-piece 'combo' would be harder to imagine (and manage). For more musical management analogies, see *Competing on the Edge: Strategy as Structured Chaos*, Shona Brown and Kathleen Eisenhardt, Harvard Business School Press, Boston, 1998.

in AKRSP (I) observes that the first Director, Anil Shah, was 'very bureaucratic and not very participatory. I am a person who likes to minimize the number of levels in an organized structure, preferring more of an egalitarian way of functioning. I need to have them if I am to function, and I found them missing. There were many silly things, like when the boss comes, you had to be there.'. The same individual admitted, however, that Anil Shah had been dealing with 'a lot of really brattish young graduates and postgraduates who would speak their mind', but who often didn't know what they were doing. Shah nevertheless placed great 'confidence and trust in the young programme coordinators in the field . . . and he backed us up fairly. Many of our projects were disasters and he may have torn us apart for that, but he never penalized us in an unfair manner. He was willing to pay the bill for us to learn. But we were not allowed to repeat a mistake.'.[19]

As noted in Chapter 3, with growth, delegation and the evolution of more complex structures, some things are inevitably lost. A Sadguru manager reminisces about the 'good old' informal days when they were a smaller, more cohesive group and each knew what the other was doing. 'I was more comfortable with the older style. When I used to go to a village and someone asked me a question, say about the forestry programme, I would feel comfortable answering the villager's question. But now we have become so large I don't even know what is going on in the other departments.'[20] Nostalgia for the good old days when everyone had access to everyone else features in IUCN as well. 'The top management has become inaccessible, with new layers of authority shoved between the programme staff and the management,' says a mid-level manager, who remembers the informality of the past as more conducive to quality and creativity.[21] A similar reorganization in Sungi, however, where a new mid-level management tier was created – went more smoothly because it was hammered out at a five-day strategic planning workshop where all managers eventually came to a consensus on the need for change. Even so, some regretted the loss of regular access to the Executive Director, perhaps feeling the burden of added responsibility that had come to them with decentralization.

A third question about delegation has to do with the need for the programming standardization that is a prerequisite for meaningful expansion. In a savings and credit operation, for example, the authority to make loans up to a certain level may well be delegated to a branch manager. But more fundamental decisions, such as altering membership criteria, interest rates and repayment schedules, may not. A decision about whether or not to begin an education or health programme may be taken by a regional manager, but anything more than minor adjustments to the content of the programme may not. Expansion to the size of an SRSC, an AKRSP or a BRAC would not have been possible if field offices had been allowed to tailor-make programme components – beyond minor refinements – to local demands.

The issue of programme alteration is less likely to arise if branch managers understand clearly how far they can go, and if they participate in programme and policy developments as they evolve. In PROSHIKA, decentralization – and deconcentration and delegation up to a point – works well because there is a 'unity of vision'. 'You have to create a culture,' says Faruque Ahmed. 'Organizational norms and culture are very important. That is one of the functions of senior managers, to create that kind of climate where people *can* participate and become part of the decision-making process.'[22] In PROSHIKA, regular staff meetings are held at all levels, but perhaps the most important is a two-day joint conference of all 120 Area Director Coordinators and senior management, held every three months.

As noted in Chapter 3, the formal organizational culture is complemented by the informal – by stories, symbols, teamwork, friendship and the bonding that can result from long journeys in cramped vehicles, from staff picnics and discussions during tea-breaks. Interaction between senior managers and field staff suggests that with good buy-in at different strata, the question of the undesirable altering of programme elements and other inappropriate expressions of managerial autonomy are not likely to arise at field level. Participatory and consultative management styles work well, not in delegating authority for programme design and policy matters, but in ensuring allegiance throughout an organization to the common design and policy needed for effective and efficient scale-up. They are also a technique for pooling an organization's intellectual capital and for synthesizing a wide variety of perspectives, bringing them to bear on a cross-section of organizational components. An IUCN educationist, for example, can offer valuable and very different perspectives on the biodiversity programme, and vice versa.

The devolution of authority to beneficiaries is the most problematic aspect of decentralization. The creation of independent and sustainable village groups is the ultimate goal of eight of the nine organizations in our study. To what extent should such groups play a role in the programme decision-making of their mentors? When should this begin to happen? Virtually all our case study organizations sing the praises of participation, or 'people's participation', or even *genuine people's participation*. Faruque Ahmed describes the latter and its application in PROSHIKA:

> *Genuine people's participation involves major stakeholders in all the critical stages of the project cycle and has the following characteristics. It involves people–*
>
> 1   *In the problem/opportunity and issue definition stage.*
> 2   *In the phase of enunciation of needs and priorities of the project.*

3   *In the design stage of the project.*
4   *In implementation, operation and maintenance of the project.*
5   *In the evaluation and monitoring stage . . .*

Pseudo participation and tokenism have to be avoided.[23]

What does this actually mean in practice, when it is known well in advance that an organization will sooner or later lead 'participants' towards savings and credit, or cattle, or non-formal primary education? Where savings and credit are concerned, participants are usually involved in decision-making from the beginning. The very nature of solidarity-group lending involves them in decisions about who gets loans and in the repayment process. In non-formal primary education projects, involvement in school construction, setting the school timetable and some aspects of teacher supervision are handled by parents. They play an invaluable consultative function. It is participatory and parents commonly feel a genuine ownership of the process. But in neither of these examples – credit and education – has there been any significant devolution of authority. Participation maximized; devolution limited.

While the word used is 'participation', some field activities go no further than consultation. In other cases, consensus among participants is absolutely necessary, while in yet others, a democratic process may be more appropriate. A senior programme officer in Sadguru says that for his organization 'it fluctuates among all three. At some points in time, one needs to consult. At another point, we need consensus. In village forest committees we go for democracy' because of the particular nature of the work.[24]

The question of devolution of responsibility for the development process – as opposed to management of the NGO's programme – is a slight but important variation on this theme, and time is inevitably a major factor. BAIF's Director, Narayan Hegde, says that when they started, 'We were acting as managers; we were the leader of the whole village; we went to every farmer and ensured that he did the same thing. They were so dependent. We realized that the more you dominate, the less they participate, the more they depend on us.'. The emphasis shifted to the building of farmers' organizations, but these, he acknowledged, could take as long as 10 or 20 years to become fully self-reliant.[25]

Structure: Formality and Complexity

Decentralization becomes more problematic as programmes become more complex. In discussing both hierarchy and decentralization in IUCN, Aban Kabraji observes that it is one thing to push responsibility down from 'level one' to 'level two', but that managers – especially new managers – can be reluctant to push it down further, in part because of the complexity of programming.

When AKRSP (I) was a small organization, there were no separate functional units or departments. All tasks were handled by the CEO. In time, various units were created – programmes, finance, administration, monitoring, human resources. As programmes grew in size and complexity, this structure too developed bottlenecks, delayed decision-making and budgetary mismatches. This led to a further delegation of responsibility for planning and budgeting after a careful review by the organization's external auditors of the appropriate levels of checks and control.

Management literature sometimes describes the structural form of organizations as variations on a continuum running between the 'mechanistic' at one end and the 'organic' at the other. Mechanistic structures are centralized and hierarchical with unambiguous lines of authority and communication, clear role definitions and the specialization of tasks. Organic structures are more collegial, more decentralized, more flexible and open; they are more encouraging of innovation, with a continual reorganization of tasks and responsibilities. It would not be difficult, given such apparently diametrically opposite forms, to speculate on which of the two the average NGO would opt for. In fact, most of our case study NGOs reflect both types of organization. For routine activities and programmes where the emphasis is on replication, mechanistic structures are most appropriate, as they are in areas where accountability and control are important: the management of money, for example, personnel matters and logistics. Where programmes are under experimentation or are changing, or where the programming environment is uncertain, organic structures are more likely to prevail.

Where our case study NGOs are concerned, their place on the continuum is a function of time as well as a function of what they do. It is a reflection of age and maturity, but it is also a reflection of the climate and the times in which they function. Most of the organizations in our study have become adept at balancing the hard and the soft, the formal and the informal. As Chapter 5 demonstrated, there may well be clear strategies and long-term programmes, but opportunism and entrepreneurial behaviour are also part of the mix. The control switch for all this is on the leader's desk. In the successful organization it is activated on the basis of the leader's judgement and knowledge, rarely on whimsy. That, of course, is a) why they are leaders, and b) why their organizations are successful. As Brinkerhoff puts it, 'real-world organizations, as opposed to pure types, tend to fall somewhere between the mechanistic-organic poles. It is rare to find an organization, either public or private sector, that exhibits all the features of mechanistic structures and none of those associated with organic ones, or vice versa'.[26]

CONCLUSIONS

While very much *de rigueur* in management literature, it is far too simplistic to say that an NGO's governing structure should be broadly based, that its board should represent a cross-section of interests and skills, and that it should focus firmly on vision and policy. These are ideal attributes found in older, more mature organizations functioning in climates where the role of trustees is well understood and where it is reasonably well regulated. Even the oldest, largest and most mature of Northern NGOs, however, have difficulty walking the thin line between the theory and the practice of good non-profit governance. Most in our study have kept their governance structures small. And until they are secure and reach a plateau of financial and programming stability, or until a leadership transition arises, their governance usually remains understandably introspective. In fact, regardless of age, only two or three in our study have expanded their initial governance structures, making them more open and inclusive of outsiders. Time is a factor in this, but the origins of the organization are equally important. Those founded and staffed by charismatic visionaries may, in fact, restrict their governance structures indefinitely, until the prospect of their retirement arises. At that point they will likely face some of the problems that are more typical of boards in Northern NGOs and of the 'premeditated' NGOs in our study: the struggle between vision and management, between policy development and implementation; between rubber-stampism and meddling.

Much management discussion among NGOs misuses the word 'hierarchy', confusing it with 'bossism'. The nine organizations in our study all have 'hierarchies'. Several have worked hard to ensure that they are as hierarchically 'flat' as possible. In some cases this was simply because the founder wanted to keep an eye on everything. In other cases it was because the literature said that 'flatter is better', and because structure was confused with process. For others, 'participatory management' was in some way seen to be inimical to a hierarchical organization. In fact, the opposite seems to be true. Hierarchy and participatory management can be compatible and complementary. This is an important finding because it goes against much of the received wisdom on the subject. Organizations in which directors' spans of control are extremely wide are probably less able to use participatory processes effectively at field level because so much authority is gathered into the clutch of managers at the top. Several of our case study organizations had to be actively pushed by their boards or by donors into the creation of additional levels of management, rethinking what they meant by participation in the process.

It is also clear from our case studies that decentralization is not the same thing as participation. A highly centralized organization may use participatory techniques to get buy-in from senior managers. Likewise, decentralization is more nuanced than is commonly recognized. An organization may have simply 'deconcentrated' its management or it may have gone much further. What our case studies demonstrate is that participatory processes will probably make decentralization more effective and that the further an organization moves towards the devolution of programming responsibility to village institutions, the more important will be the participation of villagers. What the case studies also demonstrate is that there are limits to decentralization and the use of organic management structures where consistency and replication are important organizational goals. Mid- or long-term devolution of authority and ownership to village structures may actually be more viable in operations that are planned and ordered – ie not very open to local tampering – but where village-level consultation and participation have been the key ingredients from the outset.

CHAPTER 7

LEADERSHIP AND THE THOROUGHLY MODERN MANAGER

The superior man is modest in speech
but exceeds in his actions

Confucius

The special characteristics of development NGOs create management challenges that are distinct from those faced by government and the private sector. NGOs have a social change mission: they aim to change society. In working towards this end, they engage people and communities that are often, if not usually, ignored by government and the private sector alike. The NGO mission is an ambitious one, and in carrying it out successfully, everything points to the pre-eminence of the person at the head of the organization.

Contrary to the commonly held idea – the myth, perhaps – that South Asian NGO leaders are indispensable, charismatic, egocentric and sometimes autocratic, our research reveals a completely different set of characteristics among those that have created successful organizations. In the emergence of large South Asian NGOs, in fact, a new type of professional development leader has emerged. Our study suggests that these development leaders are marked by an ability to balance – and to balance very carefully – five things: values, ambition, technical competency, the capacity to inspire and judgement. They have been able to marry sound organizational design and effective management with strong personal values, ambitious development aspirations, and an ability to understand and work within an uncertain and changing external environment.

When this study began, a major focus was the founder, and his or her role and influence; the 'top team' of senior managers; and – where there had been a change – their successors. We began with the idea that the mission, management style and the effectiveness of an NGO depends significantly, if not completely, on the personality and the ideology of a charismatic founding leader. All too often such individuals, while inspirational, lack basic management skills. Like shooting stars, they soon disappear from the scene. A private sector analogy is the family firm, dominated by an entrepreneurial figure with energy and flare, but too often without the managerial skills that are needed to grow the business. Such businesses are commonly beset by conflicts over succession, and how, if at all, power can be transferred across the generations.

The ability of the leader to influence other people and organizations is commonly used to explain the success of an organization. In the NGO community there are plenty of examples of visionary and charismatic leaders who have successfully motivated others to dedicate their lives to humanitarian ideals. On the one hand, such leaders have been criticized for dominating the organization, for being unaccountable, and for failing to adapt to changing circumstances. On the other, many have demonstrated the drive and commitment, and the ability to mobilize people and resources, that are required to convince governments and donors of the value of their work. The lessons from such cases, and usually the impact, can be contradictory and confusing.

The 'founder's trap' – sometimes called the 'guru syndrome' – is a further problem. There is plenty of anecdotal evidence of NGO leaders who have resisted change, blocked innovation and rejected the evolution of a more collective or participative management approach. Growth can threaten their personal power base, their relationships and patronage. As a consequence, many founders have suffocated their own babies. The issue here, however, is not about those threatened by growth and change, but about understanding the character and characteristics of leaders who have confronted, and who appear to have overcome, the 'founder's trap'. What is it about them and their approach to leadership that determines success? What makes them different from other leaders?

LEADERS AND LEADERSHIP

There are many ways of defining leadership. For some it is about exercising power, for others it is about achieving results, or motivating a team, or energizing followers. Winston Churchill called leadership 'the intelligent use of power'. Management author John Adair suggests that leadership is about 'holding people together as a group while leading them in the right direction'. John Harvey-Jones suggests that leadership is about 'getting extraordinary performance out of ordinary people'.

The literature and research on leadership is as voluminous as it is diverse and contradictory. Some researchers conclude that leadership style and behaviour are contingent on the circumstances and environment in which the leader operates – culture, tradition, legal and political frameworks, and organizational culture.[1] Much evidence suggests that effective leaders are highly pragmatic, flexible and capable of adapting to a variety of different leadership styles. Vroom and Yetton identify different styles that effective leaders adopt at will to suit different situations.[2] One of the critical competencies of an effective leader, therefore, is an ability to judge when to adopt the style that is best suited to a particular situation. Thus judgement becomes a key determinant of the effective leader.

Other researchers have focused on identifying and analysing innate leadership traits and skills. The bulk of this research seeks to establish the personal and psychological qualities of specific leaders.[3] This includes studies of their physical appearance, their intellectual ability, their personality and interpersonal skills. Leadership researchers have also attempted to analyse the style and behaviour of particular leaders. By implication, once these skills and behaviour can be identified, aspiring leaders can be trained to adopt them as well. More recently, researchers have focused on attributes such as charisma, visioning, emotional intelligence and the ability to promote learning.[4] Peter Senge, for example, concludes that the leader of a learning organization should have a facilitative role rather than an inspirational or a technical one. The leader should be a designer, a steward, a teacher.[5]

In short, a tremendous body of research has shaped (and confused) our understanding of what a 'leader' is. Certainly there is greater awareness of the importance of personal traits, individual behaviour and of context and culture in determining an effective leader. But behind it all, there appear to be three distinct elements of 'leadership'. First, an ability to influence the behaviour of subordinates or followers, and an understanding of the dynamics and sensitivities of such power relationships. Second, the capacity and reputation needed to motivate staff or volunteers, and to build teams. Third, the ability to think strategically, and to be able to communicate a vision in such a way that it is achievable and doable. Simply put, leadership is the process through which an individual influences group members to attain group or organizational goals.

LEADERSHIP: A DEVELOPMENTAL PERSPECTIVE

In development literature, there is limited research into the leadership characteristics and managerial capabilities of key individuals, whether they run an NGO or a rural development programme. There are, however, throughout the NGO community, anecdotal tales about the detrimental influence of 'charismatic autocrats' and the deleterious results of the 'guru syndrome'. On one hand, charismatic leaders have demonstrated drive, commitment and a remarkable ability to mobilize people and resources. On the other, they are widely criticized for dominating their organizations, for being unaccountable, and for failing to adapt to changing circumstances.

Charismatic leaders can and do resist change, block innovation and reject collaboration. This is not especially unique to NGOs, however; it is common in business and it is rampant in politics. Growth can threaten a leader's personal power base, relationships and patronage. As a result, many stifle promising initiatives. Where development leaders are concerned, Robert Chambers says it well: charismatic leaders can achieve many good things through their 'guts, vision and commitment'. But he also suggests that their power can be a disability that jeopardizes organizational effectiveness. He argues that charismatic leaders are 'vulnerable to acquiescence, deference, flattery and placation'. They are not easily contradicted or corrected. It becomes easy and tempting for them to impose their own agenda, to block change and to deny the realities and perceptions of others.[6]

Norman Uphoff presents an alternative perspective on charismatic leaders. He sees them as development entrepreneurs or social innovators. He identifies a group of unusually able and motivated individuals – commonly coming from outside the community – who have inspired, initiated and guided many rural development programmes. They have brought to rural communities simple but effective management methods, they have introduced new technologies and organizational forms, and they have encouraged experimentation and learning. What these leaders have in common is a commitment to broad-based participatory development, and the ability to persuade communities that they have something to gain from 'collective self-improvement' and working together. Uphoff concludes that the next generation of development leaders will have to develop their intellectual and interpersonal skills to play a role as facilitators and initiators.[7]

Some would say that NGO leadership is a very particular style, peculiar to the NGO community. Here, NGO leadership is seen as an inherently personal and participatory activity in which leaders interact and engage on a personal and emotional level with colleagues, staff and volunteers. Alan Fowler argues that the highly personalized management styles of many NGO leaders is a natural consequence of the attitude of staff to each other, of high levels of commitment and of a shared sense of ownership.[8] Both Fowler and Uphoff identify consistency and commitment to a moral purpose as the common characteristics of the successful NGO leader. Uphoff says that a major source of leaders' effectiveness is their 'conviction and consistency regarding the potential of rural people'.[9] Fowler suggests that a key trait is 'their adherence to moral principle' and their 'enduring, consistent drive, rather than charismatic personality' which inspires and mobilizes those with whom they work.[10]

There is also evidence to suggest that different cultures perceive leadership and the relationship between themselves and their subordinates very differently. As noted in Chapter 6, researchers have tackled the cultural aspects of management in a variety of ways. Some have observed that South Asian cultures are highly collectivist and that they accept innate social differentials more easily than the cultures of Europe or North America. Where leadership is concerned, Geert Hofstede suggests that South Asian societies have high 'power distance' scores, with the implication that less powerful members of an organization expect and accept that power will be distributed unequally. Hofstede also suggests that such societies are highly 'collectivist', with the implication that people are integrated into strong, cohesive social groups from birth.[11] Fons Trompenaars also notes the highly collectivist nature of South Asian society, and the importance of 'ascription'. He sees this as the extent to which position and power are ascribed by virtue of birth, kinship, education, networks and connections.[12]

Thus, we have a cultural context in which cohesive group relations are apparently paramount, and where it is accepted that power and status are dependent on kinship ties, personal relationships and connections. This is regarded as alien to the highly individualistic, low 'power distance', achievement-oriented meritocracies of Western Europe and North America. In organizational terms this would imply that in South Asia, strong personal relationships between the leadership and the staff, or the communities with whom they work, is essential to success and survival.

This is an issue of particular importance to South Asian NGOs, and it raises questions about whether Western concepts of leadership can be translated into a different cultural environment. Certainly the work of Hofstede or Trompenaars suggests that the collectivist, high 'power distance' cultures that are commonly associated with the developing world would promote a very different leadership style from that found in the West. This would imply that the concept of leadership is not universal, and that in reality it is contingent on different cultural norms and assumptions. The evidence from our study, however, is that while certain aspects of leadership style *are* culturally determined, there is a growing cadre of development leaders with similar competencies and outlook that transcend cultural boundaries in the increasingly interdependent world of international development.

FOUNDER-LEADERS

Each of the founder-leaders in our study appears to have a distinct character and leadership style. More detailed analysis, however, suggests a number of shared characteristics that may help to explain their success. Some of their attributes can be seen in the brief outlines of the six different founder-leaders that follow. We have used these six not because they are brighter or better (or worse) than others, but because they represent the very different leadership styles and backgrounds that are typical of many NGOs in South Asia. First, Manibhai Desai, a Gandhian activist; second, Harnath Jagawat, a bureaucrat, disciple and social innovator; third, F H Abed, a corporate manager and humanitarian; fourth, Shoaib Sultan Khan, a professional administrator; fifth, Aban Marker Kabraji, a biologist turned manager; and sixth, Qazi Faruque Ahmed, a Freirian social activist. They reflect the diversity of background and the commitment of spirit that marks so many successful development leaders in South Asia.

BAIF and Dr Manibhai Desai

The Pune-based Bhartiya Agro Industries Foundation (now simply 'BAIF') was registered by Dr Manibhai Desai in 1967 as a non-profit voluntary organization, based on his belief that research and development should go hand in hand. Manibhai had worked with, and was a close disciple of Gandhi. Although he read widely and experimented with new techniques, his work was underpinned by two key Gandhian principles. The first was that development should be labour- and not capital-intensive. The second was that local resources should be used to encourage economic self-sufficiency.

Manibhai became a disciple of Gandhi in 1945. In 1946, when he was 26, he took a vow of celibacy, pledging that he would devote his entire life to the service of the rural poor. Like Gandhi, he was concerned about economic sustainability and financial probity. This ethos is reflected in the story of a visit by Gandhi in 1946. In the middle of the visit, he was called away to Delhi for urgent discussions with the Viceroy, Lord Wavell, on the transfer of power from Britain to an independent government. Just before he left, he called Manibhai and asked for a bill. Manibhai asked him why he wanted such a thing, but Gandhi insisted. Manibhai worked out the cost of meals and accommodation, wrote a bill, and Gandhi took out his purse and paid. Then he gave the bill back to Manibhai saying, 'now frame it and put it on your wall so that, if somebody comes with all sorts of claims about being a social worker, or a philanthropist who has supported us and they will not pay, you can show them this, and say that even Gandhi paid'.[13] After that, Manibhai insisted that everything had to be paid for and that the centre had to become economically self-sufficient.

While he placed great store on economic sustainability, he also understood the importance of using science and technology to help the rural poor. By the early 1960s Manibhai had a national reputation as both a cattle breeder and a horticulturist. He was very much a self-taught agriculturist, using science to serve the rural poor. Few Gandhian organizations survived the 1980s and 1990s, but, throughout its history, BAIF drew on Manibhai's example and merged scientific approaches pragmatically with Gandhian philosophy. As a result, it has been able to adapt to the changing environment, while still keeping its core values. Much of BAIF's success can be traced to the ability of Manibhai to adapt technical advances to the needs of the poor and to his belief that 'committed people are not enough, everyone needs technical skills'.

In many ways, however, Manibhai was the classic charismatic guru, a man who ran the organization like a family patriarch. Staff recall: 'I joined because of Manibhai'; 'We used to look forward to his visits but were afraid because he would be very firm if he found the work was not being done'; 'He was like a father to us'; or 'Manibhai knew us and our families, he visited our homes, enquired after our wives and children.'[14] His style was inimitable. He was a bramachari* with no family. He made sacrifices, demonstrated commitment and hard work, political savvy and technical know-how – 'My life is my message' he said.

His leadership style was that of a paterfamilias, concerned with the work and family life of his staff, with their values and their culture, with their growth as individuals and professionals. He did not appear to manage people; people followed him. The appearance, however, was deceptive. Although he was benevolent, he was also a tough disciplinarian. He believed in rules, regulations and systems – he set standards of discipline and punctuality – 'if he saw laggards, he chased them up'. 'He set an example . . . it was his behaviour, his simplicity, his working ability that set an example to us all.'[15] In many ways Manibhai's leadership style is akin to the development entrepreneurs and social innovators identified by Uphoff . He was a highly principled and motivated individual, with a strong spiritual conviction and commitment to the rural poor. Yet he was also willing to introduce new technologies, to encourage experimentation, and to promote different ways of working and new organizational forms.

Sadguru and the Jagawats

The Sadguru Water and Development Foundation can be traced to Ranchhod Dasji Maharaj, the 'Sadguru' and his disciple Arvind Mafatlal, a wealthy industrialist. The prefix 'Sad' in Sanskrit means a great and pious teacher. Arvind Mafatlal met the Sadguru in 1967 during the Bihar famine where he was engaged in relief work. The Sadguru was a saint who believed in community development. He provided a founding vision and offered those who joined him the chance to work on 'a sublime cause'.

---

* A bramachari is an individual who has renounced marriage.

The Sadguru did not believe in constructing temples, he wanted only to help poor people and to enhance their productive capacity.

Arvind Mafatlal became a disciple of the Sadguru and offered financial support for his welfare activities in rural areas. In 1974 he helped to organize a massive eye camp at Dahod in Gujarat, which was attended by some 20,000 tribals. It was here that Harnath and Sharmistha Jagawat came into contact with Mafatlal. The Jagawats were helping at the camp, and Mafatlal, impressed by their organizing abilities, invited them to work with him to help to alleviate poverty in tribal communities.

The Jagawats agreed, on the condition that nothing would be imposed on them, and that they would be free to take time to survey the area and to build a personal understanding of local needs. Only then would they decide what intervention was most appropriate. As a result, they spent the first two years of their work walking from village to village, listening to people talk about their needs. Harnath Jagawat estimates that he walked up to 30 miles a day and visited over 200 villages. By doing this he gained a personal understanding of the immediate needs of local people. Irrigation and natural resource management were eventually identified as the priorities. As important as setting priorities, however, the time and the process allowed the Jagawats to develop friendships, build trust and gain credibility, the credibility on which their future work would be based. This two-year process of 'walking and talking' was of immense operational benefit, but it was also highly symbolic, and it is the basis on which the Foundation's relationship with the local community rests.

Looking back on 25 years of work, Harnath Jagawat says that the early period was 'full of miseries and challenges. For the first two years there was only one person, combining chief executive, typist, clerk, driver, peon, everything.'[6] He also remembers that their 'office' was one common table shared by four people, sitting one on each side in a small, one-roomed office. 'The purchase of a cheap 20-rupee chair required a lot of thinking and budget adjusting.'[17] Some aspects of this situation continued for the first ten years of Sadguru's existence. Everyone, including the Director, shared tasks and helped each other. This contributed to the strong work ethic that developed, and to the way that work continues to be shared out years later. As a former employee observes, 'We would often stay late in our office, or work Sundays and, when we went to the field, we would pay for our own food.'.[18] One should not over-romanticize this period and the relationships that developed, however. Harnath Jagawat is concerned that overly collective participatory management is too often used as an excuse for inefficiency and poor quality work.

The Jagawats were social innovators not only in the way that they worked with the local community, but also in the way that they introduced new techniques and ideas into an isolated tribal district. The early days of the organization were marked by hard work, which in turn demanded a high degree of commitment and perseverance. This legacy continues to characterize the work of Sadguru.

BRAC and F H Abed

BRAC was established in 1972 in Sylhet, following the turmoil and destruction caused by disastrous cyclones and the brutal war of independence. A small group of people, under the leadership of Fazle Hasan Abed, who came from that part of the country, banded together to provide relief to the people of an area known as Sulla in north-eastern Bangladesh. Originally called the 'Bangladesh Rehabilitation Assistance Committee', it later became the 'Bangladesh Rural Advancement Committee' and is now known simply as 'BRAC'.

Working on relief and rehabilitation in 200 villages, Abed and his colleagues rebuilt over 14,000 houses and provided tools to help craftsmen to rehabilitate their trade. It was thought that this effort would take two or perhaps three years at most, by which time the situation would return to normal. It was soon realized, however, that hopes of an early withdrawal were premature. 'Normal' was terrible. The task was huge, and government agencies were insufficiently motivated and equipped to take on longer term tasks. It was also realized that something more than relief and rehabilitation was needed, and so BRAC began to think about how to develop self-reliant village institutions.

One of the key explanations for BRAC's success is obviously its Executive Director, F H Abed. In many ways, BRAC's evolution mirrors his personality and background. Having worked internationally as an accountant for Shell Oil, he brought with him a strong belief in learning, and a keen sense of accounting, accountability and order. His confidence inspired confidence in others, to such an extent that confidence has now become synonymous with empowerment in thousands of villages throughout Bangladesh.[19]

Abed talks of BRAC as an autonomous institution that exists independently and despite him. He is deeply conscious of the many other organizations that are dependent on the charisma and public profile of the founder-leader:

> *I felt very strongly that I did not want Abed to be known; I wanted BRAC to be known. So I kept myself to myself as much as possible, away from the glare of publicity. I would not give interviews or go on talk shows . . . I felt that in Bangladesh there are just too many institutions led by individuals who patronize themselves at the expense of their workers. I wanted to make a BRAC worker feel that he or she is BRAC. This is an organization of many people who all work hard at it, and who are trying to develop a new way of doing things.[20]*

Although this sentiment is no doubt genuinely felt, the reality is that F H Abed is integral to BRAC, and, as in many other organizations, staff and external stakeholders want (and need) a focal point like him on which to hang the organization's identity. As Executive Director, Abed has a clear vision for the organization, based on an inclusive and sustainable model of collective self-help. He has the ability to communicate this vision to people not just inside, but outside the organization. He is seen, for example, as 'a master of visualizing what was acceptable to donors and government.' But he felt that it was not his role to be a leader who gives all the answers:

> *The answers came from them – the staff – more than I gave to them. Even at the beginning, I wanted to do the right thing in the most sensitive way possible, so people should be treated as people, as human beings.*

He is not unrealistic about this, however:

> *I wanted the organization to be known as a high-quality organization, so we sought a lot of people . . . but those who were not good enough were terminated. I had no qualms about that, since I did not want BRAC to be contaminated by these kinds of people. I wanted BRAC to develop into an institution that did not just* say *things but did them.*[21]

This emphasis on quality encouraged him from the beginning to introduce systems that would both encourage and monitor high-quality work. He promoted education, training and shared learning across the organization. In this sense he fits Senge's dictum that leadership is central to organizational learning, and that the leader's role is one of facilitator and educator.[22] This may also explain why most of BRAC's senior managers have been with the organization for many years, even though they could command higher salaries elsewhere. For many, the reason is the sense they have of accomplishment and mutual learning, as well as the degree of freedom they enjoy and the feeling of involvement that Abed engenders. At the recruitment interview of a long-time BRAC manager Abed said, '"I have a dream, and I need your help." He welcomed me, he didn't grill me.'.[23] A listener more than a talker, he is widely viewed as a motivator and as a source of inspiration for villagers, staff and donors alike.

AKRSP and Shoaib Sultan Khan

The Aga Khan Rural Support Programme was established in Northern Pakistan in 1982. Its founding leader was Shoaib Sultan Khan, who served the organization as General Manager until 1992. He was a former senior civil servant, a teacher and an internationally respected development professional, with many years of experience in rural development. He was heavily influenced by the work of Akhtar Hameed Khan, a renowned figure in post-colonial rural development in both Bangladesh and Pakistan.* 'Shoaib Sahib' brought a strong work ethic to AKRSP (P) and promoted a culture of disciplined, high-quality work. As its founder-director he started and expanded AKRSP so successfully that it became a respected and much copied model of integrated community-based development in Pakistan and elsewhere in Asia. Committed to the values inherent in community-based development, he applied his knowledge, administrative skills and political contacts to good effect. But he was also an inspirational leader, and he developed strong personal loyalties among villagers and AKRSP staff. There is a sense of awe and reverence in the way that many remember him.[24]

Shoaib Sultan Khan's leadership style was highly personalized. It was based on a set of personal relations, on his great ability to empathize with all sorts of people, and on his ability to generate high levels of commitment and loyalty. He had a keen political sense and had a well-developed, if diverse, power base. He was adept at building new coalitions; as he himself commented, 'it is better to have fifty power bases than only one'.[25] He had the ability to mobilize support and resources from a variety of sources – from the aid community, from government and from the commercial sector. His leadership style and his ability to work with and motivate a wide cross-section of people and organizations reflects a pragmatic, contingency approach to leadership.

IUCN and Aban Marker Kabraji

IUCN's 1985 start in Pakistan, with a half-time biologist working on a sea turtle project, hardly looked like the beginning of something big. But sea turtles were only a part of what Aban Kabraji already understood about environmental and social issues. As a child growing up in Quetta, she had always loved wild animals and nature, but as a girl and as a Parsee in a predominantly Muslim culture, she also knew something about

---

* In fact Akhtar Hameed Khan was an early inspiration for the work of many Bangladeshi and Pakistani NGOs. He served on the board of the Sarhad Rural Support Corporation and was an advisor to AKRSP(P). He was an outspoken supporter (and critic) of NGOs, and late in life he founded a very successful one himself in the slums of Karachi, the Orangi Pilot Project. An activist, writer and teacher for most of his 85 years, Akhtar Hameed Khan died in 1999.

outsiders and insiders. Later, studying in Britain during the heady days of the feminist movement, she learned about advocacy at first hand, and although her first inclination when she returned home was a career in her father's successful pharmaceutical business, she became involved as well in Pakistan's nascent women's movement. She was a founder of Shirkat Gah, one of the first feminist advocacy organizations in Pakistan, and was later involved in establishing the Women's Action Forum.

Three years working in her father's business taught Aban Kabraji a lot about management, but pharmaceuticals gave way to sea turtles when she discovered that the Sind Wildlife Department was looking for assistance in developing a project proposal. Having helped the department to obtain funding, Kabraji wound up running the project, and in the process came to know others in the conservation field. In 1984, the Government of Pakistan approached IUCN in Geneva for assistance in drafting the first National Conservation Strategy, and to anchor the process, IUCN needed a local office. Kabraji got the job – a half-time arrangement with IUCN and a half-time arrangement with the World Wildlife Fund. It was an opportune moment to join IUCN: the environmental movement was on the boil and IUCN was attracting a new breed of bright young activists who understood that environmental issues were also social issues. This is something she took forward into her new job as IUCN's Regional Director for Asia, looking for individuals in different countries of the region with broad backgrounds and high ideals.

Aban Kabraji is not shy about saying that connections are very important in South Asia, and coming from a well-known family did not hurt her at the outset. 'In Pakistan,' she says, 'the unfortunate reality is that it is who you know that counts.'[26] Her father, however, told her that connections would get her a first appointment only. After that she was on her own. Working with the Sind Wildlife Department for five years, she saw how nasty and frustrating bureaucracy could be, and how wasteful of human talent it was. This sensitized her to issues of power and mismanagement. But it taught her something else: senior officials have about as much power for bad as they do for good. But further down the ladder, mid-level bureaucrats have much more power for good than for bad. The ripple effect of positive behaviour can be enormous.

Later, with IUCN, she began to develop a theory of 'space and chaos'. Outsiders are often struck by how organizations like IUCN, Sungi and AKRSP have thrived in a hostile climate, a climate that Kabraji feels is actually meaner and more difficult than anywhere else in Asia. In an empty field, or in one dominated by chaos, she feels that there is actually a greater opportunity to create something positive – a greater space to do good – than there might be in well-ordered societies where the field is more crowded. In an open field, or in the midst of chaos, when something new begins to show promise, it can quickly attract good people who are eager to escape from the old environment. They are eager to help to build an alternative, where there is space to think and to talk and to grow, where merit and initiative are valued.

Creating something new in such an environment is not easy, however. There are detractors everywhere, and the tall poppy syndrome flourishes. Flowers that rise above the others are noticed, and many are keen to bring them down – in a reflection, Kabraji feels, of their own mediocrity and incompetence.

Kabraji is nevertheless an optimist. Despite the rampant human destruction of nature, she feels that one way or another – through good sense or because disaster will demonstrate the imperative for change – people will pull back from the brink. The issue for her is how to preserve a critical mass of biodiversity over the next 50 or 100 years in order to ensure that there is enough to build on for the longer term.

In a society like Pakistan, Kabraji feels that women who succeed do so both because they are women, and despite the fact that they are women. While women are handicapped because of the way that society perceives them, most who get ahead have taken more bruises along the way than the average man, and so are better equipped to deal with constantly changing challenges. And women may have an advantage working in NGOs that they would not enjoy in business or the civil service: NGOs may be more 'feminine' in their nature than the more aggressive worlds of business and government.

Ironically, what Kabraji feels she will wind up learning best in her professional life are lessons about management, people and organization. Her achievements here, she feels, will probably be more significant than anything she might contribute to the natural environment. Starting out with an idea about saving wild animals, she has found herself taming a social jungle instead.

PROSHIKA and Qazi Faruque Ahmed

Qazi Faruque Ahmed had a masters degree in chemistry behind him when he joined the Canadian NGO, CUSO, as a project officer with responsibility for appropriate technology in 1973. At age 27, he did not intend to stay long, and had already written examinations for the civil service. Although CUSO was predominantly a volunteer-sending organization, in Bangladesh it was experimenting with support to the fledgling NGOs like BRAC that had begun to emerge following the 1971 war of independence, and Faruque encountered some of them for the first time. In 1974, he took a leave of absence to go to North Bengal with Oxfam, to work on the provision of relief to those suffering from a devastating famine that had struck the country. He had read about the great man-made

Bengal famine of 1942, but here he had a chance to see the same thing for himself – abject human misery while there was still food in the shops and warehouses. He began to understand that *all* the country's poverty was an on-going famine, that poverty was structured and manipulated, and that it was based on inequities built into the system. Technical solutions alone would not be enough, especially when people died without protest and without the ability to protest – without organizations of their own and without other organizations that might support them.

Faruque decided not to join the civil service, perhaps making the decision when CUSO encouraged him and some of his co-workers to think about setting up an organization of their own. In fact, CUSO more or less became PROSHIKA within the next couple of years. Although it remained in Bangladesh for another decade supporting other organizations, the confluence of people, ideas and events that led to the creation of PROSHIKA are its lasting legacy.

If establishing PROSHIKA was a test, Faruque took on another test that was almost as great in 1987, when he left the organization for a year to complete a PhD in development studies at the University of Sussex. He wanted time to read and reflect, to spend more time with his young family, and to see what might become of PROSHIKA in his absence. This absence has since become one of PROSHIKA's institutional 'stories' – almost a legend – of the type discussed in Chapter 3. Everyone knew that it was a challenge fraught with risk. That they emerged unscathed and stronger for the experience still provides senior PROSHIKA management with confidence for the future.

An avid reader, Faruque is surrounded in his office by books. Asked about the greatest influences on his thinking, he talks about having read Marx and Mao, Gandhi and Nehru. Julius Nyerere provided tremendous inspiration where the role of education was concerned. 'And, of course,' he adds, 'Paolo Freire.' He is fascinated by Buddhism – its philosophical principles, the 'middle path', truth and the pursuit of truth.

He has always been interested in psychology, coming to management texts late, and then with an interest in the psychology of management, communication, the building of teams, and the theme that he refers to in almost every conversation – participation. He has become more overtly political in recent years, calling loudly for the resignation of the Ershad government in 1990 and the BNP government in 1996. Some see a politician in the making, but Faruque says that his only political aim is to make the existing parties work better – more honestly, more accountably, more transparently in the service of development. The conversation returns to the things that have influenced him most profoundly, and he talks again of the terrible famine of 1974, and of the tens of thousands of people who died needlessly and without protest

Observations

These six examples suggest a group of individuals who are so eclectic in their background that the differences at first glance seem by far to outweigh the similarities: a disciple of Gandhi, an accountant from Shell Oil, a former civil servant, a personnel manager from the private sector, a Freirian activist and an expert in sea turtles.

On closer examination, however, the similarities are striking. First, they were ideas people, not systems people or number crunchers. Each had a clear vision, a firm value-set and a strong sense of commitment to change. Each was able to share this with others and inspire them. Second, there was a willingness to experiment, to apply new technologies and organizational forms, and to draw on science or other sources of applied, professional knowledge. Third, there was an ability to analyse the environment, to follow trends and to respond to changing circumstances. Fourth, each had very effective communication talents and good interpersonal skills, enabling them to motivate staff and to engage a broad cross-section of society and donors.

If there is a central leadership competency among them, it is the ability to balance diverse demands and to play very different roles, depending on the situation and context. These leaders exhibit a hybrid of skills, insights and interests. They have a chameleon-like ability to play different roles, to use different styles and to adapt to different organizational needs. They have the ability to be a 'guru' when this is useful or important, and they have the capacity to be the thoroughly modern manager when this is more appropriate. They have the ability to combine ideals and values with analysis, technical expertise and professionalism.

COLLECTIVE LEADERSHIP

These brief sketches illustrate the style and some of the background of six founder-leaders and they shed some light on the way they have led their organizations. Whatever their day-to-day style, it is striking how they and others in our study have placed great faith in building effective teams and developing a collective leadership. Running through all our cases is a firm commitment to shared, participative leadership, or what many prefer to call 'collective leadership'.

Collectivity was especially crucial to the early development of PROSHIKA which grew out of the ideas and efforts of four individuals, two of whom would share the official leadership during the early years of the organization. PROSHIKA's leadership emphasizes shared vision, a participatory collective management style, and a willingness to listen, to learn and to guide. One of the first things that the founders developed together was a coherent strategic plan, then a team that could implement it. This was the genesis of the collective leadership that marks PROSHIKA's continuing approach to management. As one senior staff member puts it, 'If everything goes right, everyone feels happy. If things go wrong they feel that they have collectively made a mistake.'[27] The pragmatic benefits of this are that no individual feels threatened by over-burdensome responsibility, and the organization's unity and coherence is maintained.

Faruque feels that institutional development must be closely linked to a collective leadership that is shared, democratic and participatory. Management is therefore a facilitative activity with operational issues as decentralized as possible, reducing over-reliance on the centre and the senior management team. He sees humility as an essential component of collective leadership. As noted in Chapter 6, however, the collective leadership enjoyed by PROSHIKA today came at a cost, when the two founding co-directors could not agree on strategy and 'collectively' broke the organization in half.

In the case of BAIF, Manibhai's death in 1993 merely formalized the move to collective leadership. He had already been encouraging senior staff to make group decisions, and he had cultivated increased participation and greater decentralization. Collective leadership meant that staff were given more freedom and space to make decisions and carry out activities, which in turn were carefully monitored through a system of quality and performance measures. Effective collective leadership is not easy. It depends on mutual trust, a strong work ethic, clarity of responsibility and clear plans. BAIF had the advantage of a senior team that had worked together for a long period, sharing the ideals espoused by Manibhai. They knew and continue to know each other well, understanding each other's strengths and weaknesses.

In Sungi there was concern that collective leadership meant that the few staff with better managerial skills would be overburdened with responsibility, and that work would not be spread fairly throughout the organization. But Sungi's Executive Director, Omar Asghar Khan, had a clear vision of what he wanted the organization to achieve and was committed to a participative style of collective leadership. As one of the younger NGOs in our study, however, the second tier of management was still underdeveloped, and the collectivity was put to a sudden and unexpected test at the end of 1999 when Asghar Khan was asked to join the government as Minister of Environment and Rural Development, with various other responsibilities. Although only time will reveal the results of this test, the management team was forced to assume a leadership role, placing decision-making – at least initially – in the hands of a programme management committee.

While recognizing the usefulness of collective leadership, BRAC managers prefer to talk of a 'collegial atmosphere'. This they recognize is dependent on open communication among and between all levels of staff. There is a feeling that much of the organization's leadership should come from field staff working with local communities. For this to work, the organization needs good communication systems and participative decision-making structures that link area managers with other managers and staff. The leadership at BRAC sees one of the purposes of collective management as the development of a shared culture and collegial atmosphere. In other words, collegiality is not only about decision-making, it is about organizational culture and the benefits to be derived from teamwork.

Collectivity, participation and collegiality are all common elements of the leadership style in many of these NGOs. These traits do not undermine the role and responsibility of senior management. In fact, as noted in Chapter 6, they complement and enhance the quality of leadership. They ensure shared responsibility for plans and strategies; they encourage greater transparency and accountability in decision-making; they promote internal communication; facilitate learning from, and understanding of, complex issues; and generally they help to pool the knowledge and expertise of a diverse range of individuals with different perspectives and skills. Collective leadership is often an indicator of good teamwork and a sign of organizational maturity.

LEADERSHIP: TEAMS AND FOLLOWERS

There is a danger that any attempt to identify leadership traits will be little more than a long shopping list of generalities: a desire to achieve, clarity of vision, ability to solve problems, interpersonal skills, creativity, self-confidence and self-discipline, intelligence and stability, listening and communication skills.

Certainly, leadership is a combination of roles and personal traits. Leaders must balance human and professional roles. Leadership is not bossism; rather it is the ability to take people on a journey, to encourage and motivate them, whether they are staff or volunteers. Leadership expert, John Adair, argues that effective leaders intuitively understand and meet the needs of 'followers' or of the teams they create. But he suggests that effective leadership is not just about satisfying the needs of followers; it is about prioritizing their needs.[28] It is also important to recognize the ways in which 'followers' influence leadership style. There is always an element of reciprocity and accountability because the right of leaders to lead is at least partly conferred on them voluntarily by their 'followers'. Leaders become role models for their staff, establishing patterns of behaviour that their staff can emulate. Aban Marker Kabraji of IUCN sets an example through her hard work and her commitment to detail. Her impact is reflected in such staff comments as 'I wish I had a quarter of her efficiency', 'I have not seen anyone working half as much as Aban', or 'She keeps a complete grip over every emerging or existing issue in the office'. Shoaib Sultan Khan of AKRSP (P) developed a distinctive work ethic which was based on hard work, time management and a respect for local communities. He also introduced a code of conduct to define the organization's relationship with village communities. AKRSP staff were expected not to miss appointments, they were advised not to sit on chairs in the villages nor to accept food, and they were expected to keep their office doors open to villagers. Initially staff were dubious about the value of such things, but they soon realized the value of the code when the villagers began to respond positively.

Apart from being role models, effective leaders are themselves proactive and they encourage the same quality in their staff. They make things happen. For example, the rapid growth of IUCN can be traced directly to Aban Kabraji's initiative and strategic awareness. She opened the first IUCN office in Pakistan on a part-time basis in 1985, and within a decade had turned it into the biggest IUCN programme in the world. As a result, IUCN became one of the premiere environmental NGOs in South Asia. This was achieved through Kabraji's ability to establish teams, to give staff sufficient operational space and freedom, and to introduce systems and structures that support their work. It also reflects her promotional skills and her confidence in her own judgement. In most of our case-study NGOs, the personal confidence of the leader and good judgement go hand in hand. They are partly the product of experience, education and status; but they also result from the ability of a good leader to stand back from the daily grind and to reflect critically on issues of broad concern.

As noted in Chapter 3, much of the relationship between leaders and their staff is couched in the language of teams and teamworking. There is obviously no standard recipe to define this relationship. Research suggests that effective leaders have the ability to match their leadership style to the different environments in which they operate and to the different teams with whom they interact.[29] There is, therefore, a perception that leadership is primarily about the ability of leaders to work with teams and to judge the capabilities and maturity of the teams with which they work. For example, Hersey and Blanchard argue that the main purpose of a leader is to build teams effectively enough that she/he becomes redundant at a daily operational level, and can concentrate on strategic and external issues instead.[30] This places a priority on the ability of the leader to offer and communicate a strategic vision, and to let others with specialist skills get on with operational details. Inconsistent leaders with unclear visions, mixed messages or erratic management styles undermine teams and dilute efficiency.

Leaders who promote a personalized, even caring approach to team-building are open to the accusation of being paternalistic and stifling. But if Sadguru is an example, staff appreciate what they see as a 'family style of management', and they 'generally like to be asked how they are. They like to feel wanted.'. The family bond is reinforced by a five-minute prayer meeting each morning to ask for strength and energy. In addition to the importance of internal teamwork, some NGOs see team-building as an external technique for building contacts and working with different constituencies and stakeholders. In the case of AKRSP (P) this has meant developing regional capacities, working with village organizations, using volunteers and interns, and developing good contacts with religious leaders and local politicians.

In contrast, BAIF has taken a more systems-driven approach, making considerable investments in both formal and informal communication. Senior management saw teamwork as central to their success, and ensured continuity by revolving staff through various roles and enabling them to take on multifunctional responsibilities. BAIF also placed great emphasis on giving staff the freedom to plan their own work, to define work programmes and to identify their own areas of responsibility. Trust and mutual respect, and the judicious use of quality control indicators and performance measurement have helped to build organization-wide values and 'expectations of achievement'. The use of a systems approach is particularly noteworthy, considering BAIF's genesis as a 'guru-driven' Gandhian organization. The apparent contradiction works because the systems are complemented by the sense of family that Manibhai worked so hard to develop. Senior executives continue to take an interest in the welfare and families of their staff, and are committed to maintaining the familial character of the organization.

Effective leaders understand that success breeds success, and they work hard at raising the profile of their organization among community leaders, government officials and donor representatives. This is often a very political role, based on the use of personal networks to build broader constituencies and to secure the organization's power base. IUCN, for example, has benefited from Aban Kabraji's connections – what her staff view as her 'right background' and good family contacts – a very successful businessman father and an internationally acclaimed uncle in the senior echelons of the United Nations. Sungi's founder, Omar Asghar Khan, also has good family credentials. The son of a retired military officer and respected politician, his own background as a businessman and political campaigner has also helped to shape Sungi's profile and to develop its external networks. This raises a more general question about where NGO founder-leaders come from, their background and, where there are general traits, whether these are what count among their successors.

LEADERSHIP: BACKGROUND AND SUCCESS

Background

One way to explain the success of development leaders is to examine their origins. Uphoff concludes that many successful development entrepreneurs are outsiders, and many in our sample too, were outsiders. This 'finding' is not necessarily very profound, however, as the 'development community' in Bangladesh was miniscule when BRAC and PROSHIKA were formed, and the same pertained in Pakistan during the 1980s when IUCN, AKRSP, SRSC and Sungi were started. Most of the leaders in our sample were from the educated upper middle classes. Most held professional qualifications and some had more than one degree. Anil Shah and Shoaib Sultan Khan, the founders of the two AKRSPs, were respected senior civil servants, albeit with a particular interest in rural development. The founders of PROSHIKA had been student activists. Aban Kabraji has a science background. Even the classic Gandhian leader, BAIF's Manibhai Desai, had invested many years researching the science of cattle breeding, agriculture and horticulture. He read widely and experimented ceaselessly with new techniques. By the early 1960s he had achieved a national reputation both as a cattle breeder and a horticulturist.

The current leaders of BAIF, BRAC and Sadguru all came from the private sector. BRAC's F H Abed was an accountant, working internationally with the oil multinational, Shell – a background which he feels gave him a solid sense of accounting – naturally – and perhaps not so naturally, of accountability. Sadguru's Harnath Jagawat believes that his early years as a personnel manager in industry helped him to handle bureaucracy, reduce red tape and develop a greater faith in his staff. 'From industry,' he says, 'I learned to put faith in people and appreciate it when people put faith in me. Sometimes it may happen that people take advantage of you, but you have to accept it, you have to learn to handle the situation and build your own team.'[31]

Narayan Hegde, BAIF's President, spent two years working for the Indian subsidiary of the British American Tobacco Company, and then continued his management education at the Indian Institute of Management at Ahmedabad. When he finished, he was about to join another multinational company, but when he heard a lecture by Manibhai, his career took a turn in another direction. The experience he gained in the private sector, however, was invaluable in the application of management systems. He still sees management in terms of systems, the clarity of strategic plans and objectives, and an ability to address core rather than emotional and operational problems.

Succession

Managerial succession is an issue that taxes many NGOs. The process of succession from a founder-leader who has created and built an organization to the next phase of consolidation or growth is the key to long-term institutional survival. Succession often revolves around the question of whether the organization needs another leader with drive, vision and inspiration; or a manager-leader with organizational and managerial skills who can cope with increasingly complex organizational challenges.

In 2002, BRAC turns 30, but the process of institutionalizing a second generation of leadership began in the late 1990s. The second generation of leadership, in the words of its Executive Director, 'should be at least as good as I have been, or probably better – because I think that better leadership will be necessary in the future, and because BRAC is no longer a small organization'.[32] In the late 1990s, BRAC started to go outside the organization for assistance with the process of succession planning, hiring Arthur D Little & Company for advice. It has also looked at the way other large international organizations, such as the Ford and Rockefeller Foundations, have managed the issue, addressing questions of management and governance more forthrightly than in the past.

For Sadguru, the issue of replacing the individuals who founded and led the organization for 25 years is a source of some anxiety. There is a fear among staff that they will not be able to find a sufficiently capable and dedicated successor to the Jagawats. In PROSHIKA, succession planning has been based on strengthening the senior management team over time. As noted above, in 1987, the current President went overseas on a one-year study sabbatical, and his absence was used as a deliberate attempt to give others an opportunity to run the organization. That PROSHIKA survived his absence and actually continued to grow is taken as evidence that the issue of future succession will not be problematic. Similarly, Sungi has used the absence of its founder as a means for developing other staff. The success of this type of approach, however, depends very much on how responsibilities are devolved, and whether senior management capacity is actually developed. Manibhai Desai also tested possible successors, by giving them managerial responsibility for state branches. For instance, Manibhai's successor, Narayan Hegde, ran BAIF Karnataka for some years. Three years before his death, Manibhai encouraged the Central Management Group to start taking decisions on its own, with a warning: 'If you come to me for advice, then I will think that something is wrong with you.'.[33]

The actual process of succession in BAIF went remarkably smoothly. BAIF confirmed Manibhai's successor within 24 hours of his demise. Although Hegde and Girish Sohani, the new Executive Vice-President, were younger than many of the senior staff, there was general agreement that they were the most suitable candidates. This was partly because of their experience and qualifications, and partly because of their relative youthfulness would allow them to give years of active service to the organization. In addition, because Hegde had been Executive Vice-President, staff and trustees felt they were merely endorsing Manibhai's choice. Manibhai himself, however, did not name a successor. As a senior staff person put it, Manibhai had prepared 'a battery of people' who would be able to manage the organization after his death.[34]

Finding a successor can be a time-consuming process, and where time is available, this may not be a bad thing. In addition to her role as Country Representative for Pakistan, Aban Kabraji was given responsibility in the mid-1990s for IUCN's South Asia region, and then for Asia as a whole. Obviously she could not devote her full attention to two very different jobs, although she retained both titles until 2000 when she handed over responsibility for Pakistan to Mohammad Rafiq. The process of change was almost imperceptible, as she brought new and more senior managers into the organization, devolving many of her responsibilities down into sectoral departments and to programmes around the country. At the turn of the century, she retained a broad supervisory function and she was still there in person, but most of her responsibilities and interests had shifted to a different plane. She no longer kept 'a complete grip over every emerging or existing issue in the office', nor did she need to. IUCN had deliberately invested in building a second tier of new management talent, establishing a new structure, the Senior Management Group, to give them exposure to strategic decisions and wider organizational issues.

The Board of AKRSP (I) invested considerable time and effort in identifying a successor to Anil Shah. They recruited throughout India, taking a year to appoint a suitable replacement. Interestingly, they chose a foreigner – Barry Underwood. From the outset, Underwood introduced new ideas and set different management priorities. The change in management style is apparent on a number of levels. Anil Shah had played the founder role; he had been a senior ICS* administrator, and he drew on his links with government to help to establish AKRSP's reputation. His style was often paternalistic, with great emphasis on personal relations, and a willingness to use his network of government and political contacts to the advantage of the organization.

In contrast, Underwood was a professional who had worked for many years in community development. He had worked with local communities in Gujarat, had been a regional manager for OXFAM and a national manager for Action Aid. His style inclined to the participatory. He personally emphasized learning and research, and, because of the pressures for

---

* The Indian Civil Service is the most prestigious level of government service in the country.

change, he placed great emphasis on training, organizational development and strategic planning. While he delegated greater authority to field staff, he also introduced new management systems and placed greater emphasis on improved monitoring and evaluation. He says that he delegates power – he 'lets people get on with it'; he tries to communicate vision and purpose throughout the organization so that 'his vision is everyone's vision'.[35] He also established a Human Resource Department and paid particular attention to improving AKRSP's gender balance. Some say that, as an outsider, he could see AKRSP more dispassionately than others and was therefore able to adopt 'a more international and scientific approach'. The AKRSP example highlights the tensions and the advantages in appointing successors with a contrasting management style to the founder's. It may result in conflicts as the old order changes, but it does allow for innovation, diversity and greater flexibility in coping with changing circumstances.

LEADERS OR MANAGERS?

Leadership and position are not the same things. Similarly, position is not always commensurate with power and influence. However, it is clear that power can accrue to individuals because of their charisma, personality, skills or other attributes. In time, such individuals will take on a leadership role and, more often than not, they find themselves in positions with the potential to influence the direction, style and values of an organization. They thus become both leaders and managers.

Although it is common to use the term 'leader' and 'manager' interchangeably, there is a distinct difference between the two. The major difference is one of function. A leader is a person who exercises influence over another person in the attainment of organizational goals. Managerial functions, on the other hand – for example, organizing, planning or scheduling – do not necessarily involve leadership skills. In many cases, managers perform both types of function, but there is no automatic link between the two concepts. Peter Drucker argued long ago that a leader lifts an individual's 'vision to higher sights, their performance to a higher standard', while managers merely 'confirm the day-to-day practices of the organization'.[36] The distinction was later elaborated by Bennis and Nanus, who suggest that leadership is path-finding, while management is path-following. Management is about doing things right; leadership is about doing the right things.[37]

Leaders, therefore, have a view of where the organization should go and understand what is important for the success of the organization. They are ideas people. They have a vision; they are able to communicate their strategy; and they can align their staff behind it. Managers, on the other hand, are more concerned with implementing strategies and plans.

They are concerned with running their part of the organization, and ensuring that systems are followed and tasks completed. Harvard management professor John Kotter sees leadership complementing management, but not replacing it. Leadership is more than a functional skill. It is a tacit process which, he argues, creates positive feelings among staff. It emphasizes inspiration rather than control, and it unlocks potential instead of issuing demands. He argues that management is concerned with activities which are designed to produce 'consistency and order', whereas leadership is concerned with 'constructive or adaptive change'.[38]

Our research highlights some of these distinctions, but within the context of time and changing needs after the founding stage has passed. One of the most serious start-up problems for SRSC (apart from the disappearance of its major funding source) was the selection by its founding board of a manager as the first CEO. Both he and his successor, in fact, had excellent management credentials – the first one coming from government and the second from USAID. They were not, however, leaders, and they could not carry a disparate and fractious staff with them, especially in the face of a funding crisis. The third Executive Director, Feroze Shah, had a background in government, but he had also worked with AKRSP (P) and had seen SRSC from the inside at its birth. While perhaps not the most obvious candidate as SRSC's third Executive Director (especially to himself – he had to be persuaded to take the job), he rose to the occasion, exhibiting good management and strong leadership skills.

AKRSP (P) staff differentiate between the visionary role of their founding leader and the more management-oriented role of Stephen Rasmussen, who became General Manager in 1994. Shoaib Sultan Khan had the ability to balance informality with professional systems, but, as one staff member put it, his strength was 'to get people to work, knowing who to motivate when, and with what'. Like Anil Shah, his counterpart in AKRSP (I), he was a leader. There is no doubt that under Shoaib Sultan Khan's guidance, AKRSP (P) was a personality-based organization, clearly influenced by his views and experience. This style changed with the appointment of Rasmussen in 1994. Rasmussen, like Barry Underwood, was an 'outsider'. But, like Underwood, he was a development professional with many years of experience in Pakistan. His style was less personal and more technocratic than his predecessor's, at a point in the organization's history when this was precisely what was required.

CONCLUSIONS

It is clear that effective leadership is contingent upon the environment, the culture and the context in which it is rooted. In other words, leadership styles develop and evolve to suit the context in which they operate. They cannot be transferred easily. The evidence from our case studies is that decision-makers operate on a very personal level. They invest considerable time in building personal contacts and developing relationships of trust. In the field they walk and talk with villagers; they listen and learn. They place great emphasis on informal contacts, unstructured dialogue and mutual learning. Their relationships, although highly personalized and sometimes paternalistic, are rooted in a genuine commitment to helping the poor and disadvantaged. But above all, their success depends on their understanding of, and their responsiveness to, the needs of the local communities with which they work.

The leaders in our case study organizations do share common characteristics. These include a clear vision based on strongly held, well-articulated values; a fundamental belief in participative development and a conviction that, with outside encouragement, assistance and support, the poor can take control of their own lives. Despite the great diversity in their backgrounds, they are a highly capable, committed group of individuals, prepared to experiment, and to apply knowledge and contemporary technologies to the needs of the poor, and to adapt them to the reality of the circumstances in which they find themselves. They are pragmatic and ambitious. They have a strong set of personal values, but they are rational, knowledge-based individuals, willing to take the best from science and education. They value learning and relearning. They have a critical understanding and insight into the environment in which they work. They have the analytical ability to react to changing circumstances, to apply appropriate judgement and to respond to the moment. Each of them has effective communication talents and good interpersonal skills, enabling them to motivate staff and to engage a broad cross-section of society and donors.

At the beginning of the chapter we echoed some of the comments about South Asian NGO leaders that are frequently made by outsiders. These boil down to a concern that many have fallen prey to the 'guru syndrome', and that their organizations are one-man bands that will not survive their passing. On this last point, it is worth noting that six of the nine organizations in our study have actually undergone a leadership transition without falling into confusion and collapse. On the other points, we found that leaders engage in a hybrid of styles, skills, insights and interests. They demonstrate a chameleon-like ability to adapt to different roles, styles or organizational needs. They are able to combine ideals and values with analysis, technical expertise and professionalism, while remaining capable of communicating vision and motivating staff, stake-holders and beneficiaries. They depend heavily on teams and teamwork. Their leadership style is value-driven, knowledge-based and responsive. They are not charismatic autocrats. Rather they are something new to the field of development management: they are 'development leaders'.

CHAPTER 8

CONCLUSIONS

You see things and you say, 'Why?' But I dream things that never were and I say, 'Why Not?'.

George Bernard Shaw, *Back to Methuselah*, 1921

This study began with a workshop in Lahore at the end of 1997, and the last pieces of field work took place in March 2000 in Dhaka and New Delhi. In between, detailed case studies by Asian researchers were carried out on each of the participating NGOs, and hundreds of hours of supplementary taped interviews were conducted by the authors in India, Bangladesh and Pakistan. The participating organizations were extremely generous with their time and their insights, and in providing a great deal of internal documentation, studies and evaluations that complemented the material already gathered.

When we started, we had a vague idea that the South Asian NGOs would conform, at least in some respects, to the received management wisdom found in writings about both the private and the non-profit sectors. In some ways they do. Most have strategies and mission statements and personnel departments. Most espouse participatory management and teamwork, and their leaders exhibit many of the attributes and skills listed in standard reference books on management and leadership. But there were surprises as well, and a number of myths about NGO management and Southern NGOs quickly evaporated once we delved into the subject.

COMMON THEMES

Throughout the writing of this book, we were looking for common themes, similarities and explanatory events that might help us to draw conclusions that could be of use to other NGOs in the region, to NGOs elsewhere, and to others seeking to understand why some NGOs grow and succeed, while others do not. We did find some common threads. One, for example, was that most of the organizations in our study had gone through a major crisis of some sort relatively early in their evolution. SRSC and BAIF went through an unexpected and damaging withdrawal of donor support. BRAC went through an ideological crisis, and PROSHIKA survived a personality clash with ideological overtones that resulted in a bifurcation of the organization. Although these events are remembered with distaste, each organization seems to have emerged stronger for the ordeal.

One lesson we learned was that appearances can be deceptive. The formal strategy document, for example, is often much less important than informal and undocumented systems for developing and managing strategy. The formal strategy document may, in fact, be more important to outsiders than to people actually working inside an organization. Similarly, the public face of many of these organizations was commonly associated with their leadership – Abed in BRAC, the Jagawats in Sadguru or Omar Asghar Khan in Sungi. Yet the reality is that collective management and effective teamworking has been crucial to their success. Ambition and drive are important, but it is clear that without a competent team that is bound together by a shared vision and common values, seeds fall on barren ground. While many of the leaders and managers we interviewed had a chameleon-like ability to adapt to different roles, styles, skills and organizational needs, they all acknowledged the importance of their colleagues in achieving their goals.

These organizations are not solo performances; they are carefully orchestrated entities, well attuned to balancing competing demands and coping with the exigencies of a turbulent external environment. They are also more adept at managing and balancing a diverse set of relationships than expected. They have clearly developed the capability to work with, yet at the same time distance themselves from, donors and governments. At the same time they are skilled at balancing the demands and needs of local communities with those of their staff, supporters and politicians. This can be explained partly by their successful use of both informal processes and formal management systems. Organizational culture is a product of both espoused values and personal commitment, as well as strategies, systems and structures.

Strategies evolved, while decision-making was as much based on dialogue and mutual trust as on formal analysis. And organizational learning was both incremental and experimental. 'Learning' – a widely extolled but sometimes ephemeral value in management literature – takes on very concrete meaning in our case study organizations. Unlike many of their Northern counterparts, most have invested heavily in formal and informal learning systems, at both an individual and an institutional level.

These conclusions and findings can be clustered under four cross-cutting themes that run through the text. The first is the importance and the influence of context: tradition, culture, religion, current events, politics and the advice of strangers. The second is time: the moment at which an intervention is attempted; the historical period in which change is accepted or challenged; the length of time it takes for something to happen; the maturity that must be achieved before an organization will open itself to outsiders and to contrary opinion. The third cross-cutting theme relates to the trade-offs between formality and informality: the need to develop strategies, systems and structures, while at the same time remaining flexible, iterative and entrepreneurial in an uncertain economic and political climate. And the final cross-cutting theme is participation: what it really means in organizations that to some viewers appear dominated by highly charismatic individuals on whose every word the organization seems to hang. Where does leadership end and management begin? How do strong leaders and participative processes coexist within the same organization, without one damaging the other?

THE INFLUENCE OF CONTEXT AND CULTURE

It is not rocket science to say that context is everything, and yet in judging South Asian NGOs, most observers ignore it almost entirely. The context in which NGOs have formed in India, Bangladesh and Pakistan over the past 30 years has been marked by continuing poverty, by hostility from government, by confusion from donors, and by a spate of very serious natural disasters that have knocked even the best laid development plans off kilter. All this has taken place during a time of great technological and societal change which has had, and which continues to have, significant impact on the lives of ordinary people. While governments have mellowed in some ways over time, the NGOs in our study have been forced to accommodate the concerns of different regimes, the whims of civil servants, and increasingly draconian regulations and laws promulgated by politicians. In some cases governments have been supportive – as was the case with BAIF and the Maharashtra State Government in its early years – only to pull the plug, change the rules or make unreasonable demands when it suits them. More than half the NGOs in our study have been asked on bended knee by their government to drop everything and assist in a flood, a drought or with cyclone relief. But when the same NGOs are attacked by fundamentalists, government is nowhere to be seen. And when they are critical of government plans to dam rivers, cut down trees and otherwise mismanage the environment, they are accused of being the unaccountable, illegitimate lackeys of Western donors.

These donors too have a love-hate relationship with NGOs, who are never quite certain what they want them to be: developmental change agents, builders of civil society, advocates for change, or simply service delivery organizations that are available for inexpensive contract work. Donors commonly pressure governments to down-size and out-source their activities to NGOs, sometimes putting them in direct conflict with government. Although they find NGOs a more effective channel for spending their poverty budget, they rarely tire of demanding that NGOs become more professional, more accountable, more results-oriented – more, in fact, like the way the donors portray themselves. They also expect that NGOs should do this with very limited support for administrative overheads, so that the donor is not threatened by that most undevelopmental of things: dependency. Northern NGOs, once key supporters of every NGO in our study, mostly abandoned them just at the point of their greatest effectiveness. Why? Certainly it was not because they had become financially self-supporting. Mostly it was because they were felt to be 'too big' or 'too bureaucratic' or too close to the bilateral donors who were actually prepared to support the costs of scaling-up (when 'scaling-up' was what Southern NGOs were accused of not being able to do).

It would be wrong to suggest that successful South Asian NGOs have been seriously ill-treated by their Northern benefactors. All, in fact, have benefited greatly from their relationship with a range of governmental and non-governmental supporters. While much of the support has been financial in nature, the sometimes unwanted donor policy and programming pressures have not all been misplaced, especially where gender issues and financial management have been concerned. But to suggest that South Asian NGOs have simply rolled over and played dead would also be wrong. Resistance to donor blandishments and pressure may not normally be very direct, but most NGOs have developed a sophisticated set of 'buffering strategies' to keep the worst aspects of donor interference at bay.

Aban Kabraji talks about the problem of balancing two sets of constituencies, one demand-based and the other supply-based.

The demand-based constituency is the one to whom we must deliver our services – government, NGOs, the people for whom we work; the supply side is the funding agency or donors. The real challenge is to try to balance these two, matching demand with supply and still maintaining the integrity of purpose in terms of one's own organization, mission and strategy.[1]

She might well have added government as a third constituency that requires equally adroit balancing.

From a management point of view, the most important contextual consideration is not so much political or financial as cultural. We recognize that much has been written about the impact of caste, class, religion and the collectivist nature of South Asian society on management practices. But we question the notion that the leadership styles displayed in these successful NGOs is heavily influenced by an authoritarian, 'high power-distance' culture. Despite the charisma of many leaders, none would have survived their first crisis if this were actually the case. All the evidence from this study suggests that they succeeded because of their ability to involve others and their willingness to encourage collective management. On the contrary, if South Asian culture is as fatalistic, authoritarian and class-ridden as has been suggested by some writers, then the management lesson to be learned from our case study NGOs is that great success can be achieved despite these characteristics. Perhaps a more fundamental point is that there are positive attributes of South Asian leadership that may equally well be shaped by cultural norms or religious beliefs – concern for the poor; a driving ambition to improve society; an ability to adapt and change; a willingness to learn. What is obvious is that with time and the right amount of care and support, these attributes – which are abundantly evident – can be turned into powerful forces for positive change.

THE IMPLICATIONS OF TIME AND TIMING

The issue of time arises again and again throughout the case studies. The first key timing issue has to do with when an NGO is established. All the evidence suggests that an NGO formed in a hostile climate may take longer to mature and longer to come to terms with its environment than others. BRAC and PROSHIKA were formed at a time of considerable suspicion and hostility towards the non-governmental sector in Bangladesh, and it took almost 20 years before they were confident enough to begin working closely with government. Government, of course, matured during that period as well and no longer saw NGOs as a great threat to its reputation or its space.

In contrast, IUCN in Pakistan had a relatively easy relationship with government from the start. This can be partly explained because its work on the National Conservation Strategy complemented and supported similar government initiatives in this area, and partly because at that time in the early 1980s, NGOs were generally unknown in Pakistan and offered no serious threat to government. In other words, IUCN's timing was good. A few years after the creation of IUCN, Pakistan, however, things had changed. Pakistani NGOs were springing up like mushrooms in the night, and politicians found them annoying and even threatening. Sungi emerged during this time and, pitting itself against vested interests in the logging and construction industries, quickly became a thorn in the side of various government departments. Although it matured considerably over its first decade and saw that it had to make at least some strategic alliances with government, it has retained its crusading style and has developed a reputation for good development work, transparency and probity. Thus, another element to consider is the time it takes for an NGO to become sophisticated and secure enough to distinguish between one part of government and another, between one type of issue and another, between one type of donor relationship and another.

A second key timing issue is the length of time it takes to develop a distinct organizational culture, and the confidence, knowledge and wisdom that accrue from it. In the early stages of an organization's development, much depends on the leader for these attributes and skills, or the core leadership group. No amount of planning and strategizing – even in the most premeditated of the NGOs in our study – was a substitute for this. Likewise, formal management systems and strategies developed late, rather than early in the life of our organizations. Among the premeditated NGOs, there *were* strategies and skeletal systems from the start, but in most cases these changed quickly or proved not to be very useful. In their evolutionary or 'pioneering' days, most NGOs took a contingent approach to strategic planning, combining opportunism and entrepreneurial skills in ways that best accommodated their vision as well as their operational and financial limitations. However, it is important to emphasize that strategy is clearly distinct from vision. And while there is no evidence in our study that NGOs need to establish a definitive strategic plan on Day One, it is obvious that virtually all our NGOs and their leaders had a clear vision, and that this has not altered in any significant way over time.

A third issue is the role of time in determining the type of leadership required. All but one of our case study NGOs began with individuals who gradually, or even quickly, developed a capacity to lead – to articulate a vision and to inspire others with that vision, inside and outside the organization. The capacity to lead comprises a variety of attributes: compassion, ambition, the ability to listen, an ability to inspire, to speak to groups, to convince the sceptical, whether staff, government officials or donor representatives.

Leadership involves a willingness to take risks, but it requires the knowledge – and eventually the wisdom – to understand how risky a risk really is, and to hedge bets accordingly. There are two elements to consider here. The first involves the amount of time it may take a leader to develop the requisite skills. Two in our group – Shoaib Sultan Khan and Anil Shah in the two AKRSPs – already had a great deal of experience, having spent a lifetime in public service and rural development before they started working with their organizations. Although the others came from a variety of backgrounds, few of them had any deep experience of leadership, and few had more than a few years of mid- or low-level management experience. It took time for this to develop. The second element has to do with the difference between management and leadership. It would appear that while management skills are important, there is no substitute for leadership ability, especially in the early years of an organization. In this regard, SRSC stands out. Although it was no less premeditated than the two AKRSPs, its board selected as the first director a man with excellent management skills, but with limited leadership attributes. They made the same mistake in choosing his successor, and it was only on the third try that they recognized the importance of leadership in the early stages of organization building. They sacrificed curriculum vitae to drive, ambition and vision, not to mention to some of the success that up to then had been so elusive.

Strong leadership, however, may become a handicap over time if it is not tempered with good management. It is not difficult to think of South Asian NGOs that have been dragged down by a founder who was unwilling to change, unwilling to adopt modern management practices, unwilling to spread authority and responsibility away from the centre. It is interesting that the successors to Shoaib Sultan Khan, Anil Shah and Manibhai Desai were all drawn from a more technocratic background than their predecessors, and they introduced fairly major changes in the way their organizations were structured and managed. This is not so much a reflection on the founder, as it is on time and the need for different ways of doing things after an organization gets through the initial turbulence and levels off at cruising altitude.

The same is true of governance structures. In the early stages of an organization's life, it makes sense that board members are friends and supporters – honest friends and supporters – rather than policy-makers. This was particularly apparent in the accidental NGO. Here the founders needed reinforcement, not a lot of extraneous chatter about policy. The individual at the helm is taking great risks with his or her name, reputation and future livelihood. Few trustees will have any knowledge or understanding of the adrenaline rush and the sleepless nights this can cause. Few will have much useful advice to offer until the organization is a viable, going concern. A cynic may call this 'rubber-stampism', but such support and mentoring fulfils a very real need for the founding leaders in their role as social entrepreneurs and risk takers.

Worries, therefore, about the 'non-accountability' of emerging NGOs are somewhat misplaced. Their leaders – the ones that government and donors talk to most often and most directly – are personally vulnerable and are therefore highly accountable. It is only after time and experience have demonstrated an organization's viability that its leaders are likely to expose themselves to strangers as board members and to new sources of policy advice. It is only after an organization has begun to develop a cross-section of beneficiaries and stakeholders, when responsibility for programmes and money has become more diffuse, that the accountability question starts to become an issue. This is as much a function of time as anything else.

BALANCING FORMALITY AND INFORMALITY

Again and again throughout our study, we have seen trade-offs between the formal and the informal. Governance structures tend to remain informal in the early years of an organization, and, as noted above, there are excellent reasons for this. While teamwork and the development of an institutional culture may be planned out and proactively managed, it is often the informal groups, the friendships and the accidental meetings that form the backbone of genuine teamwork. Organizational culture is as much the product of history and age as it is of informal relationships and groupings, let alone the impact of formal strategies, organizational structures and systems. This echoes a much wider discussion in management literature as to whether organizations are managed more effectively through formal management systems and controls, or through informal, consensual processes that motivate staff, encourage learning and facilitate change.

Most voluntary sector management books and certainly most donor agencies argue the importance of strategic planning as a formal management process, yet the evidence from our study suggests that effective strategies are very often emergent and evolutionary. They commonly reflect immediate needs and demands, as well as opportunities or challenges arising within the context in which the organization expects to operate. While several of our case study NGOs have developed mission statements and highly professional strategic plans, these came late in their development, usually in response to pressure from donors. It is possible that strategic planning *has* become important and useful for some NGOs. It is also possible that it is a 'buffering strategy' to keep outsiders at bay while insiders figure out what to do and how to do it. Given the uncertain political and financial climate in which South Asian NGOs work, the ability to adapt and change appears to be a more important professional quality than the ability to write out a five-year plan. The point here is not that NGOs should be strategy-free. None of them are. It is that the formal strategy document has come late to many, probably because it was not very useful. In a handful of cases, it is still noticeably absent.

That said, there are some aspects of formality that clearly make sense to our participating NGOs. One example that came late to some are formal personnel policies and human resource management strategies. The later the introduction of these policies and strategies, the greater the management difficulties that are likely to be faced in an organization. When organizations are small and populated by young idealists, informal, personalized recruitment and promotion makes some sense. But as the span of a founder's control widens, systems that take achievement, training and longer term security into account become more important. As NGOs mature, so do their staff. Many NGOs have recruited the best and the brightest, giving them development skills that cannot be found on the street. The retention and enhancement of staff, therefore, become critical issues early in the life of the organization.

An important part of human resource management is training and staff development, and the way in which this contributes to overall organizational learning. One of the most striking features of virtually all our case study NGOs is the level of investment they have made in staff development. If no other aspect of their management sets them apart from their Northern counterparts and supporters, this one does. Learning new skills, concepts and attitudes, and unlearning the old, have become heavily ingrained in a very formal sense. Training begins with simple induction courses, but it continues in a wide variety of ways. All our sample organizations conduct regular management training programmes, and several have created their own management schools or institutes that are open to outsiders as well as their own staff. Secondments and scholarships are commonplace, as are thematic, organization-wide courses on computer training, environmental issues or gender awareness.

There is some debate around the idea that NGOs are unique because of their particular values and distinctive vision, and some commentators argue that the ability of NGOs to learn is inherent in their values and culture. The evidence from this study suggests quite the opposite: effective learning is a hard won goal that relies as much on targeted investment in formal training and research as on personal empowerment and informal contacts. Efforts to promote gender policies in organizations like BRAC and SRSC are an excellent example of how a formal, policy-based approach to training can move an organization beyond platitudes and into areas of genuine change management. The reality is that NGOs, as any other type of organization, need both formal management systems and controls, as well as informal and participative processes that can motivate staff, encourage learning and facilitate change.

PARTICIPATION AND PARTICIPATORY MANAGEMENT

Participatory management is a *sine qua non* of developmental NGOs. It is an essential condition that all embrace unquestioningly. Some NGOs in our group can actually be said to have written the book on participation, or at least they worked with Robert Chambers while *he* wrote the book.*

In embarking on this study, we were not overly concerned about whether an NGO used participatory management techniques; we assumed that they do. Rather we were interested in what was understood by the word 'participation' itself. There were three reasons for this. The first is that there is virtually no institution left that does not espouse

---

* Robert Chambers has written several books on rural development and has pioneered participatory rural appraisal (PRA). Books such as *Challenging the Professions* (IT Publications, 1993) and *Whose Reality Counts?* (IT Publications, 1997) reflect visits to and work with many organizations in South Asia, including AKRSP (I) and BRAC.

participatory development and participatory management. This includes
the World Bank, the Organization for Economic Cooperation and
Development (OECD) and all bilateral donors. What organization these
days would care to admit that it was *un*participatory? So our first question
about South Asian NGOs had to do with the meaning of the word itself.
The second had to do with operational issues. In organizations where
scaling up has taken place on a grand and rapid scale, and where
programmes are inevitably formulaic, how can participation happen? Do
villagers sit under a tree, as Saul Alinsky said they should, and in a totally
participatory manner decide – one village after another, in their thousands
– that the thing they really need is a savings and credit programme? And
thirdly, what does 'participation' mean in an organization that is dominated by a dynamic, charismatic leader, or a small group of managers? Are
these organizations *truly* participatory, or is it all a sham, as some outsiders
like to believe?

Where programming is concerned, there are clear boundaries to
participation. Given the nature of funding and the desire to take what
has worked in a few villages to many, the luxury of working out tailor-
made programmes from one village to the next rarely exists. Depending
on the organization, however, villagers may well have options, most of
which will deal in one way or another with a basic and urgent need –
income, health or education. There is a participative element in making
that choice. There may also be a more profound element of participation
in the way a programme is introduced and managed. Savings and credit
societies can be managed collectively and openly. Loans can be jointly
guaranteed by villagers. Primary schools may be constructed by parents;
the school calendar can be set by parents; the teacher can be selected by
and made responsible, in part, to parents. Water management can be
organized collectively; seeds can be purchased jointly; produce can be
marketed together rather than separately. Depending on the organization
and the programme, 'participation' can mean consultation, it can mean
consensus, or in some cases there will be a vote and it will mean democracy.
Maximizing, or at least optimizing, the participation of beneficiaries
conveys ownership, and in turn ownership begets empowerment.

To some, the concepts of leadership and participation seem incompatible. There is a nagging suspicion that despite effusive talk of
'participatory management', too many NGOs are essentially dependent
upon one person or a handful of individuals at best. However, if there is
one myth that we would like to debunk, it is this one. Certainly BAIF was
the creation of Manibhai Desai. Sadguru would never have existed had
the Jagawats not spent two years walking through Dahod talking to
villagers. BRAC would not have survived its first year without the skills
and drive of F H Abed. All the AKRSP strategic planning in the world
would have come to naught without a Shoaib Sultan Khan or an Anil

Shah to make it happen. IUCN might still have a part-time office in Karachi had the first manager not been Aban Kabraji. Nothing can detract from the enormous achievements of these individuals and others.

At the outset, they may very well have 'directed' events, in the full sense of that word. But to imagine that Abed could direct, much less 'manage' the details of 30,000 primary schools himself is ludicrous. That Faruque Ahmed and a small coterie of managers could successfully control events in 90,000 village groups, or that Aban Kabraji could manage IUCN's work on a national and several provincial conservation strategies, plus a dozen complicated donor contracts, plus all of IUCN's efforts across Asia, is at best nonsense. At worst it is an insult to the hundreds and thousands of very competent workers and managers who have helped to develop and manage these organizations over the years.

There is another way to look at participation, one that emerged at several levels in our study. Participatory and consultative management styles work well, not only in delegating authority for programming matters, but also in ensuring allegiance throughout an organization to a shared vision and alignment behind a mutually agreed strategy. What has emerged from these studies is that hierarchy and participatory management can be complementary and compatible. An organization with clear management hierarchies can also be participatory in style.

In fact, what our research shows is that there *are* hierarchies in South Asian NGOs, plenty of them. The issue is not so much that they exist, but how they function. What these studies demonstrate is that 'participatory management' needs a particular mind-set and specific management competencies. First and foremost, it means that successful leaders must be able to listen, and must be able to respond to what is being said. They have to be adept at managing cross-functional teams and a range of decentralized operations. Without two-way vertical respect and under-standing, without the delegation of authority, it would have been impossible for virtually all of our case study NGOs to have survived, let alone to have thrived. Six of our nine organizations have gone through significant leadership change, and while the jury may be out on one or two because the change has been so recent, several have survived for five, six or seven years without collapsing, despite predictions to the contrary. Why? Because these were and are not directive hierarchies run by authoritarian leaders. They are empowered hierarchies headed by 'development leaders' whose leadership style is value driven, knowledge-based and responsive.

Where, then, does the idea of the authoritarian, one-man NGO come from? It comes in part from the fact that casual observers too easily make the equation: BRAC equals Abed or SRSC equals Feroze Shah. Some leaders have become legendary in South Asian NGO development, partly because of their achievements and reputation, and partly because they are regularly invited to speak publicly about their work. This strengthens the equation. Donor agencies are a pernicious, reinforcing influence on the misunderstanding. Their resident representatives usually insist on dealing exclusively with the Executive Director, while visiting programme officers and dignitaries *must* see the Executive Director.* In addition, donor perceptions of a recipient NGO are derived from reports and evaluations that rarely mention individuals. Consequently the Executive Director remains uppermost in their minds. This situation is aggravated by the fact that often only senior managers are fluent in spoken English. The insistence of donors and other outsiders on dealing only with senior managers has created imaginary personality cults and sustained the idea of the indispensable 'guru'.

Participatory management is not about making every decision by consensus, no matter how long it takes. It is not about worker control. It could be, but in our nine successful South Asian NGOs, it involves a considerably more sophisticated process of trust, mutual respect, dialogue and commitment to a shared vision and strategy. Participatory management is about blending formal and informal systems, old cultures and new cultures, ambitions and hopes and needs, with the very serious business of changing the face of poverty in countries where it is as entrenched as deeply as anywhere else on earth.

Managing for Change: Future Challenges

NGO managers have to balance personal commitment to a vision with the urgent needs of local communities, the demands of donors, and the vested interests of politicians and local pressure groups. In response, they have adopted a hybrid leadership style in order to cope with the ever-changing demands of the sector, and they have learned how to devise strategies that can meet the real needs of the poor while still satisfying donor requirements and staff concerns. They work in poor, vulnerable communities with limited resources, and they have to make choices that are cost-effective while remaining true to the values of the sector and the vision of their own organization. They have meagre management budgets and limited spare cash to cover more than basic administration and the high costs associated with running numerous projects in difficult conditions. They work in a sector that expects managers to promote caring

---

* In the early 1990s, the problem of visiting donors was so bad at AKRSP (P) – coincidentally located in one of the most scenic mountainous parts of the world – that Shoaib Sultan Khan was forced to build a visitor centre and hire a manager with excellent English language skills to run it and physically block the route to his office.

staffing policies, to encourage participatory decision-making and to promote shared learning, but which does not have the systems or structures, let alone surplus money, to embed such processes.

It is clear that management in this sector is different from management in others. Yet there are very few training centres or universities that focus on developing the management capacity of NGO staff. There has been limited research in this area, and few institutions offer specialist management training for the next generation of development leaders. The alternative is for aspiring or potential NGO leaders to join an MBA programme or some such course, on the assumption that management practices and organizational challenges transcend sectors. Such courses are dominated by a private sector mindset, with examples and case studies commonly derived from the business community. Where development issues or NGOs are mentioned, they are treated as a specialist elective or lumped together in the area of social responsibility or ethics. The reality is that some strategic and operational challenges facing NGO managers are specific to the sector, and to the kind of work that they do. This book has identified some of the specific management issues involved. It highlights the intrinsic importance of further research and the need for training material that can be used to enhance the skill base of a new generation of NGO managers.

Apart from the need for more relevant training and research into NGO management, what of the future? This book offers some indicators as to the challenges that may be faced by NGOs in the South. Clearly there are major issues around management succession and how organizations will have to adapt to a new generation of NGO managers. The challenge is not merely one of changing personalities or scaling up. It is about responding to change, introducing new management systems and structures, adapting to new information and communication technologies, decentralizing responsibility and authority, and evolving fundamentally different organizational cultures that are designed to cope with new development challenges and different partners. There are signs that this trend is already in train. The expansion of BAIF has taken place through administrative decentralization and the devolution of power to different autonomous entities. BRAC is becoming increasingly involved in sophisticated income-generating operations – Internet services, publishing, printing and agro-processing. All NGOs in our sample stressed the importance of increased investment in organizational learning, staff development and affirmative action gender policies in order to create more inclusive, creative, flexible and therefore more effective organizations.

These initiatives respond partly to pressures for the more effective use of resources in the light of a changing aid environment, changing donor priorities and increasing competition for development funds. It may also be partly the consequence of the changing role of NGOs in society, and changing relationships between communities and government. There are debates as to whether large, successful NGOs such as those in our study can remain independent, sustainable entities, or whether the changing financial climate and funding exigencies will mean closer contracting relations with government, as has begun to happen in many industrialized countries. Alternatively, if NGOs are to remain independent, they will need to generate a higher proportion of their own budget through income-generating operations, local philanthropy or through new financing relationships. Already we are seeing large players like BRAC moving into private sector-type operations in order to support their development work. This trend may result in an increasing bifurcation between 'soft', long-term development work and 'hard', project-based income-generating activities, or the creation of new subsidiaries or even completely new independent entities.

One clear weakness that was apparent in our study was the failure of many NGOs to collaborate with other NGOs or to form new relationships. Pressure, however, from a changing financial and political environment may encourage greater cooperation, promoting new forms of strategic alliances or joint ventures, and possibly leading to the merger of key NGOs. Such new organizational forms will put great pressure on the leadership style and management skills of the senior staff involved. Traditional management practices will have to be reconsidered, a more facilitative leadership approach will need to be adopted, and there will have to be genuine clarity of purpose and alignment behind a common strategy. The make-up of boards and the role of governance structures will have to be renegotiated. This could result in changes to the legal status of NGOs or to the introduction of completely new governance structures. This in turn could result in pressure to adapt the legislation that defines the NGO sector, allowing for more innovative organizational forms. Managing an NGO is already a demanding process; it could well become even more so, and, as change occurs, it will require a very different set of strategic competencies and skills than has hitherto been appreciated.

At the beginning of this book we suggested that some of our findings might be surprising. Those working in NGOs or close to them may not appreciate in fact, just how much some of what we found deviates from received management wisdom. For the record, some of our most important findings are worth repeating.

First, context and culture are hugely important, but they should not be seen only as constraints or barriers to change. NGO managers can and do use them as levers for change. Similarly, timing and maturity are crucial determinants of an NGO's management style and of the effectiveness of its systems and structures. Second, leadership, hierarchy and participation are not incompatible. An organization with clear management hierarchies can also be participatory in style. The real issue for

NGOs is not whether they have a flat organizational structure, but whether they have systems and processes in place that will encourage teamworking, promote learning and facilitate decentralization. The issue is not participation for its own sake, but the use of participatory processes to spread information and knowledge, and to build consensus around organizational objectives and vision.

Third, NGOs depend as much on formal systems and policies as they do on informal, participative processes and personal commitment. Effective NGO management is about recognizing the complementarity of the formal and the informal. Fourth, effective NGO leadership is not the domain of one individual; it is dependent on good teamwork, joint responsibility and collective accountability. The strong, risk-taking, charismatic leader has a clear role in the formation of an NGO, but if the organization is to survive and thrive, the single leader has to give way to many leaders, or to new leaders. Thus, the development of a collective leadership and the creation of a clear succession plan are crucial determinants of future success. A final important observation has to do with the surprisingly high levels of investment that South Asian NGO managers have made in training, research and learning. This has created new kinds of institutional knowledge about development and about how to manage effectively for development. It has transformed early experiments into substantial and substantive weapons in the fight against poverty.

South Asian NGOs are of interest to many in the field of management studies because many have grown up so rapidly and so successfully in such a very short period of time. They have grown despite the challenges of the social, political and economic climates in which they emerged. And because of their success, they have captured the imagination of their counterparts in other regions of the world. They are also of great interest because they offer hope for the future in the fight against debilitating poverty and injustice. There is no one reason for their growth and there is no single reason for their success. As this book has shown, there are many reasons, and they depend to varying degrees on individuals, on time and on context.

In conclusion, the most important lesson from our case study organizations, perhaps, is that something new and important is happening in the field of international development and voluntary action. Where development and NGOs are concerned, the experience of the last third of the 20th century in South Asia demonstrates great potential for the 21st century. This potential began with a handful of people, but it grew from the work of thousands: impatient and ambitious people who obtained and used the best tools and management practices they could find to make good things happen. They are people who are tired of hearing others look at things and ask 'Why?'. They dream of things that never were and they ask 'Why Not?'. And then they make them happen.

NOTES

CHAPTER 1

1 Wood, Geof (1997) 'States Without Citizens: The Problem of the Franchise State', in Hulme, D and Edwards, M, *NGOs, States and Donors: Too Close for Comfort?* SCF and Macmillan, London, p84
2 Hashemi, Syed (1996) 'NGO Accountability in Bangladesh: Beneficiaries, Donors and the State', in Edwards, M and Hulme, D, *Beyond the Magic Bullet: NGO Performance and Accountability in the Post-Cold War World*, Kumarian, West Hartford, p127
3 Edwards, M (1999) 'NGO Performance – What Breeds Success? New Evidence from South Asia', *World Development*, vol 27, no 2, p366
4 Hashemi, op cit, p130
5 First expounded in Korten, David C (1987) 'Third Generation NGO Strategies: A Key to People-centered Development', *World Development*, vol 15, supplement, pp145–159

CHAPTER 2

1 Chambers, R (1988) 'Poverty in India: Concepts, Research and Reality', *IDS Discussion Paper*, no 241, Sussex, pp8–9; see also Chambers, R (1983) *Rural Development: Putting the Last First*, Longman, Harlow, Essex, Chapter 5
2 Narayan, D, Chambers, R, Shah, M and Petesch, P, (1999) 'Global Synthesis; Consultations with the Poor', Poverty Group, World Bank, 20 September
3 Mahbub ul Haq Human Development Centre (1999) *Human Development in South Asia 1999*, Oxford University Press, Oxford, p2
4 Mohanty, Manoranjan (ed) (1996) *Foreign Aid and NGOs*, Voluntary Action Network India, New Delhi, p15
5 Society for Participatory Research in Asia (1991) 'Voluntary Development Organizations in India', New Delhi, p45
6 ibid, p47
7 *The News*, Islamabad, 10 May 1999
8 *The News*, Islamabad, 6 November 1999
9 *The News on Sunday*, Islamabad, 7 November 1999
10 Annis, S (1987) 'Can Small-Scale Development be a Large-Scale Policy? The Case of Latin America', *World Development*, vol 15, supplement, autumn, p129
11 Edwards, M and Hulme, D (1992), *Making a Difference: NGOs and Development in a Changing World*, Earthscan, London, p16

12   Ahmed, Sara (1998) 'Navinchand Mafatlal Sadguru Water and Development Foundation: Managing for Growth and Change', South Asian NGO Management Project, Ahmedabad

13   Salamon, L and Anheier, H (1992) *In Search of the Nonprofit Sector II: The Problem of Classification*, Working Papers of the Johns Hopkins Comparative Nonprofit Sector Project, no 3, The Johns Hopkins Institute for Policy Studies, Baltimore

14   Morgan, Peter et al (1993) *Capacity Building for the Environment: A Review of IUCN, The World Conservation Union, in Pakistan*', IUCN, Karachi, April, p3

15   Quoted in Oza, Apoorva (1998) 'Case Study of BAIF Development Research Foundation', South Asian NGO Management Project, Ahmedabad

16   John Hailey interview with Dr Hegde

17   Fatmi, Mohammad N E, Kabir, A, Sabri, Asgar Ali, (1998) 'A Case Study of BRAC', South Asian NGO Management Project, Dhaka

18   Buffering strategies are discussed in Alnoor Ebrahim (1999) *The Making of NGOs: Global Influences and Local Responses from Western India*, PhD dissertation, Stanford University, Chapter 5

19   Ebrahim, op cit, p166

20   ibid, p193

21   Zafar Qureshi interview with Aban Kabraji, Karachi, December 1998

22   Correspondence with Stella Jafri, January 2000

23   Edhi, Abdul Sattar (1996) *A Mirror to the Blind*, National Bureau of Publications, Islamabad, p306

24   Zafar Qureshi interview with Aban Kabraji, Karachi, December 1998

25   Putnam, Robert D (1993) *Making Democracy Work: Civic Traditions in Modern Italy*, Princeton University Press, Princeton, p164. The prisoner's dilemma is a recurring theme in management writing. See, for example, Mintzberg et al, 1998, pp110–111

26   ibid, p175

27   Putnam, op cit, p177

28   Hussain, Saneeya (1998) 'Managing Growth and Change: A Case Study on Sungi Development Foundation', South Asian NGO Management Project, Karachi, p23

CHAPTER 3

1   Handy, C (1988) *Understanding Voluntary Organizations*, Penguin, London

2   Peters, T and Waterman, R (1982) *In Search of Excellence*, Harper Row, New York

3   Schein, E (1992) *Organizational Culture and Leadership*, Jossey-Bass, San Francisco

4   John Hailey interview with Harnath Jagawat, July 1998

5   M G Sattar interview with Qazi Faruque Ahmed, January 1998

6   Pettigrew, A (1987) *The Management of Strategic Change*, Blackwell, Oxford

7   Hudson, M (1995) *Managing Without Profit*, Penguin, London, p94

8   John Hailey interview with Barry Underwood, July 1998

9   John Hailey interview with Dr Mangurkur, July 1998
10   Greiner, L (1972) 'Evolution and revolution as organizations grow', *Harvard Business Review*, July
11   Korten, D (1990) *Getting into the 21ˢᵗ Century: Voluntary Action and the Global Agenda*, Kumarian Press, West Hartford, Connecticut
12   Kaplan, A (1996) *The Development Practitioners Handbook*, Pluto Press, London
13   Schein, E, op cit
14   Fowler, A (1997) *Striking a Balance: A Guide to Enhancing the Effectiveness of NGOs in International Development*, Earthscan, London
15   Ian Smillie interview with Salehuddin Ahmed, June 1998
16   Beer, M and Spector, B (1984) *Managing Human Assets*, Free Press, New York
17   Hudson, M, op cit, p160
18   AKRSP, Organization Manual, Ahmedabad, March 1996, p45
19   Ian Smillie interview with F H Abed, June 1998
20   Ian Smillie interview with Salehuddin Ahmed, June 1998
21   Ian Smillie interview with Qazi Faruque Ahmed, June 1998

CHAPTER 4

1   Chowdhury, A M R and Cash, R A (1996) *A Simple Solution: Teaching Millions to Treat Diarrhoea at Home*, University Press, Dhaka
2   Revens, R (1983) *The ABC of Action Learning*, IFAL, Manchester
3   Fowler, A (1997) *Striking A Balance: A Guide to Enhancing the Effectiveness of NGOs in International Development*, Earthscan, London, p64
4   Edwards, M (1996) 'Becoming a Learning Organization, or, the Search for the Holy Grail', paper presented to AKFC Round Table on Systematic Learning, Ottawa
5   This is discussed at length in Smillie, I (1995) *The Alms Bazaar*, IT Publications, London
6   Handy, C (1994) *The Empty Raincoat*, Hutchinson, London
7   Drucker, P (1993) *Post-Capitalist Society*, Butterworth, Oxford
8   World Bank (1998) *World Development Report: Knowledge for Development*, Oxford University Press, Oxford
9   Korten, D (1980) 'Community Organization and Rural Development: A Learning Process Approach', *Public Administration Review*, vol 40, pp480–511
10   Fowler, op cit
11   Korten, op cit
12   Lovell, C (1992) *Breaking the Cycle of Poverty*, Kumarian, West Hartford, Connecticut, p15
13   Smillie, I (1997) *Words and Deeds: BRAC at 25*, BRAC, Dhaka
14   Senge, P (1990) *The Fifth Discipline: The Art and Practice of the Learning Organization*, Century Business, London
15   Pedler, M, Burgoyne, J and Boydell, T (1991) *The Learning Company*, McGraw Hill, London
16   ibid
17   Harrison, R (1995) *The Collected Papers of Roger Harrison*, McGraw-Hill, London

18 Fowler, op cit
19 Swieringa, J and Wierdsma, A (1992) *Becoming a Learning Organization*, Addison Wesley, Wokingham
20 Ahmed, Sara (1998) 'Navinchand Mafatlal Sadguru Water and Development Foundation: Managing for Growth and Change', South Asian NGO Management Project, Ahmedabad, p27
21 Khan, Shandana (1998) 'Case Study of Aga Khan Rural Support Programme, Pakistan', South Asian NGO Management Project, Islamabad, p33
22 Ian Smillie interview with Sadia Choudhury, June 1998
23 Fatmi, Mohammad N E, Kabir, A, Sabri, Asgar Ali (1998) 'A Case Study of BRAC', South Asian NGO Management Project, Dhaka, p7
24 John Hailey, interview with Barry Underwood, July 1998
25 Khan, op cit, p18
26 Fatmi, op cit, p12
27 Ian Smillie interview with Dr Samdani, June 1998
28 Ian Smillie interview with Quazi Faruque Ahmed, June 1998
29 Ahmed, op cit, p28
30 BRAC, *Annual Report*, Dhaka, 1997, p7
31 ibid
32 Mohammed Fatmi interview with F H Abed, March 1998
33 PROSHIKA, *Scaling Up Participatory Development*, Dhaka, 1997, pp7–11
34 Hussain, Saneeya (1998) 'Managing Growth and Change: A Case Study on Sungi Development Foundation', South Asian NGO Management Project, Karachi, p67
35 Chowdhury and Cash, op cit, p87
36 PROSHIKA, *Activity Report 1998–1999*, PROSHIKA, Dhaka, pp90–91
37 Oza, Apoorva (1998) 'Case Study of BAIF Development Research Foundation', South Asian NGO Management Project, Ahmedabad, p31
38 Khan, op cit, p17
39 NOVIB, 'Evaluation of SRSC', May 1998, NOVIB, The Hague, p30
40 ibid, p14
41 John Hailey interview with Ravi Shankar, August 1998
42 Howes, M and Roche, C (1996) 'How NGOs Learn', paper to DSA NGO Study Group, Oxford

CHAPTER 5

1 Brinkerhoff, D (1991) *Improving Development Program Performance: Guidelines for Managers*, Lynne Rienner, Boulder, p65
2 Korten, D 'Strategic Organization for People-Centred Development' *Public Administration Review*, vol 44, no 4, p344, cited in Brinkerhoff, op cit, p65
3 Drucker, P (1992) *Managing the Non-Profit Organization: Principles and Practices*, Harper Business, New York, p59
4 Kelleher, D and McLaren, K (1996) *Grabbing the Tiger by the Tail: NGOs Learning for Organizational Change*, Canadian Council for International Cooperation, Ottawa, p63

5   Hudson, M (1995) *Managing Without Profit: The Art of Managing Third Sector Organizations*, Chapter 4, Penguin, London
6   Van Crevald, M (1991) *The Transformation of War*, The Free Press, New York, p96
7   Hilmer, F and Donaldson, L (1996) *Management Redeemed: Debunking the Fads that Undermine Our Corporations*, Free Press, p185
8   Mintzberg, H, Ahlstrand, B, Lampel, J (1998) *Strategy Safari*, Free Press, New York
9   Borst, D and Montana, P (1977) *Managing Non-Profit Organizations*, Amacom, New York
10   Ian Smillie interview with F H Abed, Dhaka, 14 June 1998
11   For the scientific origins of chaos theory, see Gleick, J (1988) *Chaos: Making a New Science*, Penguin, New York. An example of its application to management can be found in Brown, S L and Eisenhardt, K M (1998) *Competing on the Edge: Strategy as Structured Chaos*, Harvard Business School Press, Boston
12   IUCN Pakistan (1993) 'The Way Ahead', IUCN (P), Karachi, p18
13   Ebrahim, Alnoor (1999) *The Making of NGOs: Global Influences and Local Responses from Western India*, PhD dissertation, Stanford University, p26
14   Hashemi, S and Hassan, M 'Building NGO Legitimacy in Bangladesh: The Contested Domain', in Lewis, D (1999) *International Perspectives on Voluntary Action*, Earthscan, London, p126
15   Fatmi, Mohammad N E, Kabir, A, Sabri, Asgar Ali (1998) 'A Case Study of BRAC', South Asian NGO Management Project, Dhaka, p4
16   Ian Smillie interview with Faruque Ahmed, Manikganj, 15 June 1998
17   BRAC interview with Faruque Ahmed, Dhaka, January 1998
18   Oza, Apoorva (1998) 'Case Study of BAIF Development Research Foundation', South Asian NGO Management Project, Ahmedabad, p24
19   Sungi Mission Statement, quoted in Hussain, Saneeya (1998) 'Managing Growth and Change: A Case Study on Sungi Development Foundation', South Asian NGO Management Project, Karachi, p5
20   ibid, p8
21   ibid, p10
22   ibid, p14
23   Correspondence from Stella Jafri, 19 January 2000
24   Carruthers, I, Chambers, R, Hanson, A J, Jackson, C and Joshi, D (1988) 'Promoting New Development Processes: An Institutional Assessment', Agrarian Development Unit, Wye College, p4
25   ibid, p5
26   Sohani, Girish (1998) 'Case Study of the Aga Khan Rural Support Programme (India)', South Asian NGO Management Project, Ahmedabad, p3
27   Smillie, I, Gohar, B and Rowe, B (1996) 'The Sarhad Rural Support Corporation: A Mid Term Review', Peshawar, p4
28   See, for example, Caruthers et al, op cit
29   Satish, S and Kumar, N P, 'Are NGOs More Cost-Effective than the Government in Livestock Service Delivery?' in John Farrington *et al* (1993), *NGOs and the State in Asia*, Routledge, London, pp169–171

30   Ian Smillie interview with Mushtaque Chowdhury, 16 June 1998
31   Ian Smillie interview with Faruque Ahmed, op cit
32   John Hailey interview with Ravi Shankar, August, 1998
33   IUCN Pakistan, op cit, p18
34   Ebrahim, A (1999) 'The Making of NGOs: Global Influences and Local Responses from Western India', PhD dissertation, Stanford University, Palo Alto, Chapter 3
35   Quoted in Ebrahim, op cit, Chapter 3, p27
36   Smillie (1996) et al, p20
37   ibid
38   SRSC (1998) 'Harnessing People's Potential: Mini Review, January–June 1998', SRSC, Peshawar, p47
39   Holloway, R (1998) *Supporting Citizens' Initiatives: Bangladesh NGOs and Society*, IT Publications, London, p155
40   Hashemi and Hassan, op cit, p130
41   Khan, Shandana (1998) 'Case Study of Aga Khan Rural Support Programme, Pakistan', South Asian NGO Management Project, Islamabad, p15
42   ibid, pp19, 22
43   ibid, p15
44   Carver, J (1990) *Boards that Make a Difference*, Jossey-Bass, San Francisco, p10
45   Quoted in Carver, op cit, p10
46   Mintzberg, Henry (1994) *The Rise and Fall of Strategic Planning*, Free Press, New York, p110
47   Handy, C (1988) *Understanding Voluntary Organizations*, Penguin, London, pp6–7
48   Kay, J (1993) *Foundations of Corporate Success: How Business Strategies Add Value*, OUP, p357
49   Paton, R (1999) 'The Trouble With Values', in Lewis, op cit, p137
50   ibid, p139
51   Jafri, op cit
52   Fowler, A (1997) *Striking A Balance: A Guide to Enhancing the Effectiveness of NGOs in International Development*, Earthscan, London, p47
53   John Hailey interview with Barry Underwood, Ahmedabad, August 1998
54   Sattar, M G, Afreen, Neena, Fakir, M G Samdani, interview with Faruque Ahmed, Dhaka, 24 January 1998

CHAPTER 6

1   Harnath Jagawat was Personnel Manager at Banco India Ltd before joining Sadguru. Anil Shah had a distinguished career in the Government of Gujarat before joining AKRSP (I). Javed Majid, SRSC's first CEO, was also recruited from a senior government position. Shoaib Sultan Khan had been a senior civil servant in Pakistan before undertaking international development assignments.
2   Hudson, M (1995) *Managing Without Profit*, Penguin, London, pp44–45

3   Hussain, Saneeya (1998) 'Managing Growth and Change: A Case Study on Sungi Development Foundation', South Asian NGO Management Project, Karachi, p18

4   Smillie, I, Gohar, B and Rowe, B (1996) *The Sarhad Rural Support Corporation: A Mid Term Review*, October

5   Fowler, A (1997) *Striking A Balance: A Guide to Enhancing the Effectiveness of NGOs in International Development*, Earthscan, London, p70

6   Abecassis, D (1990) *Identity, Islam and Human Development in Rural Bangladesh*, University Press, Dhaka, quoted in Holcombe, S (1995) *Managing to Empower: The Grameen Bank's Experience of Poverty Alleviation*, University Press, Dhaka, pp82–83

7   Salamon, L and Anheier, H 'The Third World's Third Sector in Comparative Perspective', in Lewis, David (1999) *International Perspectives on Voluntary Action*, Earthscan, London, p76

8   ibid, pp16–17

9   Holcombe, Susan (1995) *Managing to Empower: The Grameen Bank's Experience of Poverty Alleviation*, University Press, Dhaka, p141

10   David Billis describes the three cultures – personal, associational and bureaucratic – in 'A theory of the voluntary sector: implications for policy and practice', Working Paper 5, Centre for Voluntary Organisation, London School of Economics, London, 1989

11   Lovell, C (1992) *Breaking the Cycle of Poverty*, Kumarian, Hartford, Connecticut, p125

12   See, for example, Bolman, L G and Deal, T (1998) *Reframing Organizations: Artistry, Choice and Leadership*, (2nd edition), Jossey-Bass, San Francisco, and Mintzberg, Henry, Ahlstrand, Bruce, Lampel, Joseph (1998) *Strategy Safari: A Guided Tour Through the Wilds of Strategic Management*, The Free Press, New York, Chapter 8

13   World Bank (1987) 'AKRSP: An Interim Evaluation', The World Bank, Washington, p21

14   'PROSHIKA Poverty Alleviation Phase V; Mid Term Review' (1997) vol 1, Dhaka, pxi

15   Hilmer, Frederick and Donaldson, Lex (1996) *Management Redeemed: Debunking the Fads that Undermine our Corporations*, Free Press, New York, p22

16   Ian Smillie interview with F H Abed, 14 June 1998

17   ibid, p33

18   Many writers have discussed the hierarchies of decentralization in development programming. Dennis Rondinelli was one of the first ('Administrative Decentralization and Economic Development: Sudan's Experiment with Devolution', *Journal of Modern African Studies*, vol 19, no 4, 1981). More recently, Alan Fowler, op cit, has discussed the deconcentration/delegation/devolution hierarchy in the context of NGO management

19   John Hailey interview with Shashi, Ahmedabad, August 1998

20   Ahmed, Sara (1998) 'Navinchand Mafatlal Sadguru Water and Development Foundation: Managing for Growth and Change', South Asian NGO Management Project, Ahmedabad

21   Risvi, Wasif A (1998) 'Case Study of IUCN Pakistan', South Asian NGO Management Project, Karachi

22 Ian Smillie interview with Faruque Ahmed, 15 June 1998
23 Ahmed, Q F (1997) 'People's Participation: Democratization of the Development Process', *Discourse*, vol 1, no 1, p60
24 John Hailey interview with Ravi Shankar, August 1998
25 John Hailey interview with N G Hegde, August 1998
26 Brinkerhoff, D (1991) *Improving Development Program Performance: Guidelines for Managers*, Lynne Rienner, Boulder, p106

CHAPTER 7

1   See Hofstede, G (1992) *Cultures and Organizations, Software of the Mind*, McGraw Hill, UK; Schein, E (1992) *Organizational Culture and Leadership*, Jossey-Bass, San Francisco
2   Vroom, V and Yetton, P (1973) *Leadership and Decision Making*, University of Pittsburgh Press, Pittsburgh. (They identify different leaderships including the autocratic leadership style, the consultative style, and the collective or group style.)
3   Adair, J (1990) *Great Leaders*, Talbot Adair, Brookwood
4   There is extensive literature in this area including: Goleman, D (1996) *Emotional Intelligence*, Bloomsbury, London; Lynch, R (1993) *Lead*, Jossey-Bass, San Francisco; Peters, T and Waterman, R (1983) *In Search of Excellence*, Harper Row, New York
5   Senge, P (1990) *The Fifth Discipline*, Doubleday, New York
6   Chambers, R (1997) *Whose Reality Counts: Putting the First Last*, IT Publications, London, p76
7   Uphoff, N, Esman, M and Krishna, A (1998) *Reasons for Success: Learning from Instructive Experiences in Rural Development*, Kumarian Press, West Hartford
8   Fowler, A (1997) *Striking A Balance: A Guide to Enhancing the Effectiveness of NGOs in International Development*, Earthscan, London
9   Uphoff, op cit, p50
10 Fowler, op cit, p75
11 Hofstede, op cit
12 Trompenaars, F (1993) *Riding the Waves of Culture*, Brearley, London
13 Quoted in interview by John Hailey with Girish Sohani, July 1998
14 Oza, Apoorva (1998) 'Case Study of BAIF Development Research Foundation', South Asian NGO Management Project, Ahmedabad
15 John Hailey interview with Dr Mangurkur, July 1998
16 Sadguru Annual Report, 1998, Sadguru, p1
17 John Hailey interview with Harnath Jagawat, July 1998
18 Ahmed, Sara (1998) 'Navinchand Mafatlal Sadguru Water and Development Foundation: Managing for Growth and Change, South Asian NGO Management Project, Ahmedabad
19 Smillie, I (1997) *Words and Deeds: BRAC at Twenty Five*, BRAC, Dhaka
20 Mohammed Fatmi interview with F H Abed, March 1998
21 Fatmi, Mohammad N E, Kabir, A, Sabri, Asgar Ali (1998) 'A Case Study of BRAC', South Asian NGO Management Project, Dhaka

22   Senge, op cit
23   Ian Smillie interview with Salehuddin Ahmed, June 1998
24   Khan, Shandana (1998) 'Case Study of Aga Khan Rural Support Pro-
      gramme, Pakistan', South Asian NGO Management Project, Islamabad
25   ibid p6
26   Ian Smillie interview with Aban Kabraji, New Delhi, March 2000
27   Sattar, M G, Afreen, Neena, Fakir, M G Samdani (1998) 'Proshika Case
      Study', South Asian NGO Management Project, Dhaka
28   Adair, op cit. He identified three distinct types of needs displayed by
      'followers': 'task needs' (planning, briefing, controlling, etc); 'group needs'
      (motivating, organizing, communicating); 'individual needs' (inspiring,
      empowering, enthusing)
29   Fiedler, F E (1967) *The Theory of Leadership Effectiveness*, McGraw-Hill, London
30   Hersey, P and Blanchard, K (1969) *Management of Organizational Behaviour*,
      Prentice Hall, Englewood Cliffs
31   Quoted in Ahmed, op cit
32   Quoted in Fatmi et al, op cit
33   Quoted in Oza, op cit
34   John Hailey interview with Dr Gokhale, July 1998
35   John Hailey interview with Apoorva Oza, July 1998
36   Drucker, P (1955) *The Practice of Management*, Heinemann, London
37   Bennis, W and Nanus, B (1985) *On Becoming a Leader*, Addison-Wesley,
      Reading, Massachusetts
38   Kotter, J (1990) *A Force for Change: How Leadership Differs from Management*,
      Free Press, New York

CHAPTER 8

1   Zafar Qureshi interview with Aban Kabraji, Karachi, December 1998

BIBLIOGRAPHY

CASE STUDIES CARRIED OUT FOR THIS BOOK

Ahmed, Sara (1998) 'Navinchand Mafatlal Sadguru Water and Development Foundation: Managing for Growth and Change', South Asian NGO Management Project, Ahmedabad

Fatmi, Mohammad N E, Kabir, A, Sabri, Asgar Ali, (1998) 'A Case Study of BRAC', South Asian NGO Management Project, Dhaka

Hussain, Saneeya (1998) 'Managing Growth and Change: A Case Study on Sungi Development Foundation', South Asian NGO Management Project, Karachi

Khan, Shandana (1998) 'Case Study of Aga Khan Rural Support Programme, Pakistan', South Asian NGO Management Project, Islamabad

Khan, Zia Ahmad (1998) 'Cruising in Turbulence; Case Study of SRSC', South Asian NGO Management Project, Peshawar

Oza, Apoorva (1998) 'Case Study of BAIF Development Research Foundation', South Asian NGO Management Project, Ahmedabad

Risvi, Wasif A (1998) 'Case Study of IUCN Pakistan', South Asian NGO Management Project, Karachi

Sattar, M G, Afreen, Neena, Fakir, M G Samdani (1998) 'Proshika Case Study', South Asian NGO Management Project, Dhaka

Sohani, Girish (1998) 'Case Study of the Aga Khan Rural Support Programme (India)', South Asian NGO Management Project, Ahmedabad

OTHER

Adair, J (1990) *Great Leaders*, Talbot Adair, Bloodwood

Arguers, C (1990) *Overcoming Organizational Defences: Facilitating Organizational Learning*, Allyn & Bacon, London

Beer, M and Spector, B (1984) *Managing Human Assets*, Free Press, New York

Bennis, W and Nanus, B (1985) *On Becoming a Leader*, Addison-Wesley, Reading, Massachusetts

Borst, Diane and Montana, Patrick (1977), *Managing Non-Profit Organizations*, Amacom, New York

Brinkerhoff, D (1991) *Improving Development Program Performance: Guidelines for Managers*, Lynne Rienner, Boulder

Brown, Shona L and Eisenhardt, K (1998) *Competing on the Edge: Strategy as Structured Chaos*, Harvard Business School Press, Boston

Carver, John (1990) *Boards that Make a Difference*, Jossey-Bass, San Francisco

Chambers, R (1997) *Whose Reality Counts: Putting the First Last*, IT Publications, London

Drucker, P (1955) *The Practice of Management*, Heinemann, London

Drucker, P (1992) *Managing the Non-Profit Organization: Principles and Practices*, Harper Business, New York

Ebrahim, Alnoor (1999) *The Making of NGOs: Global Influences and Local Responses from Western India*, PhD dissertation, Stanford University

Edhi, Adbul Sattar (1996) *A Mirror to the Blind*, National Bureau of Publications, Islamabad

Edwards, M (1996) 'Becoming a Learning Organization, or, the Search for the Holy Grail', paper presented to AKFC Round Table on Systematic Learning, Ottawa

Edwards, M (1999) 'NGO Performance – What Breeds Success? New Evidence from South Asia', *World Development*, vol 27, no 2

Edwards, M and Hulme, D (1992) *Making a Difference: NGOs and Development in a Changing World*, Earthscan, London

Edwards, M and Hulme, D (1996) *Beyond the Magic Bullet; NGO Performance and Accountability in the Post-Cold War World*, Kumarian Press, West Hartford, Connecticut

Farrington, John and Lewis, David (1993) *NGOs and the State in Asia*, Routledge, London

Fiedler, F (1967) *The Theory of Leadership Effectiveness*, McGraw-Hill, London

Fowler, A (1997) *Striking A Balance: A Guide to Enhancing the Effectiveness of NGOs in International Development*, Earthscan, London

Goleman, D (1996) *Emotional Intelligence*, Bloomsbury, London

Greiner, L (1972) 'Evolution and revolution as organizations grow', *Harvard Business Review*, July/August

Handy, C (1988) *Understanding Voluntary Organisations*, Penguin, London

Hersey, P and Blanchard, K (1969) *Management of Organisational Behaviour*, Prentice Hall, Englewood Cliffs

Hilmer, Frederick and Donaldson, Lex (1996) *Management Redeemed: Debunking the Fads that Undermine our Corporations*, Free Press, New York

Hofstede, G (1991) *Cultures and Organisations, Software of the Mind*, McGraw Hill, London

Holcombe, Susan (1995) *Managing to Empower: The Grameen Bank's Experience of Poverty Alleviation*, University Press, Dhaka

Holloway, Richard (1998) *Supporting Citizens' Initiatives: Bangladesh NGOs and Society*, IT Publications, London

Hudson, M (1995) *Managing Without Profit*, Penguin, London

Hulme, D and Edwards, M (1997) *NGOs, States and Donors; Too Close for Comfort?* Macmillan, London

Kaplan, A (1996) *The Development Practitioners Handbook*, Pluto Press, London

Kay, John (1993) *Foundations of Corporate Success: How Business Strategies Add Value*, Oxford University Press, Oxford

Khan, Mahmood Hasan (1998) *Climbing the Development Ladder with NGO Support*, Oxford University Press, Karachi

Korten, D (1980) 'Community Organization and Rural Development: A Learning Process Approach', *Public Administration Review*, vol 40

Korten, D (1990) *Getting to the 21st Century: Voluntary Action and the Global Agenda*, Kumarian Press, West Hartford, Connecticut

Kotter, J (1990) *A Force for Change: How Leadership Differs from Management*, Free Press, New York

Lewis, David (1999) *International Perspectives on Voluntary Action*, Earthscan, London

Lovell, C (1992) *Breaking the Cycle of Poverty*, Kumarian Press, West Hartford, Connecticut

Lynch, R (1993) *Lead*, Jossey-Bass, San Francisco

Mintzberg, Henry (1994) *The Rise and Fall of Strategic Planning*, The Free Press, New York

Mintzberg, Henry, Ahlstrand, Bruce, Lampel, Joseph (1998) *Strategy Safari: A Guided Tour Through the Wilds of Strategic Management*, The Free Press, New York

Mushtaque, A R Chowdhury, and Cash, R (1996) *A Simple Solution: Teaching Millions to Treat Diarrhoea at Home*, University Press, Dhaka

Pedler, M, Burgoyne, J, and Boydell, T (1991) *The Learning Company*, McGraw Hill, London

Peters, T and Waterman, R (1982) *In Search of Excellence*, Harper Row, New York

Pettigrew, A (1997) *The Management of Strategic Change*, Blackwell, Oxford

Putnam, Robert D (1993) *Making Democracy Work: Civic Traditions in Modern Italy*, Princeton University Press, Princeton

Revens, R (1983) *The ABC of Action Learning*, IFAL, Manchester

Schein, E (1992) *Organizational Culture & Leadership*, Jossey Bass, San Francisco

Senge, P (1990) *The Fifth Discipline: The Art and Practice of the Learning Organization*, Century Business Books, London

Smillie, I (1995) *The Alms Bazaar*, IT Publications, London

Smillie, I (1997) *Words and Deeds: BRAC at 25*, BRAC, Dhaka

Trompenaars, F (1993) *Riding the Waves of Culture*, Brearley, London

Uphoff, N, Esman, M and Krishna, A (1998) *Reasons for Success: Learning from Instructive Experiences in Rural Development*, Kumarian Press, West Hartford, Connecticut

Vroom, V and Yetton, P (1973) *Leadership and Decision Making*, University of Pittsburgh Press, Pittsburgh

INDEX